THE CASE AGAINST
BARACK
OBAMA

THE CASE AGAINST
BARACK OBAMA

The Unlikely Rise and Unexamined Agenda
of the Media's Favorite Candidate

DAVID FREDDOSO

Since 1947
REGNERY
PUBLISHING, INC.
An Eagle Publishing Company • Washington, DC

Cataloging-in-Publication data on file with the Library of Congress

ISBN 978-1-59698-566-7

Published in the United States by
Regnery Publishing, Inc.
One Massachusetts Avenue, NW
Washington, DC 20001
www.regnery.com

Manufactured in the United States of America
10 9 8 7 6 5 4 3 2 1

Books are available in quantity for promotional or premium use. Write to Director of Special Sales, Regnery Publishing, Inc., One Massachusetts Avenue NW, Washington, DC 20001, for information on discounts and terms or call (202) 216-0600.

To my parents, Alfred and Deborah.
Honora patrem tuum et matrem tuam ut sis
longevus super terram quam Dominus Deus tuus dabit tibi.
Exodus 20:12

CONTENTS

THE RHETORIC VS. THE REALITY

Barack Obama is a mere man. Even worse, he is a politician.

Obama claims to be a new kind of politician—a candidate who will rise above petty partisan divides and bring us a new era of "change."

That is his rhetoric, anyway.

Here is what he really is: A shrewd, Machine-aligned politician from Chicago—the kind who "won't make no waves and won't back no losers."[1] A left-liberal politician in the mold of Hillary Clinton, John Kerry, and Walter Mondale. A charismatic, smooth-talking politician whose words make people faint.

Our press normally fixes a critical eye on ambitious politicians who promise us the world. That eye just seems to well up with tears whenever it falls upon the junior senator from Illinois.

As the least experienced politician in at least one hundred years to obtain a major party nomination for President of the United States, Obama appears to be escaping the appropriate examination that any man (or woman) who covets the Oval Office deserves. Too many of those criticizing Obama have been content merely to slander him—to claim falsely that he refuses to salute the U.S. flag or was sworn into office on a Koran, or that he was really born in a foreign country. Such spurious criticisms have given rise to an intellectual laziness among the very people who should be carefully scrutinizing Obama.

That is why this book needed to be written.

It took only a couple of years covering Washington and Congressional politics for me to learn a sad, simple fact: A disappointingly small number of those who run for office from either party are true reformers. The ones who are reformers usually lose.

Obama has crafted himself an image as one of those rare reformers who succeeds. This is what prompted me to begin work on this book. As it became clear that he was going to win the Democratic nomination for president, it seemed irresponsible to stand by as so many were offering admiration, piety, even worship to—of all things—a politician. Because the idea of Barack Obama as a reformer is a great lie.

Obama has not pursued true reform in any of the offices he has held. He has silently and at times vocally cooperated with Chicago's Democratic Machine to preserve one of the most overtly corrupt political systems in the nation. He maintains his silence now, even though he has the political capital to do something about the problem, because his political allies in Illinois *are* the problem. These are the allies who drafted and gave him popular, must-pass bills to herd through the state legislature; the allies who openly take credit for making him a senator; the allies who control Chicago's political money. In Washington, his commitment to reform has been no greater—not even this year, as he runs for office promising "change" and "hope."

Obama's ethnic pedigree understandably attracts much interest and fascination. But it is far less interesting than his unusual political pedi-

gree. He is the product of a marriage between two of the least attrac-
tive parts of Democratic politics—the hard-core radicalism of the
1960s era and Chicago's Machine politics. Obama plays hardball and
knows when to look the other way. But he also surrounds himself with
political, social, and spiritual mentors who are so far to the left that
many push the envelope on ideological respectability. The interesting
result of this mix is that Obama can engineer a high-minded drive to
register thousands of voters in Chicago's black wards, only to turn
around and throw all of his opponents off the ballot on a technicality,
so that those voters have no choice but to elect him. This is precisely
how he first won his state Senate seat in 1996.

It also means that despite his capacity for such political savvy,
Obama was still so attracted to the startling radicalism of the Rev. Jere-
miah Wright that he continued to attend the Trinity United Church of
Christ in Chicago. Oprah Winfrey, recognizing the problems with
Wright that Obama has since experienced, had much earlier abandoned
the same congregation in part out of concern for her public image.

Barack Obama is a candidate for the presidency of the United States.
It is appropriate to consider his character, his record, his background,
and his proposals. It is not appropriate for anyone who takes his role as
a citizen seriously to weep at Obama's message of "hope" and
"change,"[2] or to shake hands with someone, just to touch the hand that
touched the hand that touched Obama's.[3] It is imprudent to entertain
false hopes about what Obama stands for and what he can accomplish
in the way of changing history and American attitudes. It is foolish to be
caught up in an orgiastic frenzy over some non-existent "new politics,"
or over that campaign chant of "Yes, We Can!"—a theme that Obama
himself considered vapid and mindless in 2004, when his campaign advisors first imposed it on him over his objections.[4] Even respected, experienced opinion writers display irrational behavior when touched by the

Obama phenomenon. It can cause a principled left-wing magazine like *The Nation* to argue in bad faith for a massive corporate giveaway of taxpayer money—the 2008 farm bill—because Senator Obama voted for it and his opponent voted against.[5] It can drive Obama's liberal supporters, normally opponents of unilateral military action, to support military strikes within the territory of an American ally without that nation's permission. They take this position because Obama apparently made a slip of the tongue in August of last year and advocated such incursions into Pakistan.[6]

Barack Obama has demonstrated great skill in fundraising and in delivering speeches that have been carefully written, parsed, and tested in advance to achieve maximum emotional impact.[7] But even if the money helps, the goodwill of good oratory cannot last forever. At the Cannes Film Festival in May 2008, Sean Penn, the liberal Hollywood actor, may have made the wisest (if the hardest to follow) statement on the Obama phenomenon: "I hope that he will understand if he is the nominee the degree of disillusionment that will happen if he doesn't become a greater man than he will ever be."[8]

Whether in victory or defeat, Barack Obama's supporters will be the last ones to understand that he is just another politician. He is not and never will be worthy of such adulation.

Barack Obama is an impressive man—he would never have gotten this far if he weren't. But he is not the force for "Change" or "Unity" that many naïve individuals believe he is. He is simply another liberal Democratic politician who will divide America along the same lines as it has been divided for decades.

As a policy-maker, Obama has very bad ideas that would hurt America—they are the same ideas that have been floating around Washington for years, though in some cases more extreme. The same ideas espoused by Hillary Clinton, Nancy Pelosi, Ted Kennedy, Barbara

Boxer, or any of Obama's other liberal ideological soulmates on Capitol Hill.

On abortion, he stands to the left of even these liberals—once you understand his position, you see that he is to the left of almost everyone in America. His understanding of foreign policy is unsurprisingly thin for someone who was still a member of the Illinois Senate as recently as November 2004.

Obama's irregular land deal with a felon later convicted of corrupting public officials deserves more than a superficial examination of whether the transaction itself was corrupt. We ought to ask why in the world Obama had a seventeen-year friendship with a figure whose livelihood depended on sapping the taxpayer for subsidies and corrupting public officials—officials like Barack Obama. What did Obama ever do to help Rezko? Quite a bit, as we shall see.

When those close to him become stained by scandal, Obama suddenly shows a level of cognitive dissonance unworthy of the obviously intelligent, reflective author of *Dreams from My Father*: "This isn't the Tony Rezko I knew..."[9] "The [Rev. Wright] that I saw yesterday was not the person I met 20 years ago..."[10]

Obama speaks of the days when his family was making $240,000 per year as if he had been suffering poverty. Meanwhile, he argues that the wealthy need to pay more in taxes, and in March he voted to raise yours if your taxable income is greater than $32,500 per year.[11] That is a very different measure of wealth.

Prior to this year, Obama has run in just one seriously contested election—for Congress, in 2000. He lost in a landslide. His victories, right up until his foray into the presidential primaries, have come almost effortlessly, owing largely to incredible good luck and the fact that his opponents' faults were much greater than his own. This makes him an unknown quantity, even now as he runs for president.

I believed that by writing this book I could fill in the picture—to shine a spotlight on some relatively unexplored and some completely new aspects of Obama's career. In this I believe I have succeeded. This book contains some new and many buried stories that the media has mostly ignored. They puncture the image Obama has created for himself.

I hope that this book will do voters a service by telling the story of the man's political life in one place, in a manner that is appropriately critical and free of hyperbole. This book obviously takes a conservative presumption against the candidate—just look at the title—but I hope that you also find it to be respectful and realistic, even if it is unavoidably shaped and shaded by my own views.

Even a conservative who rejects his policies can rest assured that an Obama presidency will not mean the end of America, an Islamic takeover, or an American Bolshevik Revolution. Nonetheless, hidden in Obama's shapeless rhetoric about "Change" and "Hope" is a dangerous agenda that will take on real substance if he is given power.

America will not end under a President Obama, but it might be a very different place from the one we know now: a place ruled by a Supreme Court full of young judges enthralled by the notion of a "living Constitution" that says pretty much whatever they want it to say; a place burdened by the higher taxes Obama has promised; an America in which the car you own today becomes illegal to make, but even the slightest restriction on abortion would be wiped away in all fifty states.

I hope that readers of this book will move beyond both the rhetoric and the smears, and learn more about the man whose "audacious hope" sweeps America.

CHAPTER ONE

OBAMA AND THE CHICAGO MACHINE: NOT A REFORMER

Most accounts of Barack Obama's political rise begin on the convention stage in Boston in 2004, or at Harvard in 1990, or even in Indonesia in 1970.

This one begins in Chicago on a cold, gray, windy day—January 2, 1996. Obama's campaign volunteers and staffers had gathered in a grim hearing room of the Chicago Board of Election Commissioners.[1] Obama was making his first run for elective office, which was to be the first in a nearly unbroken line of victories.

At the beginning of *The Audacity of Hope*, Obama attributes his 1996 election victory to the message he brought to the neighborhoods of Chicago's South Side—telling people to drop their cynicism about politics, because *yes, they can* make a difference through voting, activism, and advocacy.

"It was a pretty convincing speech, I thought," Obama writes. "Although I'm not sure that the people who heard me deliver it were similarly impressed, enough of them appreciated my earnestness and youthful swagger that I made it to the Illinois legislature."[2]

But Obama's telling leaves out an important part of the story. For it did not matter what he said on the stump. It did not matter whether the South Side voters were "impressed" or not. All that mattered was what his campaign staff did in the elections office on that chilly January day.

Ronald Davis was a paid consultant for Obama, who called him the "guru of petitions."[3] Davis's job on January 2, 1996 was to look at each of the nearly 1,600 signatures that state senator Alice Palmer's campaign had collected in order place her on the ballot for re-election. Davis was supposed to find a way to challenge and disqualify as many signatures as possible. The goal was to throw her off the ballot.

Palmer, the long-time South Side activist and state senator since 1991, had gathered 1,580 signatures, more than twice the 757 required to get on the ballot. But Davis and his team, over a few days, disqualified hundreds of them, one at a time. Obama says he was uneasy with this hardball tactic. In the end, however, he would say of the five-year incumbent Palmer: "If you couldn't run a successful petition drive, then that raised questions in terms of how effective a representative you were going to be."[4]

With that justification, he approved the project, and he checked up on its progress nightly. One by one, Obama's "petitions guru" disqualified Palmer's signatures for one reason or another. According to one local newspaper at the time: "Some of the problems include printing registered voters name [sic] instead of writing, a female voter got married after she registered to vote and signed her maiden name, registered voters signed the petitions but don't live in the 13th district."[5]

Soon enough, Davis and his crew had brought Palmer below 757 valid signatures.

They had thrown an incumbent state senator off the ballot.

While they were at it, Obama's campaign got the other three candidates disqualified as well.

One of them was Gha-is Askia. He never had much of a chance of winning anyway, but he had gathered 1,899 signatures, and Team Obama took the time to challenge them as well.[6] Askia spoke to the *Chicago Tribune* in 2007 about it:

> "Why say you're for a new tomorrow, then do old-style Chicago politics to remove legitimate candidates?" Askia said. "He talks about honor and democracy, but what honor is there in getting rid of every other candidate so you can run scot-free? Why not let the people decide?"[7]

Thanks to his shrewdness and his willingness to play hardball, Barack Obama had made the first step in his astonishingly rapid political ascent.

This was the man who just a few years earlier had run "Project Vote." According to a 1993 article in *Chicago Weekly*, the registration campaign reached every part of the city with its slangy slogan—"It's a power thing." Obama had trained hundreds of activists and flooded the streets with posters and the airwaves with radio advertisements, apparently producing the first black voting majority in the city's history. His work even had people mentioning him as a possible candidate for elected office—the kind who could run against opponents and win.[8] Three years later, he would be a candidate—thanks to the work of his "petitions guru," the *only* candidate. Obama would explain his tactics years later:

"If you can win, you should win and get to work doing the people's business."[9]

OBAMA'S FIRST POLITICAL SPONSOR

There had been happier days between Obama and Palmer, who in 2008 backed Senator Hillary Clinton for president. Palmer had been serving as a state senator in 1995 when a rare congressional vacancy had opened up—the incumbent Mel Reynolds had been indicted for sexual misconduct with a minor (he would later be convicted, but eventually pardoned by President Clinton).

Palmer had jumped into the special election race early. Obama had backed her for the U.S. House seat, and she in turn endorsed him to be her replacement in Springfield. (Obama had been so close to Palmer that around this time the socialist newsletter *New Ground* misidentified him as her chief of staff.[10]) But then a young man by the name of Jesse Jackson Jr. entered the Congressional race, as did the state senate Democratic Leader, Emil Jones, who would later become Obama's mentor.

Palmer raised only $257,000 to Jackson's $430,000.[11] As the line goes from one famous Chicago-based movie, she had brought a knife to a gunfight. She finished a distant third in that November 28 special election. She might have even cost Jones the victory.

After her embarrassing loss, Palmer did not want to give up her safe state Senate seat. She asked Obama to step aside, wait his turn, and give it back. Obama said no. His surrogates told the *Chicago Tribune*, the *Chicago Reader*, and other news outlets at the time that she was reneging on a promise. The *Reader* wrote at the time: "She promised Obama that if she lost—which is what happened on November 28, 1995—she wouldn't then run against him to keep her senate seat."[12] She claimed that she was running because of popular demand—that a groundswell had formed to keep her in office.

Obama was well within his rights to stay in the race. State Senate seats do not "belong" to anyone but the voters who live in the district, even if it sometimes seems otherwise in Chicago. And besides, he had already made preparations for the campaign, among other things calling on fundraiser Antoin Rezko (more about him later). Rezko raised roughly $15,000 for him in that election[13] as he built his war chest.

As an incumbent with the backing of the new congressman, Jesse Jackson Jr., Palmer was considered the early favorite in this contest.[14] She went out and collected nearly 1,600 petition signatures in just ten days and submitted them ahead of the December 18 deadline.[15] She would still need to defeat Obama and two other Democratic challengers, but as an incumbent with the backing of the popular new congressman, Palmer was the early favorite. Until Obama kept her from running, that is.[16]

Downtown, Chicago Mayor Richard M. Daley must have smiled when he learned that some "skinny kid with a funny name" had just ended Alice Palmer's career. According to contemporaneous news reports, Daley considered Palmer a serious threat, a potential mayoral rival.[17] The black press had also raised the possibility of Palmer's husband running for mayor.[18] Chicago was a majority-minority city with a white mayor. Both Palmers represented precisely the kind of black candidate around whom others might have united against Daley, as they had united around Chicago's first and only black mayor, Harold Washington, in 1983.

By clearing the ballot, Obama had done more than just elbow his way into power without a real election—he had also erased any doubt of Daley's path to his next term.

There was nothing illegal in what Obama did in the primary. It was typical Chicago politics—"*If you can win, you should win.*"

And that is the point. Barack Obama promises to smooth over the bitter divides of American politics. He promises hope and an end to bitter partisanship. He frames himself as someone who rises above Clintonian or Rovian tactics. Contrast his promises today with what he did in 1996. He was not even a state senator yet, and he had already done enough to make Karl Rove, Bill Clinton, or Niccolo Machiavelli proud. He got his start in politics by denying voters a choice.

Does this betray Obama's professed ideals? Does it clash with the "new politics" he is supposed to herald? Was he really serving South Side's voters with his tactics?

When asked this in 2007, Obama smiled. "I think they ended up with a very good state senator."[19]

COOK COUNTY POLITICS

Everyone says that Chicago politics is dirty, but what exactly does that mean? Here is one story about how politics is dirty in the Windy City—and about how Barack Obama helped keep it that way.

Imagine working in the Cook County government. What's it like? If you have the right political connections, you get the job. You get the raise. You get the promotion. No qualifications necessary—just campaign contributions.

If you don't have the political connections, then you don't get the raise. You languish at the same desk for years without a promotion. You watch unqualified political stooges sent from "downtown" take the best jobs. You suffer the indignity of training them to take the supervisory job for which you applied and for which you were qualified.

This is how John Stroger, the former President of the Cook County Board of Commissioners, ran things until his retirement in 2006. According to court papers, his successor—his son, Todd Stroger—has not changed the system much, despite federal court-ordered supervision that began in January 2007. The federal investigation revealed several stories from John Stroger's reign that capture perfectly the environment inside the Cook County civil service, including this one about a loud-mouthed county employee who was allegedly hired through illegal patronage:

> On his first day in the department, he told a number of his new co-workers he was a "soldier for Stroger" and he was going to become their supervisor... One witness claims after working at the department for a total of five hours, the employee had already identified co-workers he intended to impose severe discipline upon when he became supervisor.[20]

Sure enough, that employee was promoted to supervisor, just as soon as "downtown" could change the job qualifications to make them less stringent.

This was not an unusual occurrence, but a regular one, much like these others:

> "The applicant was granted the position days after she made a monetary donation to Citizens for Stroger..."[21]
>
> "The allegedly politically connected applicant was given... a job the applicant was not qualified for and did not receive an interview..."[22]
>
> "Despite his qualifications, claimant did not receive the promotion. The position was filled by an individual connected to an Alderman. The promoted individual does not have the required experience and does not appear to have the required B.S. degree in a related field."[23]
>
> "Claimant... was told 'a personal lieutenant to President Stroger blocked (claimant's) application.' The position was subsequently filled by an allegedly politically connected individual."[24]

"A document found in the application file, dated after the conclusion of the interviews, states the position is not to be filled by the current crop of applicants because 'downtown' wished to fill the position."[25]

"... pressure to perform political work in exchange for job advancement."[26]

"'Downtown' changed the minimum qualifications for the position..."[27]

Like every politically involved Chicagoan, Barack Obama knew exactly how the Stroger Machine worked in 2006. The County government was not only paying for John Stroger's standing political army of door-knockers, it was also sending out the salary checks that would eventually make their way to his campaign account.

Obama knew all of this. He knew how Chicago's county government works. And he worked that year to keep the Stroger Machine running when it faced a potential election loss.

Did Barack Obama engage in illegal patronage hiring and the other corrupt practices of Cook County's government?

Absolutely not.

Has he repeatedly and knowingly enabled those who do?

Absolutely.

Had Obama lifted even his pinkie finger in the name of "Change we can believe in," there would be no Strogers in power today. There would be no more "Soldiers for Stroger," abusing civil servants and pocketing taxpayer cash.

But he did not. When Veteran Cook County Boss John Stroger faced a strong and credible challenge in the 2006 primary election from a reform-minded liberal Democrat, Obama said nothing. Local politicians on the left and right, sick of the corruption, lined up against Stroger. Senator Obama stayed silent, and the reformer narrowly lost.

When John Stroger soon fell ill, and his son Todd took his place on the ballot (under suspicious circumstances) for the general election, many Democrats refused to back their own party's candidate. Some even announced they would vote for the Republican. That's when Obama found his voice. He endorsed the young Stroger, going so far as to call him—to the absolute horror of Chicago liberals—"a good progressive Democrat."[28] As we shall see, Barack Obama has never stood up for "change" in Chicago. "Change" and "reform" are for people who *lose* elections.

The charming "Soldier for Stroger" story and the other employee complaints quoted above are just a handful of those that appear in a scathing 54-page report on the two Stroger administrations, submitted in March 2008 by retired County Circuit Judge Julia Nowicki. She is the federal court-ordered Compliance Administrator investigating the past and present hiring practices of the Stroger Machine. Her appointment came after an FBI raid of the Cook County office building in September 2006, when the feds finally put their foot down on Cook County corruption.

Nowicki received more than two hundred complaints of illegal cronyism and patronage hiring. She found evidence of employees using county time and resources for political activity. She found county employees who were harassed for not joining their ward's political organization. She wrote that young Todd Stroger's human resources staff still appears to keep multiple sets of personnel files in order to "cover" patronage employment.[29] In her judgment, she writes, all of the complaints she discusses are backed by "reasonable evidence,"[30] although no final rulings on the county's civil liability had yet been made.[31]

Eventually, when the county government settles the employee claims, Cook County taxpayers will be the ones to pay for the Strogers' sins.

Nowicki also wrote that "in the last six months, there has been little change in the *status quo* since the last report..."[32] She told the county commissioners in April 2008 that Todd Stroger's administration has been less than fully cooperative in her investigation, that patronage hiring continues, and that more employees would likely come forward with complaints except that they fear retaliation from Todd Stroger and his allies.[33]

Like father, like son.

After the elder Stroger's death in early 2008, his obituary would read:

> President Stroger has also been accused of padding the county payroll with political cronies and relatives, being more open to tax increases than cutting waste and installing political pals in high-paying jobs in the Cook County Forest Preserve District while laying off the people responsible for picking up the garbage and cleaning the toilets.[34]

For more empirical evidence of how the Stroger Machine worked, the non-partisan, Chicago-based Better Government Association provided this breakdown:[35]

- Between early 1999 and the middle of 2005 President Stroger raised approximately $2,413,246 million in itemized contributions.
- During that period, at least $615,078.99 (25.5%) in itemized contributions was raised from county contractors, their owners, agents and employees.

- At least $624,543 (25.8%) in itemized contributions was raised during that time from Cook County employees who ultimately report to his office.

In other words, more than half of Stroger's campaign cash came from people whose pockets he was lining with taxpayer money. That's not even counting the money Stroger directed them to donate to other Machine politicians and ward organizations. The county employees who gave money would also form Stroger's squad of foot soldiers in the days and weeks leading up to elections, getting out the vote for him and his allies. He didn't have to pay them through his campaign— Cook County was paying them.

Patronage is part of the typical cycle of Machine politics. Politicians hand out tax dollars to friends, who return the favor. With tax dollars serving him so well, it's no wonder Stroger liked high taxes. Just in his final two years in office, John Stroger endorsed: a 2 percent hotel-motel tax; a 2 percent "prepared food and beverage" tax; a $200 "automatic amusement device" tax; an 8.5 percent property tax increase; a $1-per-pack cigarette tax increase; and a tripling of court fees from $5 to $15. Before that, Stroger had tried to triple the property-transfer tax, and he had helped create a variety of special "tax districts" that could assess special-purpose taxes. This money was the fuel for his patronage machine.

After inheriting his office, the younger Stroger kept the family tradition alive by loading the payroll with family members and cronies according to what is known as the Chicago "friends and family" plan. He gave his own cousin—at this point the county's chief financial officer—a sudden 12 percent pay hike, to $160,000. He hired his best friend's wife for a $126,000 job.[36] He hired his childhood friend as his spokesman.[37] He hired an unqualified friend to a top health job apparently created just for him.[38]

Around the same time, claiming a lack of funds, he shut down several health clinics, laid off hundreds of nurses from the county hospital that is named after his father, and gave the axe to forty-three prosecutors in the state's attorney's office. In total, he got rid of 1,700 county workers, barely touching a hair on the heads of any "Soldiers for Stroger."[39] In order to support both legal and illegal political hiring—and over the objections of both conservatives and progressives—he rammed through the Cook County Board of Commissioners a regressive sales tax increase that makes Chicago's the highest sales tax burden of any major city in the United States today.

Todd Stroger denounced Judge Nowicki's report on patronage hiring, insisting that there was no patronage hiring in Cook County. He later admitted that he had not read the report he was denouncing.[40]

"I never really expected Todd Stroger to do much about cleaning up the county government," says Jay Stewart, executive director of the Better Government Association. "He has succeeded in meeting my low expectations."

OBAMA: SOLDIER FOR STROGER

It did not have to be this way. Barack Obama, the reformer, was by then a member of the United States Senate. He had a chance to change things in Cook County government forever. He passed it up. Then he had a chance at least to keep his mouth shut rather than throw his good name behind a corrupt system. He passed that up, too.

Everyone knew how the Stroger Machine worked. Media outlets Left and Right assailed the corruption of Cook County politics. Politicians, both liberal and conservative, joined forces against

Stroger. By 2006, after a long climb, reformers had briefly built an "anti-Stroger majority" on the seventeen-member County Board of Commissioners, consisting of six Republicans and three liberal Democrats.

So when good-government liberal Forrest Claypool announced a primary challenge to John Stroger for the 2006 election, he immediately attracted support from reform advocates. It was a clear case of Clean versus Machine. Republicans and progressive Democrats found a reason to unite in the name of Change—in the very mode of post-partisanship that Obama extols today.

Chicago Sun-Times columnist Neil Steinberg framed the voters' decision thus:

> Isn't it enough that Stroger has turned Cook County government into a bog of waste, cronyism and incompetence? Isn't it enough that a solid, respectable, smart alternative exists? Claypool is a longtime reformer who has fought heroically to make Cook County better and more effective—if you are voting to try to improve the vital Cook County services, the vote is for Claypool. If you vote your race, for any clown, no matter how ignored and betrayed you are year-in, year-out, then go for Stroger.[41]

Claypool, who in 2002 had narrowly unseated a Stroger ally to become a commissioner, was walking exactly in sync with Obama's campaign rhetoric of 2008: Kick out the entrenched interests. Reach across the standard political divides. Provide hope and reform.

Liberals around Chicago were energized. Republicans made plans to cross over and support Claypool in the primary. The other anti-Stroger candidate, board member Michael Quigley, dropped out of the race to present a unified reform campaign—Quigley even became Claypool's campaign manager.

The *Chicago Tribune* at the time wrote:

> [C]ounty government works for Stroger's pals, not for the people and businesses that pay taxes. And it certainly doesn't work for the impoverished people who have nowhere else to turn. On Monday, Quigley correctly said Stroger's fiefdom "cynically abuses their trust by wasting precious resources on the hangers-on—the contractors and the patronage workers."[42]

Chicago's voices of reform were speaking in unison, but Obama's was not among them. He did not campaign for John Stroger or even endorse him, but he certainly didn't lift a finger for Forrest Claypool, even though Claypool was his personal friend.

Imagine the splash Obama could have made: In early 2006, he was the most popular politician in Illinois and the star of the national Democratic Party. Had he gone into Chicago to play a role in that race, the national press would have followed him. The local press would have been glued to him. Obama could have yanked out a keystone of the corrupt Machine that has plagued his city for decades.

He did not. At one point, it appeared that Claypool would win, but Stroger, who suffered a stroke shortly before the election, gained sympathy. Mayor Daley cut ads for him and urged a Stroger vote.[43] His campaign recovered near the end. He won by seven percentage points—42,000 votes of 600,000 cast.

Obama's silence had probably saved Cook County's political kingpin.

It might have been difficult for Obama to stand up for principle and support "change," but it was certainly not impossible. John Stroger had backed one of Obama's rivals in the 2004 primary that brought him to the U.S. Senate. Some attribute Obama's deference in this case to his fear of alienating the black community. John Stroger was black, and Claypool is white. As political writer Tom Bevan would put it:

> Obama's calculus in protecting his interests meant first and foremost showing deference to the Chicago machine, and also not making a move that would cost him support within the African-American community.[44]

This explanation probably overstates the racial angle, though. Obama was certainly not on the verge of losing support from black voters. The real problem was the Machine. Had he endorsed Claypool, Obama would have really rocked the boat, alienating Emil Jones, his patron in the state Senate. He would have upset Mayor Richard Daley, and every alderman and County Supervisor and Machine politician who had (and still has) political stooges on the Cook County payroll.

Two years later, Claypool was supporting Obama for President, and Jeff Berkowitz, a respected television journalist whose weekly show *Public Affairs* is Chicago's local equivalent of *Meet the Press,* asked him about Obama's silence in 2006:

> **Berkowitz:** You could have seen reform...You could have done a great many things that I know Barack Obama would like to do, to improve health care and so forth for people in Cook County. Why couldn't he make that move?
>
> **Claypool:** I don't know. I mean—look, politics is complex. People have multiple relationships and they do the things they have to do and believe in.[45]

Obama had "multiple relationships." "Change" and "Hope" could wait.

In the general election that November, Obama would compound his omission with active support for the Machine.

John Stroger had suffered his stroke on March 14, seven days before his narrow primary victory.[46] He disappeared completely from the public view.

For months, the media and the public were left to guess about his health. His critics in politics and the media were already speculating that his cronies were hiding from the public his mental incapacitation—perhaps even his death.[47] There was some serious uncertainty throughout the spring and early summer about whether the governmental decisions emerging from his hospital room—for example, the 408 new hires from June 11 to July 8, when the county was technically on a hiring freeze[48]—were actually being made by Board President Stroger himself, or by his staff, or his son. In a May 4 interview with the *Chicago Tribune*, Todd Stroger had "said flatly that his father was not running the county government."[49]

The *Tribune* editorialized:

> For 117 days since he suffered a stroke, Cook County Board President John Stroger has been incommunicado, with aides and family members asserting that they are relaying his wishes. The record suggests that those surrogates have misled citizens about Stroger's health.
>
> The plain goal of this unethical—if not illegal—fraud on voters and taxpayers is for Democratic politicos to keep control of the county patronage and contracts that cement their own power. The surrogates and politicos have exploited John Stroger, manipulating information about the infirmity of a man evidently unable to speak publicly for himself. They've said whatever they had to, first so a reform challenger wouldn't beat

the impaired Stroger in a Democratic primary race, then to dis-
courage any third-party candidate from running in the November general election.[50]

Indeed, the announcement of John Stroger's incapacitation was delayed
until well after June 26, the deadline for independent candidates to
enter the race. By the time his father finally dropped out on July 8, his
son Todd Stroger was angling to take his place on the Democratic line.

After some intra-party wrangling—even an attempt by Democratic
congressman Danny Davis to block the young Stroger by taking the job
himself—the Machine won again. The Cook County Democratic Party
placed Todd Stroger on the November ballot.

Criticized as an unqualified underachiever, Todd Stroger held forth
the promise of several more years of the same corrupt patronage
racket that his father had run for more than a decade. Progressive
Chicagoans were not happy. Conservatives were fuming. Claypool
said openly that he would not vote for Stroger.[51] Some Democrats—
such as Frank Coconate, chairman of the Northwest Side Democratic Organization—went so far as to endorse the Republican, Tony
Peraica, rather than support the Strogers in this electoral stunt. The
press gave Peraica a genuine chance of being the first Republican
Cook County board president in thirty-six years.

But come November, Todd Stroger won. And he did it with the
enthusiastic endorsement of United States Senator Barack Obama.
Obama, together with fellow Illinois senator Dick Durbin, sent a letter
to their Cook County supporters:

Today we write to urge your attention to one race in particular. Our friend, Todd Stroger, former state representative and
alderman, is candidate for president of the Cook County

Board. Please consider voting for Todd...Todd is a good progressive Democrat, who will bring those values and sensibilities to the job.[52]

"A good progressive Democrat." One can almost imagine the two senators laughing as they wrote it. As one liberal Chicago commentator wrote at the time:

> Todd Stroger was a "strong voice" in Springfield, the letter says. He has "worked assiduously" for the poor as an alderman. Yet, of course, the record reveals that Stroger is an unimaginative legislative drone whose reform credentials are wholly imaginary—an unlikely trailblazer to a new era.
>
> Then Obama and Durbin take an epistolary dive into the mud and start yammering in the letter about Republican challenger Tony Peraica's conservative stance on social issues that almost never come before the County Board. In particular, they raise the fear that Peraica would unilaterally put a halt to abortions at county hospitals, even though Peraica has repeatedly pledged that he will not.
>
> "We've come too far for that," says the letter.
>
> And Obama has come too far as an inspiring new breed of politician on the national scene to muck around in local politics, endorsing machine hack candidates and substituting party for principle. Or so you'd imagine.[53]

Welcome to the "new, post-partisan politics" Obama has promised. Stroger may have been a symbol of corruption, but he was a Democrat, and his opponent was a Republican. Obama endorsed him, employing what even liberals called misleading scare tactics.

It was not his first collaboration in Chicago's corruption, and it would not be the last in his long record of un-reform.

SAVIOR, OR SAVVIER?

How involved is Barack Obama with the seedy world of Chicago Machine politics? As he told the *Chicago Tribune* in April, hardly at all.

"I think I have done a good job in rising politically in this environment without being entangled in some of the traditional problems of Chicago politics," he said.[54]

Tribune columnist John Kass, an expert on Chicago's political scene, views it differently:

> Why is Obama allowed to campaign as a reformer, virtually unchallenged by the media, though he's a product of Chicago politics and has never condemned the wholesale political corruption in his home town the way he condemns those darn Washington lobbyists?...He has endorsed Daley, endorsed Daley's hapless stooge Todd Stroger for president of the Cook County Board. These are not the acts of a reformer, but of a guy who, as we say in Chicago, won't make no waves and won't back no losers.[55]

That's not entirely true. Obama did back one loser in 2007, Alderman Dorothy Tillman. Tillman was no Daley ally, but she was certainly no reformer, having enriched her family through contracts with the Harold Washington Cultural Center, which she had been entrusted to run.[56] Tillman's most important legislative initiative was a city ordinance to provide reparations for slavery. She once demanded that two white waiters at a downtown banquet she was hosting be replaced with black waiters.[57]

In 1991, witnesses said Tillman had brandished "a .38-caliber, snub-nosed, nickel-plated pistol" during a contentious ward redistricting session.[58] Obama endorsed a marginally sane, self-dealing politician on the grounds that she had endorsed him in 2004. She lost anyway, by 665 votes.[59] It was a small victory for sanity and for Chicago, no thanks to reformer Obama.

Richard M. Daley, however, is no loser. He has been Chicago's mayor for nearly twenty years, and for good reason—he knows political organizations, and his puts the Stroger family to shame. Unfortunately, much of the Machine's workings have been revealed in federal investigations of the underlings in his office. Indictments and convictions have already been secured, details revealed in court papers and news articles.

But even when things got tough, at least Daley could count on Barack Obama, the reformer, to endorse him for re-election in 2007.

Distrustful of the Democratic Party's regular ward organizations, many of which had not supported him in his 1989 run for mayor, Daley built his own Machine organization of party irregulars. It consisted of such groups as the ironically named Coalition for Better Government, the Hispanic Democratic Organization (commonly called the "Hispanic Daley Organization"), and a few trustworthy ward organizations.[60]

And every political soldier needs his pay—a place on the city payroll, no qualifications necessary. You can be a former gang member and still be appointed to oversee a $40 million program, as long as you belong to one of the right political organizations.[61] If you have the right connections, the city will hire you even after you've stolen $4 million in quarters from the city's toll booths.[62] That's the Chicago version of "change you can believe in."

In 2005, U.S. Attorney Patrick Fitzgerald began picking apart this Machine, uncovering the same kind of illegal patronage hiring in which Cook County was engaged, but on a larger and far more sensational scale. The biggest difference between Stroger and Daley is that Daley has managed to avoid being directly implicated.

Daley aides Robert Sorich and Timothy McCarthy were indicted in 2005 and convicted in 2006 on mail fraud charges related to their organizing this patronage army and rewarding the mayor's political allies with jobs and promotions.[63] The U.S. Attorney's office alleged that interviews for city jobs were routinely faked and interview scores inflated for candidates who appeared on the "blessed" list of those who worked on the campaigns of Daley and his allies. One applicant was in Iraq on the day his interview supposedly took place—his absence did not prevent him from scoring a perfect five out of five in that interview.[64]

Federal agents also seized papers and computer files that Daley's men were using to track "thousands" of political hires[65]—"a color-coded document reflecting the winners' names at the end of a hiring sequence, as well as the political organization or union sponsor associated with the particular winners." Completely unqualified candidates—some described as "goofballs"—were hired for jobs they had no business doing. Of one candidate, described as "a drunk," Sorich had demanded he be hired anyway and said, "Do the best you can with him."[66]

As his men were being indicted for this illegal arrangement, the mayor said he was "saddened by these charges for these individuals and their families." He said that the federal investigation "has uncovered practices that plainly demand reform." He said, "I cannot change the past, but I have learned from it and have taken aggressive steps to address these issues, and I will continue to do so."[67]

No one knows for sure whether he was trying to be funny.

None of this stopped presidential candidate Barack Obama from endorsing Daley's re-election in 2007. But that's not to say that Obama never had doubts. In August 2005, with indictments flying in the illegal patronage scandal, Obama *almost* said something mildly critical of Daley when asked whether he would endorse him for re-election.

"What's happened—some of the reports I've seen in your newspaper, I think, give me huge pause," Obama told a reporter from the *Chicago Sun-Times*.[68]

Obama must have thought this went too far, though, because an hour later he was already calling back to "clarify" his comments:

> Obama said the mayor was "obviously going through a rough patch right now." But he also said Chicago has "never looked better" and that "significant progress has been made on a variety of fronts." The senator said then it was "way premature" to talk about endorsements because the mayor had not yet announced his candidacy.

In January 2007, when Obama finally endorsed Daley for re-election, a reporter asked how his "concerns" from 2005 had figured into his endorsement. Again, Obama hedged. "There is no doubt that there remains progress to be made...But ultimately you want to look at the whole record of this administration...The city overall has moved in a positive direction."[69]

Obama's endorsement of Daley was as disappointing as the Stroger endorsement. But it was perhaps less incomprehensible. Considering the power that the mayor has over Chicago's political money, no one planning a run for president could afford to disappoint him. Obama's wife had also worked very briefly in the mayor's office.[70]

But of even greater importance in the Obama-Daley relationship is Obama's chief political strategist, David Axelrod. Since 2004 he has been Mayor Daley's man in the Obama circle.

It was Axelrod who had been trying to spin reporters away from the patronage operation in Daley's office, just one month before the feds began handing down the indictments of summer 2005. Reporters from the *Chicago Sun-Times* had asked Axelrod that June how it was that nearly 500 members of the Hispanic Democratic Organization (one part of the political Machine) were on the city payroll, more than a dozen of them with top-paying positions. "The mayor believes strongly a city work force's only mission is the job of doing taxpayer business and nothing else," Axelrod said. "He's committed to take any step necessary to make sure that happens anywhere if and when it hasn't."[71]

After the indictments were handed down, Axelrod told another reporter, "The so-called 'machine' doesn't exist anymore."[72]

When a no-name candidate had challenged Mayor Daley in 2003, charging that "this city is being stolen dry," and giving examples of apparent fraud in the awarding of minority contracts (such fraud was later revealed), Axelrod had brushed off her complaints: "I don't think anyone who says that either knows the mayor or has paid attention to what's happened in the city."[73]

Again in 2005, Axelrod had been defending Daley against completely separate corruption allegations involving special treatment of Daley friends and contributors, who had been caught defrauding the city, taking bribes and shaking down contractors for political contributions.

"They aren't his friends," Axelrod had told the Associated Press. "I've worked for him for 15 years and I know that what he cares about more than anything is this city. And these people who have besmirched the city—they aren't his friends."[74]

But a lot of them *were* Daley's friends—and family. One was James Duff, a local businessman whose family had raised money for Daley. Duff pleaded guilty to using his 76-year-old mother and a black friend as a phony front for his janitorial business in order to secure $100 million in city contracts set aside for businesses owned by women or minorities.[75]

Another was John Briatta, brother-in-law of the mayor's brother, County Commissioner John Daley. Briatta was sentenced to eighteen months for taking bribes to steer city business to a trucking company.[76]

Briatta was a small-time crook caught up in a big scandal—the so-called hired truck scandal. At the center of it was Donald Tomczak, the man Daley appointed as First Deputy Commissioner of the city Water Department. Tomczak sold contracts to trucking companies in Daley's $40-million-a-year hired-truck program. The payments came in the form of nearly $400,000 in bribes and political contributions—some to an unspecified ward organization referred to in the indictment, and some to candidates for alderman, judge, and other offices.[77]

Where did the contributions go? According to news reports, Mayor Daley and the 11th Ward organization (controlled by the mayor's brother, Cook County Commissioner John Daley) reaped substantial contributions from the companies that had been paying bribes.[78] Tomczak was notorious for all of the typical Machine tactics, such as using promotions and raises to reward his political foot soldiers.

Daley may not have personally known John "Quarters" Boyle, another big player in the truck scandal, but someone in Daley's "Coalition for Better Government" clearly did, according to videotapes obtained by *Chicago Tribune* reporter John Kass.[79] "Quarters" had gained fame when he embezzled $4 million, mostly in coins, from Chicago toll booths in 1992. For reasons that remain unclear, Boyle was hired as a $33-an-hour engineer for the city Department of Transportation after he got out of prison. From there, he showed a similar lack of restraint as he and another city official allegedly shook down the truckers for a combined $200,000. (He returned to jail on fraud and tax charges.)[80]

James Laski, the former city clerk who served eleven months in prison for his role in the scandal, would later say that the mayor "knows more than he says he does."[81]

Everything about Daley's hired truck program was crooked. Tax-payers were shelling out millions to well-connected trucking companies, whose trucks often sat idly all day.[82] City workers were even stealing asphalt from city projects and bribing truck drivers to take it to private job sites.[83] It was so bad that Daley was forced to promise that his campaign would take no more contributions from city contractors.[84] Not to worry, though—he also made it clear that his political Machine organizations would still take their money.[85]

It was in this context—multiple corruption investigations and trials, implausible denials, convictions obtained and the promise of more to come—that Barack Obama endorsed Mayor Daley "as somebody who is constantly thinking about how to make the city better."[86]

Ryan Lizza of *The New Republic*, calling Daley "the symbol of machine politics, corruption, and racism for Hyde Park progressives and Obama's old organizing friends," quoted an Obama ally who framed the situation in the most sympathetic light possible:

> That's part of [Obama's] political savvy...He recognizes that Daley is a powerful man and to have him as an ally is important. While he was a state senator here and moving around in Chicago, he made sure to minimize the direct confrontational approach to people of influence and policymakers and civic leaders. These are the same people now who are very aggressively supporting his campaign.[87]

The idea is that deep down, Obama is a reformer—he's just undercover for now, so that he can advance and *then* show his true colors later. Until then, he has to be "savvy." Remember Obama's words: "If you can win, you should win and get to work doing the people's business."

Here's another way of putting it: If Barack Obama is a reformer, he may be the first reformer ever to become president of the United States before doing anything serious in the name of reform.

Mayor Daley probably could have won without Obama's endorsement, but it saved him from any further headaches at a time when he was dealing with indictments and federal probes. Daley was facing two black opponents in the mayoral primary of 2007.[88] Again, he had survived five terms as the mayor of a racially divided, majority-minority city only by preserving an uneasy truce with the black community's leaders—preventing them from uniting around a credible black opponent.

Ahead of Daley's 2003 re-election, the *Chicago Tribune* gave indications of just how extensive his efforts were in this field:

> Critics have accused Daley of buying off the clergy by awarding them contracts and selling them vacant city lots for $1. They also contend he has co-opted black aldermen with governmental largess and a new ward map designed to protect incumbents.[89]

It also helped to have a popular black senator like Barack Obama at his side, too. Despite having the independence and political capital that came with his popularity, Obama became Daley's newest tool in maintaining the *status quo*.

In Chicago, Barack Obama denied the voters a choice and backed the Machine. He still does. He has never rocked the boat. That is the real-life story of "Change we can believe in."[90]

CHAPTER 2

OBAMA GAMES SPRINGFIELD

I n January 2003, state senator Barack Obama approached his mentor, Senate President Emil Jones, and presented him with an intriguing offer:

"You can make the next U.S. senator."

"Wow, that sounds good!" was Jones's reply. "Got anybody in mind?"

"Yes," Obama said. "Me."[1]

How could Jones "make" a senator? He could do quite a bit, and he did it all. As Jones put it in early 2008, Obama was a smart enough guy to succeed, but "he needed someone who could give him credibility."[2]

Before explaining how Jones punched Obama's ticket to Washington, we should get to know Emil Jones, another Chicago Machine politician who is described as Obama's "political Godfather."[3]

MAKE ME A SENATOR

Jones is portrayed, but not named, in *Dreams from My Father* as "an old ward-heeler who had made the mistake of backing one of the white politicians in the last mayoral election." (Jones had endorsed Jane Byrne for mayor in 1983.[4]) In that book, published before Obama entered the state Senate, Obama was fairly critical of Jones as a man whose main ambition was to take credit for just about everything and get his picture taken with Mayor Harold Washington.

Jones was a product of the patronage system—a far more extensive system when he was young, before the federal courts had established limits. Back then, Jones had been hired as a sewer inspector. His first political volunteer job came in 1960, when Democratic ward-heelers were turning out the populations of entire Chicago cemeteries to vote for John F. Kennedy.

Today, Jones still takes care of his own through the state payroll. His son, Emil Jones III, does not have a college degree, but this did not stop him from landing a $57,000 job with the Illinois Department of Commerce last April.[5] The job had not even been advertised, but it went to young Jones when his father agreed to back the governor's budget plan.[6]

Jones's stepson, John Sterling, owns a technology firm called Synch-Solutions, which received a contract for $700,000 of work for the state budget office in 2007.[7] In that same year, many people were wondering why Jones was so vigorously backing Commonwealth Edison, the utility company, in its fight against lower electricity rates—he went so far as to use a rare legislative procedure to circumvent a majority Senate vote to lower rates.[8] The following month, reporters from the *Chicago Sun-Times* discovered that Synch-Solutions had been on the payroll of Com-Ed's parent company since 2004.[9]

Governor Rod Blagojevich, a Democrat and Jones's close ally, in 2005 rescinded the requirement that the director of mental health at the state's Department of Human Services be a medical doctor. This allowed Jones's wife, Lorrie, to take the position, with a salary of $186,000—an $80,000 raise over her previous salary.[10] That was not enough money for Jones, though, who was reported earlier this year to be giving himself interest-free loans out of his campaign fund.[11]

Again, it is not just Republicans complaining about Jones's self-enrichment, but anti-Machine Democrats as well. State representative Jack Franks, Democratic chairman of the House State Government Administration Committee, is among those who have criticized Jones's participation in the "Friends and Family Plan," suggesting that the families of legislative leaders at least be barred from state and city contracts.[12]

Emil Jones doesn't mind. In Springfield, he's in charge, far more powerful than he would have been if he'd won that congressional race in 1996. He says that Obama "feels like a son to me."[13] And, in fact, the Obama-Jones alliance is key to understanding Obama's time in Springfield. It accounts for nearly all of Obama's legislative accomplishments and explains how he was in any position to become a U.S. senator in 2004.

THE MACHINE-MADE SENATOR

How did Emil Jones "make a U.S. senator" out of Obama?

Jones gave Obama high-profile legislation in its late stages, sometimes taking bills away from their original sponsors. He gave Obama committee assignments that would cement key constituencies for his Senate primary. The most important thing Jones gave Obama was probably the coveted chair of the senate's health committee in 2003, shortly after their conversation. This placed Obama in charge of legislation that affected the Service Employees International Union, which has more than 100,000 members in Illinois.

As his biographer David Mendell puts it, from this position Obama "carried SEIU's water" in Springfield on a wide variety of bills. He would increase benefits for SEIU hospital workers and even force hospitals to post mortality statistics on the Internet along with statistics on staffing levels—it was a way of bullying hospitals into hiring more SEIU staff.[14] As a result, Obama would receive that union's endorsement in his Senate race. It was a very significant development, because most other unions endorsed one of his opponents.[15]

Obama's colleagues at times expressed bitterness about Jones's habit of taking popular, high-profile, must-pass bills away from their writers and champions in the late stages and giving them to Obama to manage in the Senate. Referring to this phenomenon, state senator Rickey Hendon once told a young reporter named Todd Spivak that "no one wants to carry the ball ninety-nine yards all the way to the one-yard line, and then give it to the halfback who gets all the credit and the stats in the record book." Years later, in the *Houston Press*, Spivak wrote that Hendon had been the original sponsor of two bills that Obama often writes and speaks about as if they had been his own. One required the taping of murder interrogations to help eliminate mistakes in the Illinois's death penalty system, and the other was designed to reduce the incidence of racial profiling by the police.[16]

As Jones's political godson, and even long before the conversation about the United States Senate, Obama had the privilege of stealing important bills. Other senators had a name for this practice: "bill-jacking."[17]

Mendell records that as early as 1998, Jones had already done such favors at the prompting of Obama's liberal friends. Abner Mikva, a former congressman and federal judge, had recommended to Jones that he give Obama a popular piece of legislation barring political fundraising on state property and barring lobbyists and contractors from giving gifts to legislators. The bill had enough loopholes to be relatively harmless, but it was a step in the direction of reform. Jones gave it to Obama. Obama proposed it. It passed, 52–4.[18] The "Friends and Family" man, the old ward-heeler, was even capable of making Obama look like a reformer.

After the Democrats' takeover of the Illinois Senate in 2003, and Obama's conversation with Jones about becoming a U.S. senator, Obama's legislative output increased exponentially. He sponsored some 800 bills. Mendell calls Obama's glut of legislative activity in 2003 and 2004 "a consequence of Jones's patronage."[19]

The murder interrogation bill—requiring videotaping of interrogations in all capital cases—was an excellent example of something with a broad bipartisan consensus in all but the minutest details, coming as it did after thirteen death row inmates were found to have been falsely convicted in Illinois.[20] The *Chicago Tribune*, known as the town's more conservative newspaper, had been campaigning vigorously for this bill for more than a year by the time it passed. Jones appointed Obama as the chief Democratic negotiator of its final details.

The alliance between Jones and Obama also had immediate and obvious consequences. Part of the Chicago Machine's work in Springfield is to spread the money around the city, through earmarks and "targeted" grants. Obama did this. In 2003, for example, he and Jones together obtained a $4.5 million earmark for the Chicago-based Muntu Dance Theater to build a cultural center. Obama's wife Michelle sat on the non-profit dance group's board.[21]

Another way Jones could help Obama in his U.S. Senate race was to give him a free pass on more controversial issues. He could remain uninvolved in nasty debates. He always had a habit of voting "present" instead of taking a real recorded vote, and he could now do it without even getting a dirty look.[22] He voted that way about 130 times while serving in the state Senate, and as we shall see in a later chapter, he would sometimes absent himself from tough votes altogether.[23]

OBAMA RETURNS THE FAVOR

All of Jones's investments in making Obama have since paid great dividends. For example, in 2007, Obama requested $11 million in earmarks for Chicago State University, which is one of Jones's pet projects.[24] Jones, who steers millions in state funds to the university, has received about $55,000 in contributions from its trustees, foundation directors, and administrators since 2001.[25] CSU even named their convocation center after Jones and his late wife, Patricia.

More importantly, Jones is suddenly the "godfather" of the Democrats' presidential nominee.

In Springfield, Obama attached himself directly to the same kind of dirty politics he had been endorsing in Chicago. He did what he was told, and they made him a senator.

And he still does what he's told.

Since last year, Jones has been blocking a package of anti-corruption bills, some of which passed the Democrat-controlled Illinois House unanimously.[26] One of them is a gift ban for members of state boards, such as Stuart Levine—the man who helped convicted felon Antoin Rezko steer investments from the state teachers' pension fund toward firms that would give him illegal kickbacks.[27]

The reform bills that Jones is blocking mirror several reform proposals that Obama has promised as a presidential candidate, and so Republican state senator Christine Radogno wrote Obama on July 31, 2007, urging him to talk to Jones and get these reform bills moving. She wrote:

> This list only highlights the proposals that are identical or nearly identical to ideas contained in your proposal. Numerous other

ethical and governmental reforms have been proposed in the Illinois General Assembly and without exception all have been blocked by your longtime mentor Senate President Emil Jones.[28]

Obama did not even respond. His spokesman told a reporter that Radogno's suggestion—the idea that Obama should make a five-minute phone call to his mentor in the name of reform—was "irregular." The Illinois Senate eventually passed a weakened version of just one of the seven reform bills, governing campaign contributions by state contractors.[29] Radogno informs me that the other six bills[30] are still bottled up in the state Senate committees—right where Jones wants them.

Call it filial piety. Senator Obama has not forgotten where he comes from.

"A LOT OF NERVE"

Being the teacher's pet in the state Senate did have some negative consequences for Obama, it seems. For one, it added to his strained relationship with that chamber's black caucus.

This tension helps explain the one recorded incident in Barack Obama's adult life when he nearly got in a fight.

The incident of June 11, 2002 is widely known by those who have studied Obama, but in the course of researching Obama's story, I obtained what I am told is a very rare audio record of what happened on the Senate floor—perhaps one of two in existence. The proceedings of the Illinois Senate are not broadcast on C-Span. The Senate does make audio recordings of the chamber's proceedings, but they are typically destroyed once the transcripts have been typed up. And so this sixteen-minute tape offers a short and rare insight into Obama's career in Springfield.

The clip begins with a typically dull legislative back-and-forth. Conservative senator Steve Rauschenberger, the budget floor manager, argues for senators to sustain Governor George Ryan's budget cuts. Senator Rickey Hendon responds with a passionate speech about the need to override the governor's veto and keep a welfare office open in his district, despite the governor's desire to cut off funding for it.

> Why can't we close some of these corporate loopholes for the rich and powerful, instead of closing places that are needed, like this little DCFS office in my district?... Instead of closing facilities that are needed, that can keep children—children that we all claim to love in this Senate—from being out there on the street, living with people who don't love them and don't care, and just generally suffering through life in Illinois?... Bipartisan cooperation is more than rhetoric, my friend... You have to work with this side of the aisle...

A routine vote takes place, and Hendon's side loses, as expected.

Obama's supporters say that Obama was outside the room when this happened—that he had a proxy vote on his behalf (the importance of this fact will become clear momentarily). But Senator Obama was indeed there, for in this recording he is recognized to speak seconds after that vote concludes.[31] He introduces a group of schoolchildren to the chamber (the lawmakers applaud). After Rauschenberger speaks again, Obama delivers a long, halting and slightly repetitive speech about budget cuts. It sounds very little like the eloquent Obama of 2008.

> The point I think I do want to make, though, is that—you know, there has been a tendency to rhetoric in both sides of this debate. Ah—I would say that although Senator Rauschenberger has

done um, uh, an able job of presenting that side of the aisle's position in this debate, there has been a tendency in this discussion for, uh, just a trace of sanctimony to creep in. . . . In fact, I think, when we start looking at the votes, it will turn out that the governor's office has his favorites, that side of the aisle has its favorites, and it's looking after the—its favorites. And that's fair, that's the nature of the political beast. But I don't want the public to be fooled into thinking somehow, uh, Senator Rauschenberger, despite your able representations, uh—that uh—the uh—y'all have the monopoly, uh, on responsible budgeting.

If this was not the most eloquent speech, it was at least a perfectly respectable representation of his point of view. But no sooner has Obama finished speaking than an irate Hendon has already returned to the microphone, demanding to be recognized:

I just want to say to the last speaker—you've got a lot of nerve to talk about being responsible, and yet you vote to close the DCFS office on the West Side when you wouldn't vote to close the one on the South Side. So I apologize to my Republican friends for my bipartisanship comments, because there are clearly some Democrats on this side of the aisle that don't care about the West Side either, especially the last speaker.

At first, the entire chamber is shocked and silent. The chair asks Obama whether he would like to respond, and shouts suddenly become audible in the background. He finally addresses the chamber, calmly:

I understand Senator Hendon's anger. Actually, it turns—the, uh—I was not aware that I had voted No on that last piece of

> legislation. I would have the Record record that I intended to
> vote Yes. On the other hand I would appreciate the next time,
> my dear colleague Senator Hendon, ask me about a vote before
> he names me on the floor.

Obama ends that sentence with a descending tone of voice. He sounds
just slightly upset. This may have contributed to what happened next.
According to other accounts of this exchange, the two men took their
grievances off the Senate floor. It became very heated—Obama reportedly had to be restrained.[32] Hendon has since made his peace with
Obama and does not discuss the incident with the press anymore.

Obama's relationship with other black politicians in Springfield had
already been tense. In Hendon's case, some of it could be chalked up
to the fact that he was a West-sider and Obama was a South-sider—
these two parts of the black caucus suffered some mutual distrust.[33]
Many of them viewed Obama as an elitist who, as one Springfield
writer put it at the time, "likes people to know he went to Harvard."[34]
Part of it might even stem from the way Obama had thrown Alice
Palmer off the ballot in 1996.

Whatever the reasons, the tension manifested itself in accusations by
some of his black colleagues that Obama was not "authentically black."
Congressman Bobby Rush, the incumbent Democrat whom Obama
challenged for Congress in 2000, told the *Chicago Reader* during that
race that Obama "went to Harvard and became an educated fool...
We're not impressed with these folks with these Eastern elite degrees."[35]
His much meaner criticism may have been his statement that "Barack is
a person who read about the civil rights protests and thinks he knows all
about it... I helped make that history, by blood, sweat, and tears."[36]

The cruelest and most unfair barb of all came from Senator Donne
Trotter, who was also in that 2000 congressional race: "Barack is

viewed in part to be the white man in blackface in our community," he said. "You just have to look at his supporters. Who pushed him to get where he is so fast? It's these individuals in Hyde Park, who don't always have the best interests of the community in mind."[37] By "these individuals," Trotter was referring to white liberals, especially in the University of Chicago academic community.

OBAMA'S CLIMB

Barack Obama does not often talk about Alice Palmer, Todd Stroger, Richard Daley, or Emil Jones. The stories of their roles in his life do not reflect the image Obama has crafted for himself. But they do explain the story of Obama's climb. His shrewdness, hard work, and well-placed patrons, along with an awful lot of luck, would lead him to where he is today.[38]

CHAPTER THREE

THE ACCIDENTAL CANDIDATE

C OUNCIL BLUFFS, Iowa, January 3, 2008—"What do you guys hang from the ladders at firefighters' funerals?"

This may not seem like the most diplomatic question to ask a crowd of firemen, but anything goes tonight in the auditorium of Kirn Junior High School in Council Bluffs, Iowa. The man asking the question is a supporter of John Edwards for the Democratic presidential nomination. He is trying to win converts to his cause during the heated caucus in Council Bluffs' 9th Precinct.

His interlocutors, muscular and culturally conservative public servants, are wearing yellow t-shirts and standing below signs for Senator Chris Dodd's doomed presidential campaign. They are baffled and offended by the question. They are also speechless, and the awkwardness prompts the questioner to answer it himself.

"The American flag!" he says. This exercise in the Socratic method does nothing to dispel the firefighters' confusion. And so he points to the back corner of the room, where a large crowd of Barack Obama's supporters are gathered. They are chanting and clapping, urging the supporters of Dodd and other non-viable candidates to join them in the second round of the caucus.

"Obama doesn't salute the American flag," the man says, with the self-assured air of an expert. *"And"*—he continues as if he's letting them in on a big secret—*"he was sworn in on the Koran!"*

This Edwards backer is doing little to help his cause, as the firemen remain completely unpersuaded. In fact, when it's clear that Dodd won't reach the 15 percent threshold in this precinct for "viability," all of the firefighters ultimately realign with Obama, save one who simply leaves the building in disgust, announcing that he will vote Republican in the fall. Maybe these firemen are angry to hear such lies told about the senator from Illinois. Or perhaps it is because their leader, Chris Sorensen, happens to be married to Obama's precinct captain.

As the debating, cajoling, and negotiating over the last undecided caucus-goers winds down, the realignment process in the 9th Precinct tells the whole story of the 2008 Iowa caucuses. After the first ballot, Clinton has a huge lead with 52 votes, followed by Edwards with 43 and Obama with 39. But of the 31 minor-candidate supporters to realign, only 3 of them go into Clinton's section, just in front of the stage. Edwards gets 12 of them, while Obama gains 15 in the second round.

And then Elle Jacobs—a twenty-year-old first-time voter and the last person in the room to decide—goes over to Edwards instead of staying with her parents in a neutral corner. She tells a reporter in the room why she made her decision: *I just don't like Hillary.*

The bottom line: Clinton is nobody's second choice—her negatives are just too high.[1] If you weren't for her at the beginning of the night, you weren't going to support her at all.

Because of one young woman's decision, John Edwards carries this precinct by a single vote over Hillary, 56 to 55. Obama finishes with 54 votes. It's as close a finish as you can possibly get.

Edwards gets 7 county delegates from the precinct, while Clinton and Obama get 6 each. That single delegate, while it does not change the statewide result, does mean Clinton's final total of county delegates will *not* be rounded up to 30 percent (a virtual tie for second place with Edwards) but instead is rounded down to 29 percent—firmly in third place.

Elle Jacobs has killed Hillary Clinton in Iowa.

As this scene unfolds in western Iowa, the same thing is happening throughout the state, and mostly to Obama's benefit. He is winning a huge upset victory because, if the supporters of Dodd, Joe Biden, Bill Richardson, and Dennis Kucinich have to settle, they're not going to settle for Clinton. Were this a primary, where no voter is ever asked his second choice, Hillary might have won—certainly, the polls suggested, it would be much closer. Had the Democrats not established the "viability" rule for minor candidates, or had the threshold been set lower than 15 percent, Obama wouldn't have had all these second-choice votes to pick up. Iowa's caucus process makes the difference.

By the time voters reach their cars to drive home, the radio announces Obama's improbable and improbably large victory. Clinton has lost the January 3 Iowa caucuses to Obama, 38 to 29 percent, despite having led him by 8 points in surveys taken as late as December 29.[2] And for Obama's long race to the nomination, the third-place Clinton finish is nearly as important as his own victory.

It is his dream come true and her worst-case scenario. It was not supposed to happen this way.

The night ends any practical hopes John Edwards ever had of becoming president, but it is also the beginning of the end for Hillary

Clinton, after all her hard work over the years and her undying desire to win the nomination.

Thanks to another stroke of bad luck, the exclusion of two states where she was bound to do well (Michigan and Florida), she would never hold the lead in the media's count of estimated pledged delegates to the Democratic National Convention.

Barack Obama, just three years removed from the obscurity of the Illinois state Senate, is the frontrunner for the Democratic nomination for president of the United States. It is an occurrence so unlikely that MSNBC's Chris Matthews attributed it to divine intervention: "He's almost *delivered to us* through Indonesia, through a Kenyan father."[3] Earlier in the night, Matthews put it even more directly: "The biblical term for it, since we're in a biblical era, is 'deliverance.' We're being picked up and moved to where we have to be."

But if your eyes aren't so misty, Obama's path to the presidential nomination looks less divine and more serendipitous.

"I'M NOT ONE OF THOSE PEOPLE"

Senator Clinton must still be wondering how this could have happened. How could she have lost the nomination that was hers? Things should have turned out differently. If only the Democratic Party's rules had not been the precise blend of arcane and populist that they are.

Some of Hillary's supporters still object that she deserved the nomination. Their claims are flimsy, but not meritless—and they're worth examining as we track Obama's lucky turns. Just like Al Gore in 2000, Clinton won the popular vote (if you include Michigan and Florida, whose January primaries violated national Democratic rules). Alternatively, had the Democrats' system of picking a nominee more resembled that of the Republicans—with winner-take-all primaries—she would have won the pledged delegate race 1,784 to 1,469, without even counting her wins in Florida or Michigan.[4]

But playing by the established rules of the game, which both candidates knew ahead of time, Obama won, fair and square.

He was smart about it, too.

It helped that one of his aides, Brandon Neal, opened the channels to Oprah Winfrey, allowing Obama to bring the nation's highest-profile television celebrity into his camp.[5]

Obama also showed he understands the American maxim that "money is the mother's milk of politics." Since the 2006 elections, according to the Center for Responsive Politics, Obama has spread around more than $380,000 from his leadership PAC, Hopefund, to Democrats in key primary states and to other superdelegates.

He gave $30,000 each to the Iowa Senate Majority fund and the Iowa House Truman Fund. In New Hampshire, he gave $15,000 each to the state-level Committee to Elect House Democrats and Friends of a Democratic Senate. Both of New Hampshire's congressmen got $9,000 from Obama, as did all three of Iowa's Democratic congressmen.[6]

Obama's campaign originally and implausibly denied that the Hopefund donations had anything to do with his presidential campaign—a denial they had to retract one week later, as Obama's presidential campaign staff had carefully picked out the recipients. But there was nothing illegal or immoral about any of this—it was just smart politics.

It was the same old way everyone does it.

As the campaign neared its end, Obama graciously—and wisely—asked his donors to pay off the Clinton campaign's $11 million debt, rather than leave the Clintons to pay it themselves.[7] The knowledge that this would happen probably helped ease her out of the race, so that there would be no floor fight and no bitter, contested convention.

Not only did Obama do all of the right things, but he was also genuinely lucky—luck has in fact characterized his career. Surely he must be surprised by his success. He would not have believed it in 2004, when, right after his election to the United States Senate, he said, "I can unequivocally say I will not be running for national office in four years, and my entire focus is making sure that I'm the best possible senator on behalf of the people of Illinois."[8]

Four days later, he would give blunt answer to a reporter who asked why he had "ruled out" a 2008 run for president: "I am a believer in knowing what you're doing when you apply for a job," Senator-elect Obama had said. "And I think that if I were to seriously consider running on a national ticket, I would essentially have to start now, before having served a day in the Senate. There might be some people who are comfortable with doing that, but I'm not one of those people."[9]

Obama was until recently just another friendly face in the Hyde Park neighborhood—the kind of guy who wanders the aisles at 57th Street Books and waves to the neighbors as he ducks out onto his back porch for a cigarette.[10] Now he has become his party's presidential nominee, an unprecedented feat for a freshman senator who is just halfway through his first term. Even if he did not think himself fit for the job, Iowa caucus-goers considered him fitter than his chief rivals.

The Iowa caucuses were not the first time Obama has enjoyed success due to the failures of others. In fact, if not for two men and their messy divorces, Obama might be giving speeches and chairing committee hearings in Springfield, Illinois to this very day.

"GOD'S PLAN": OBAMA WINS BY DEFAULT

Can accidents happen often enough and at just the right times and places to propel a man all the way to the presidency? In the case of Barack Obama, the answer might turn out to be yes. If the extent of corruption in Chicago seems hard to believe, Obama's rise in just the last five years seems even more extraordinary.

Step back to Obama's election to the U.S. Senate in 2004. Democratic congressman Bobby Rush of Chicago, once a bitter rival but now an Obama supporter, speaks about that race in terms of Divine Providence. "I would characterize the Senate race as being a race where Obama was, let's say, blessed and highly favored," Rush told the *New York Times* earlier this year. "That's not routine. There's something else going on...I know that that was God's plan."[11]

In January 2003, Obama was a state senator representing Hyde Park and several poor, black neighborhoods on Chicago's South Side. Despite being discouraged by several of Chicago's leading Democratic lights, he threw his hat into the ring for a run at the Senate seat being vacated by Republican senator Peter Fitzgerald.

Fitzgerald was a fairly conservative (and certainly independent) senator who never played nice with Illinois's Republican establishment or with the so-called "Illinois Combine"—the bipartisan group of public officials who ran a statewide operation resembling Chicago in its disregard for good government. Fitzgerald could afford to be independent—he had won his seat in 1998 by spending $13.5 million of his own money[12] against embattled incumbent Democrat Carol Moseley Braun. Even then, he had won by less than three percentage points.[13] Illinois was already turning "blue."

Peter Fitzgerald rejected the ethical and legal truce that several Democrats and Republicans of the Combine had established. Key to the Combine's survival had been the bipartisan assurance that the state's U.S. senators were "part of the gang"—that they would recommend pliant, "see-no-evil" individuals for the position of U.S. Attorney for the Northern District of Illinois. That way, business could continue as usual. If an outsider, a determined non-Illinoisan were appointed as U.S. Attorney, it would open a floodgate of prosecutions.

In September 2001, the Combine's nightmare came to pass. Senator Fitzgerald demanded and secured from President Bush the appointment of U.S. Attorney Patrick Fitzgerald (no relation), who has since initiated scores of public corruption investigations and sent several officials from both parties to prison.

The politicians fear Patrick Fitzgerald. If you can't tell just from watching Mayor Daley's aides marching handcuffed into the gray-bar hotel, then the trial of Antoin Rezko, Obama's friend and fundraiser, should give you some idea. A witness testified that Rezko had assured him in February 2005 not to worry about a subpoena he had received, because former Speaker of the House Dennis Hastert (a Republican) was going to get Fitzgerald replaced as U.S. Attorney.[14]

As for *Senator* Fitzgerald, the political classes of both parties were less than pleased with him for bringing prosecutor Fitzgerald into town, and for a few of his unpredictable votes. GOP luminaries such as Peoria-based Congressman Ray LaHood and GOP chairwoman Judy Baar Topinka made it known prior to the primary that Fitzgerald would have little party support in the next election. Lacking the will to take on the Combine politically, Fitzgerald bowed out gracefully rather than seek re-election in 2004.

His decision was very encouraging for the national Democratic Party, which already seemed certain to lose ground in the U.S. Senate that year thanks to several seats that were opening up in the South. Illinois is one of the states that has turned from "purple" to "deep blue" in the last decade. On the same night in 2002 that Republicans had enjoyed nationwide victories, seizing control of the U.S. Senate, expanding their House majority, and winning state-level races everywhere else, the Illinois GOP had unraveled. They lost the governorship and control of the state Senate (Democrats already controlled the state's House of Representatives), as well as just about every statewide office. As the 2004 election began, the disgraced former governor, Republican George Ryan, was facing a future in prison because of a massive bribery scandal. And President George W. Bush was guaranteed to lose Illinois again by a large margin.

Republicans had not completely given up on the state, though. In their primary they chose a promising young conservative, whose personal wealth and connections would surely be an asset in the campaign. More about him in a moment.

Several ambitious Democratic politicians saw that the chances were excellent for a pickup, including, Dan Hynes, the state comptroller; state senator Barack Obama; Gery Chico, chief of staff to Mayor Richard M. Daley; and liberal talk radio host Nancy Skinner. And then there was eccentric multi-millionaire Blair Hull.

Early on, Hynes looked like the clear favorite. He had already been elected statewide. People knew his name. In a different race, Hynes could have led wire-to-wire. But when one of your opponents is willing to spend $28.7 million of his own money on a primary, your frontrunner status becomes a bit precarious. And that is just what Hull did, blanketing the state with television spots and running ads all around the Internet, according to Chicago journalist David Mendell.[15] The media saturation sucked the wind out of Hynes's campaign, dragging him down into a second-place tie in the polls with Obama.

In the final weeks, everything was pointing toward a Hull victory. He was about to buy himself a Senate seat. On February 22, 2004, he led the race, with 27 percent, to 17 percent each for Obama and Hynes.[16] If the primary had been held on Tuesday, February 24, instead of Tuesday, March 16, Barack Obama might have remained in relative obscurity.

But then, on February 27, 2004, all Hull broke loose. Hull's divorce files were released to the public.[17]

Twelve days earlier, the *Tribune* had reported that Hull's ex-wife had filed for an order of protection against him. After this report, Hull had kept his lead in the polls, but the paper kept pressuring him to release the divorce file. When he finally gave in, the results weren't pretty.

Hull's second ex-wife had called him "a violent man." Here's one unpleasant story from his ex-wife that made it into the *Tribune*: Hull "hung on the canopy bar of my bed, leered at me and stated, 'Do you want to die? I am going to kill you...'."[18]

This was news to most Illinois voters, but it wasn't really news to Obama advisor David Axelrod. Axelrod had originally learned of Hull's Achilles heel in 2002, when he considered working for the wealthy former professional gambler. He had heard rumors that Hull had gone through a messy divorce, complete with allegations of abuse. He asked Hull whether there was anything to it, and Hull admitted that there had been accusations of "physical and mental abuse." Axelrod then asked him the key question—were they true?

The multimillionaire gave Axelrod a look that Axelrod would later describe as "glacial." Then Hull simply said, "There's no paper on that."

Hull's answer, Axelrod would later tell David Mendell, was deeply unsatisfactory.[19]

Axelrod then became Obama's consultant. He insists that he never used the abuse story against Hull—that he considered the information "privileged."[20]

There's no evidence Obama's campaign was the force behind dragging down Blair Hull, but there is this set of facts:

- Axelrod knew about Hull's marital problems
- Axelrod's former employer, the *Chicago Tribune*, unearthed Hull's marital problems just weeks before the primary, and not until Hull had already sucked the wind out of Hynes's sails
- Obama benefited—immensely—from these revelations

By primary day, Hull was a goner. He had sunk from frontrunner status to a pathetic third-place finish with 10.8 percent. His support, it appears, mostly transferred to Barack Obama, who surged to a stunning 52.8 percent finish and became the Democrats' Senate candidate.

WHIPS, CAGES, AND . . . ALAN KEYES

Barack Obama's history of effortless wins in significant elections tempts one to search for some divine or astrological explanation.[21] The real reason, however, is that Obama was lucky. And as his first, unopposed election had demonstrated, he also knew how to make his own luck.

After Hull's self-destruction in the 2004 Senate primary, Obama's streak of luck continued. He probably could have won the race—he began that race twenty-two points ahead of his Republican opponent.[22] But had Obama been engaged in a tough race, he could never have gained national fame as quickly as he did. If he had been busy all summer campaigning in Illinois, he would never have been able to do what he did that summer, which would lead to the situation in which reporters could seriously ask him about a presidential run before he had even been sworn in as a U.S. senator.

Obama did not face a serious race in November 2004, for lightning was about to strike a second time. I was there to see part of this amazing story unfold.

On the same day Democrats chose Obama, Republicans had settled a heated primary of their own. The winner was Jack Ryan (no relation to the former governor), whom one could almost call a conservative Barack Obama—smart, youthful, handsome, and eloquent, a Harvard alumnus. Ryan knew his issues, and he spoke like a limited-government conservative who could hold together the entire Republican coalition: voters who cared about taxes, government spending, abortion, gun rights, national security—the whole package.

Like Obama, he was impressive. He lacked the abrasiveness and baggage that career politicians usually bring to a race. He had a Rolodex full of financial services colleagues who were likely to help raise money for his campaign. He was willing to spend some of his own money as well, and he did spend some of it on amusing advertisements during the primary—they featured a bureaucrat furiously chasing after dollar bills in a whirlwind. His biggest liability seemed to be that he shared the same last name as the corrupt former governor.

Ryan was also the ex-husband of actress Jeri Ryan, who is famous for her roles on *Boston Public* and *Star Trek: Voyager*. Their divorce was a potential problem for his candidacy—as I headed to a lunch interview with candidate Ryan, a California judge had already announced his intention to release Ryan's divorce file. The *Chicago Tribune* (again) had sued, successfully, to have the file released. At that time, I was a cub reporter for the conservative magazine *Human Events*. My experienced colleague John Gizzi and I lunched with Ryan and one of his political consultants in early June at The Monocle, which stands in the shadow of the Senate office buildings. We chatted with Ryan about policy, Illinois politics, his campaign and his career over an expensive lunch of steak and potatoes.

John and I had agreed in advance that he would ask the big question: Is there anything embarrassing in that divorce file that could hurt your candidacy? The question was (perhaps unnecessarily) asked off the record, for, more than anything else, we just wanted a straight answer to inform our own analysis of the race. We did not want to overestimate his chances, only to appear foolish later. The divorce file would be available to the public within days, so we did not see why he would be anything but fully honest about it. Especially *off the record*.

Ryan did not hesitate for one moment in giving his answer: Absolutely not. The file contained nothing to worry about whatsoever.

At that point, his consultant[23] sent Ryan off to the restroom. ("Just get out of here, Jack, will you?") He then spoke to us in a hushed voice. "When that file is opened," he said, "all you're going to see is what a wonderful guy he is, and how much he loves his autistic son. Jack values his privacy, and he didn't want all of the details about his son leaked out to the press. That's all it is. There's nothing to hide. You will be positively edified by what's in there."

I left that lunch feeling that Ryan had as good as chance as anyone of keeping Fitzgerald's seat in Republican hands. At least he would put up a real race against Obama. And the divorce file must really not be a problem. Why would he lie to us when it was to be released any day? His consultant had actually gone so far as to say: "When you see that file, *you're almost going to think this guy is Mother Teresa.*"

On June 22, 2004, Ryan's file was made public, and it did not bring to mind any aspect of Mother Teresa's life that I am familiar with. Jeri had accused Jack of taking her to sex clubs described as having whips and cages. He made her cry by pressuring her to have sex with him in public.

Given its lewd nature, this revelation was bound to create weeks of bad press. It might not have ended Ryan's career had he been a sitting senator—in fact, by today's Washington standards, it is a rather pedestrian scandal (it *was* with his wife). But for a young wannabe at the beginning of his political career, it was fatal. Even worse was the way he had handled it—he had lied to the public, to the voters, to members of his own party.

He had lied to us, too. As soon as we found out, John and I agreed that all of the material from our conversation was now fair game. We co-authored a piece describing the experience, and at the end predicted an easy win for that guy with the funny name.[24]

Ryan was eventually forced to relinquish the nomination, and Republicans failed to find a suitable replacement. For a brief time there was a chance that former Chicago Bears coach Mike Ditka would run—perhaps one of the few Republicans who could carry Illinois. But Ditka's wife reportedly vetoed this undertaking,[25] and the state party could find no one else interested in cleaning up Ryan's mess. They finally dredged up Alan Keyes, a perennial all-purpose candidate who was particularly ill-suited for this race. Obama wrote that Keyes was "an ideal opponent; all I had to do was keep my mouth shut and start planning my swearing-in ceremony."[26]

Keyes went on to lose by the largest margin in Illinois history. As Obama describes it, "My campaign had gone so well that it looked like a fluke."[27]

THE ROAD TO BOSTON

The long, lopsided contest did more than simply guarantee Obama's election to the United States Senate. It also propelled his rise within the party and led to his being chosen as the 2004 convention keynote speaker.

For months, lacking any opposition, Obama devoted his time to helping Democratic candidates in other states, raising money and campaigning for his Democratic colleagues. He would contribute and raise over $1 million for the Democratic Senatorial Campaign Committee in the lead-up to the 2004 election, including $262,000 that his campaign contributed directly to help Democratic Senate candidates in thirteen states.[28] He stumped for Senate Minority Leader Tom Daschle in South Dakota, for Senator Russ Feingold and presidential nominee John Kerry in Wisconsin, among others. Obama contributed $12,500 to the Nevada Democratic Party (home of Senate Whip Harry Reid), $12,500 to the Kentucky Democratic Party, $10,000 to the South Dakota Democratic Party, $5,000 to the Georgia Democratic Party, and $10,000 to help the Senate campaign of Betty Castor in Florida.[29]

Obama was already becoming a hot commodity in Democratic circles before even taking office. He writes in *The Audacity of Hope* that he knows nothing of how he came to be chosen to give the keynote address at the Democratic convention that summer,[30] but the monetary help he gave other Democrats in that cycle surely played a role in the decision. His July speech would make him a national figure and a representative of his party's future. Further, Obama's spectacular 2004 would in turn make possible his 2008. Just call him the luckiest man alive—and a man who knew how to exploit his luck.

What lesson is to be taken from Barack Obama's good fortune? It would make waste of a good political story to conclude simply that he is touched by a beneficent God, or even guided by some evil power. The relevant conclusion is that Obama is currently running the first real political campaign of his life. Yes, he did make a run for Congress in 2000, in which he had a Democratic opponent, but that had been completely hopeless from the start. By the end, he was just going through the motions.[31]

This time, it is for real. This is his first campaign ever, and it's for the highest office in the land.

TABULA RASA

Obama writes that in 1983, when he decided he wanted to be a community organizer, "There wasn't much detail to the idea ... When classmates in college asked me just what it was that a community organizer did, I couldn't answer them directly. Instead, I'd pronounce on the need for change. Change in the White House ... Change in the Congress ... Change in the mood of the country."[32]

One cannot help but compare this to Obama's decision to run for president. There isn't much detail to the idea, so he pronounces on the need for "change." Somehow, it works for him.

This is partly because, as one writer put it in January, Obama has entered this race as "an idealized candidate unsullied by political competition."[33]

Politicians in America are not generally well regarded. They almost necessarily pick up their unflattering (and often accurate) image when they pass through the gauntlet of the adversarial campaign process. They start to look like liars and cheats and fools because of all the bitter accusations and counter-accusations, gaffes and lies. It's the way the system works at its best. We remember "POTATOE," not Dan Quayle's seven-point defense plan. We remember Howard Dean's scream and John Kerry's "I actually did vote for the $87 billion before I voted against it," and Bob Dole's angry "Stop lying about my record!"

Not everyone can be as lucky as Obama and avoid competition. He hasn't really had to play the game. He's never been the bad guy who throws elbows in public. And he has never had to campaign on a record of ideas or accomplishments, either. This sets him apart from nearly every politician who reaches the pinnacle of political life, at which he now finds himself.

Once luck had put him in the right place, Obama worked hard at Iowa's retail politics and succeeded—again, fortunate to have the opponents he did. His victory at the Democratic convention this summer will not have been a result of mere luck, but Obama still won his pivotal Iowa victory because Clinton was no one's second choice. Once her inevitability had been shattered, the geography and mechanics of the process (for example, the use of caucuses instead of primaries in key states, the dominance of black voters in Southern primaries) worked heavily in his favor.

Given the unusual nature of Obama's victories, the Clinton campaign's reference to him as an "unvetted" candidate has merit. He has few political accomplishments, and the ones he does have remain relatively unknown. His personal life is largely unknown as well, save for what he himself has written. As one Democratic operative told *Rolling Stone*, "People don't come to Obama for what he's done, they come because of what they hope he can be."[34]

Obama's ambiguity has given rise to many false ideas and expectations, both negative and positive. All of the preposterous negative ideas about Obama—that he is a closeted Muslim sworn in on a Koran,[35] that he does not salute the flag[36]—have the same origin as the surprisingly widespread and false idea that he is a reformer, or that he espouses some "new politics" that will revolutionize the country and change the way things are done in Washington.

Finally, Obama has never had to attack or demonize Republicans in public, because he has never faced a credible one in any election. Before very recently, the closest he comes is the occasional disparaging remark about the sitting president, whom even Republicans are hesitant to defend at this point. Obama even enjoys the luxury of being able to praise and refer favorably in his speeches and debates to President Ronald Reagan—the man whom he blames as mostly responsible for hardening the political divisions in America.[37] Obama's public praise for Reagan gives him an opportunity to gain respect or at least understanding from conservative voters.

Because of his winning rhetoric, Obama is at times compared to Reagan, the man they called "The Great Communicator." But the comparison is facile, ignoring the decades that Reagan spent articulating a clear philosophy, or the time that he spent as governor of the nation's most populous state.

Long before he sought the presidency, Reagan wrote extensively on policy, demonstrating a comprehensive view of governance that clashed with the established thought of his day.[38] He also appeared in public to

debate and discuss matters of policy, both outside of the political context—as in his debate with William F. Buckley Jr. over the Panama
Canal Treaty—and within it, most famously in his televised speech on
behalf of Barry Goldwater in 1964. That address, "A Time for Choosing," was unlike anything we see in politics today, replete with policy
content and pointed attacks on government interference with the economy and liberal weakness in the face of Communism. Reagan's overt
ideological rigor forms an essential part of his story. It helped him create a new conservatism that later severed the Republican Party from
the nostrums of the Nixon era. It formed a large part of his appeal to
voters.

Obama's appeal is of the opposite nature. Biographer David Mendell
cites "his ingenious lack of specificity" as one of the virtues that has
"most abetted his career in politics... While talking or writing about a
deeply controversial subject, he considers all points of view before cau-
tiously giving his own often risk-averse assessment, an opinion that
often appears so universal that people of various viewpoints would
consider it their own."[39] It is for this reason that a Democratic operative has called him "a kind of human Rorschach test."[40]

The Reagan era created today's divisive politics, Obama writes.
After him, "[n]o longer was economic policy a matter of weighing
trade-offs between competing goals... You were for either tax cuts or
tax hikes, small government or big government... In politics, if not in
policy, simplicity was a virtue."[41]

Of course, this is because Reagan had a clear philosophy that everyone understood, even those who disagreed. It held that government
needed to *stop* trying to weigh goals as a step toward engineering a
solution, *stop* choosing winners and losers, and to *stop* causing the
social and economic problems that liberal policies—however thoroughly weighed-out—had created.

Obama has a philosophy too. He writes about it, as we will see in a later chapter, but he does not speak about it very often. In writing, he also candidly explains the effect of his opacity and lack of specificity on voters: "I am new enough on the national political scene that I serve as a blank screen on which people of vastly different political stripes project their own views. As such, I am bound to disappoint some, if not all, of them."[42]

Obama's campaign has adopted a conscious strategy of sticking to rhetoric over issues and winning an election based on personality—it is a feat that Obama may well pull off. As the *Washington Post* noted, Obama's message of unity and hope "did not come out of nowhere." David Axelrod, the Chicago campaign consultant, long ago hatched the idea that Democrats' campaigns "should revolve more around personality than policy."[43]

So far, Obama's campaign has worked hard not to forfeit this advantage of ambiguity. But as Obama predicts, the disappointment will come as soon as his amorphous political rhetoric crystallizes into something of substance. At the very least, it has to happen if he becomes president. That may be where the dream ends for his enthusiastic following.[44]

CHAPTER FOUR

OBAMESSIAH

W hen I mentioned that I might write a book about Barack Obama, a liberal friend warned me that such a project could adversely affect our close relationship. Knowing me to be a practicing Roman Catholic, she asked how I would feel about a lengthy hatchet job on Pope Benedict XVI.

Not sensing the underlying gravity of the conversation, I laughed and remarked that that sort of piece is published every day. "Besides, why stop with the pope?" I asked. "Would you compare it to an attack on Jesus Christ?"

"Maybe."

I laughed, but she was giving me a stern look.

She was serious.

It was through conversations like this one that I first began to appreciate just how much Barack Obama means to so many people. Quite a bit, I learned, and the impression was reinforced by all of the hate mail I got when news leaked that I was writing this book.

To put so much stock in a politician is to invite disappointment. My time covering Congress reinforced in my mind the Psalmist's adage: "Put not your trust in princes."[1] Politicians are far less impressive people than the pageantry of congressional proceedings or cable television news would suggest. Most of them are just bad people. As Occam's Razor exhorts us to consider the simplest explanation to be the best, so do Washington reporters often presume that the most corrupt explanation of legislative and political activity is also the truest. It's a good way of being right most of the time.

As bemused as I was by my friend's naïve and inordinate faith in the young senator—by the idea that this man is somehow unlike all the others—the comparison between Obama and Christ was a bit jarring. It says quite a bit about how a good number of Obama's followers view him. He inspires visceral emotions, creating such scenes as the following, from newspaper coverage of his early April trip to Montana:

> Many people left the arena quickly after Obama did, but one man was so moved by the possibility of hope and change that he sat quietly in the stands and cried.[2]

It is hard to tell from the story whether Doug Frandsen was the man crying, but his name begins the following paragraph, and he offers an equally humorous quotation:

> Doug Frandsen said Obama represents hope that there's something better for this country. The Missoula man said Obama is charismatic, but it isn't his charisma that speaks to him. It's his message.

"I don't think I've experienced anything quite like it. I
thought the Rolling Stones was [sic] good. This is better,"
Frandsen said.[3]

There is undoubtedly a religious component to "Obamania." The
Reverend Jesse Jackson, himself a former presidential candidate, com-
mented that Obama is running a "theological campaign"—that "[a]t
some point, he took off his arms and grew wings." At the University
of Texas, crowds sang "Obama-leluja" at his approach.[4] Onlookers
faint at his speeches with alarming frequency compared to other campaigns.[5] In Dallas, 17,000 people applauded when he stopped a
speech to announce that he had to *blow his nose*.[6]

"It changes the whole world," is how film director Spike Lee
described Obama's nomination and the chance of an Obama victory.
"It changes the way America is looked upon. It changes the whole par-
adigm."[7]

David Yepsen, the *Des Moines Register's* dean of Iowa political journalism, wrote a piece beginning with the words "Oh, Oh, Oh Obama"
to mark the senator's September 2006 visit to the town of Indianola.
"Nobody's got anything bad to say about Obama. Whenever any of the
other candidates show up, you hear grumbling about their being too
old, too green, too liberal, not liberal enough, had their turn, can't win
or been there and done that."[8]

MSNBC anchor Chris Matthews has been unapologetic in his
Obama-cheerleading, professing on air that when he sees Obama he
gets "a thrill going up my leg." In an interview with the *New York
Observer*, Matthews compared Obama to Mozart. And then he compared him to Christ:

> I've been following politics since I was about five…I've never
> seen anything like this. This is bigger than Kennedy. [Obama]

comes along, and he seems to have the answers. This is the New Testament.[9]

Some have jokingly called him "Obamessiah." A blog titled "Is Barack Obama the Messiah?" exists to document the fawning press coverage he receives, and it is an invaluable resource for finding many and diverse—and really, really funny—examples of Obama delusions.[10] Click here and you find something merely unrealistic. Click there and you'll find something delusional. Click over there, and you find comparisons between Obama and Jesus Christ. Serious comparisons, not joking ones like the one Chris Matthews made.

Ezra Klein, associate editor of *The American Prospect*, is a talented liberal writer. He probably got too caught up in the moment when he wrote:

> Obama's finest speeches...enmesh you in a grander moment, as if history has stopped flowing passively by, and, just for an instant, contracted around you, made you aware of its presence, and your role in it. He is not the Word made flesh, but the triumph of word over flesh, over color, over despair...Obama is, at his best, able to call us back to our highest selves, to the place where America exists as a glittering ideal, and where we, its honored inhabitants, seem capable of achieving it, and thus of sharing in its meaning and transcendence.[11]

Martin Snapp of the Bay Area *Contra Costa Times*, after comparing Obama to Moses, King David, and Luke Skywalker all in the same column (and no, none of it is in jest), gets to the really good part. He writes that the candidate's followers "love him because he's taught them to love themselves." He then explains why Obama is unlike every other politician:

Clinton's supporters think she would be the best president. Ditto for McCain's. But the Obamaphiles want something more: They believe the country is going down the tubes, and they consider it their patriotic duty to lay aside all the old differences that have divided us for the past 40 years and work together for the common good.[12]

More extraordinary than the suggestion that Obama is the first presidential candidate in four decades to work for the common good is the news from singer-songwriter-violinist Lili Haydn, writing in the *Huffington Post*. She reports (one must wonder who her sources are) that Obama has found his way into America's bedrooms and is spicing up sex lives across the nation:

> Barack Obama is inspiring us like a desert lover, a Washington Valentino... [C]ouples all over America are making love again and shouting "yes we can" as they climax![13]

Mark Morford of the *San Francisco Chronicle* begins his June 6, 2008, column in a way that makes you *think* he isn't being serious. But after several paragraphs like the following, the reader cannot be certain:

> Many spiritually advanced people I know... identify Obama as a Lightworker, that rare kind of attuned being who has the ability to lead us not merely to new foreign policies or health care plans or whatnot, but who can actually help usher in *a new way of being on the planet*, of relating and connecting and engaging with this bizarre earthly experiment. These kinds of people actually help us *evolve*.[14]

Wow.

Obama's followers provide further gems when they write letters to the editor in praise of their political savior. Take this one, for example:

> I'm taking a special look at Barack Obama because he's a lot closer to a Jesus-type than the other candidates, by quite a bit. What if God decided to incarnate as men preaching "hope and change." And what if we didn't recognize them, because we are so dull, and let them slip away, not availing ourselves of the opportunity to be led by God![15]

Lest anyone think that Obama's followers merely compare him to the Word of God, a pastor in Jamaica did the opposite—comparing God's word to *him*:

> Obamian hope moves beyond the past and seeks to proactively conceptualise and create the future. It does not just wait for the future to come; it contributes to its shaping and coming. It pulls the future to itself and pushes itself towards the future.

Biblical hope is similar.[16]

By quite a bit, these Obama-reactions outdo any praise the Luo tribesman could confer upon him during his 2006 visit to his father's clan in Kenya:

> A handful of the older women danced and pranced in song, at one point showering Obama with these words in Luo: "It's not just God we praise, but Obama too."[17]

God and Obama. At least the Kenyans have the good sense to distinguish the two. I know that anyone can make blog posts on Obama's website, but will someone at the campaign *please* take down that picture of the grey piece of sheet metal, spray-painted in black: "Obama Is God"?[18]

And does Obama really need his own national seal, produced by his campaign, complete with the eagle, arrows, and fascia, plus an *ad hoc* attempt at the Latin for "Yes, we can!" in place of the national motto? "*Vero, Possumus!*"

Another blog on the campaign website begins with the writer witnessing someone shake Obama's hand. It goes on to resemble the Gospel stories of sick people hoping to touch even the hem of Christ's garments,[19] or hoping that Saint Peter's shadow might pass over them and bring healing:[20]

> As the guy drew back his hand I asked him, "You shook his hand didn't you?" Happily the guy said "Yes." I then said, "give me some of that" and the guy shook my hand with the same hand he had just clasped with Barack's. A woman friend of mine who was standing next to me saw me shake hands with the guy. I turned to her and said "He [the guy] just shook hands with Barack," to which she responded... "Hey, give it up." We then shook hands. She then turned to the person next to her and shook hands. This chain of hand shakes went on for about five or six more persons.[21]

Obama's sister, meanwhile, tells crowds,

> To get to know him is to fall in love with him... They're not just falling in love with him, but they're falling in love with themselves, and with their country.[22]

A younger and more sober-minded liberal writer worried in the *Harvard Crimson* about the "Ron Paulization" of Barack Obama. He feared that Obama's supporters were beginning to look foolish as his campaign subtly encouraged his establishment as an icon rather than a political candidate. He also feared that in their reverence for Obama, his supporters were beginning to divide the Democratic Party by demonizing Hillary Clinton.

> Although much of this Obama-obsession has been a grassroots phenomenon, out of Obama's control—as in the case of Ron Paul—the Obama campaign has done little to quell the tide of Obama hero-worship and Hillary bashing... While "change" is indeed a fundamental part of Obama's platform, failing to adequately link this message to genuine political issues laid the groundwork for the kind of character-over-substance mentality of many Obama supporters.[23]

But there is an important distinction, even if a significant and vocal minority of Paul's followers came close to such adulation for their candidate. They were usually throwing themselves stridently into obscure, wonkish debates. Right or wrong—in some cases just plain crazy—they were passionate about a set of *ideas*. Many of them will engage heated policy discussions for hours, defending the gold standard with such convictions that you would almost think they had themselves invented gold.

Ron Paul and Obama are similar only in that both have passionate supporters. Obama's supporters, however, are not necessarily passionate about ideas. Perhaps they do like the idea of "free" health care, but the ins and outs of policy details are not the point, in their minds.

Obama does not present ideas in any fashion comparable to Paul. Not in public, anyway—his books and record are much better resources for understanding his ideology, as we shall see. Obama presents not ideas but *feelings*. He is the candidate of emotivism. Obamian passion is based on the persona that his followers have created for Obama in their own minds. Many don't know who the man really is. They certainly don't know about Chicago.

Many admit they have never cracked either of his books. Tell them that he did not grow up as an underprivileged child, and they become confused. Mention that he threw all of his opponents off the ballot in 1996 in order to win his first election, and they won't even believe you. He leaves so much to the imagination. No wonder people write of him as a "desert lover," as "the triumph of word over flesh," or even as an incarnation of God himself.

HOW DARE YOU?

When news emerged that I was writing a book critical of Obama (the title must have given it away), I began to receive e-mails from his supporters. The more civil ones expressed the same charming naïvete about the candidate that my friend had displayed. This one came from a fellow graduate of Columbia's Graduate School of Journalism:

> I am ashamed that someone with intelligence from my generation would go to this length, potentially spoiling the first and only honorable political moment of our time...

The first and only honorable political moment of our time! This one was in the same vein:

> Without knowing, you could very well quell an opportunity for this country to gain some real vision. Of which, we all benefit...Do you really want to risk repeating that history again?

Another from overseas:

I am sure that many people in the US, when hearing you are writing a book about Barack Obama, feel anger/scorn/contempt toward you, but I don't. I feel pity. Your thinly disguised attack on Obama is nothing else than an attempt to continue the politics of hate that the right continues to this day. I feel badly for minds like your [sic] as they do NOTHING to advance the intelligent dialogue that this country needs to have...I hope you get the help you need.

"Obama has this almost irrational following and I myself can't sometimes explain why I'm supporting him," one of his younger followers candidly told the *Washington Post*.[24] "He's all things to all men.[25] At least that's how I put it."

That phrase, too, is biblical, and very descriptive. Biographer David Mendell, writing months before Obama's presidential campaign began in earnest, spelled it out more clearly: "He is an exceptionally gifted politician who, throughout his life, has been able to make people of widely divergent vantage points see in him exactly what they want to see."[26]

TURNING THE LEFT ON CLINTON

If Barack Obama is a secular Messiah, his first miracle has to be the turning of so many liberal Democrats against former president Bill Clinton. These are often the same people who unscrupulously defended everything untoward in Clinton's two-term administration—the hoarding of political enemies' FBI files, the firing of the White House travel office, the philandering, the lies under oath, the last-minute pardons, *everything*. Not only could Clinton do no wrong at that time, but he had also been responsible for the benefits of peace after a Cold War that had ended without his help. He had been responsible for the low unemployment of a dot-com bubble that would burst, conveniently, just before he left office.

If Obama does nothing else to bring the nation together, he has already created this new point of agreement between liberals and conservatives: that the Clintons are a dangerous and cutthroat pair that will do absolutely anything to win and cling to power.

Conservatives almost want to shout it out: "I *told* you so!"

Thanks to his ruthless but unsuccessful efforts to secure the presidential nomination for his wife, Bill Clinton's name is now uttered with contempt, at times even with expletives, in the same circles where he was once held in high regard.

Spike Lee, who voted for him twice, told *Uptown* Magazine that "both of [the Clintons] would lie on a stack of Bibles and sleep well doing it." He added, "I love Toni Morrison, but when she said that Bill Clinton was the first black president, that sh-t went to his head. He actually believed it. No one ever explained to me why that statement was made. Because he played saxophone?"[27]

Most frequently cited is Bill Clinton's attempt to racialize Obama by comparing him to Jesse Jackson after the South Carolina primary.[28] Democrats may forgive Bill Clinton by November, but this, more than anything else, has destroyed his reputation as a racial healer, a reputation that had been created for him in the first place as pure myth.

As Clinton decreases, so Obama increases.[29] And he is not just taking over the role that "Bubba" once played as an object of liberal admiration. Obama's appeal is truly messianic—something far beyond the "likeability" that Clinton exemplified.

Obama's second miracle—the more important one that continues as this fall's general election approaches—is his ability to turn opponents' criticisms back upon them. He has so far enjoyed cooperation from a press corps that shows toward him a different sort of reverence than that shown by his followers—a reverence of omission.

This had to be particularly frustrating for Hillary Clinton, who saw all of her attacks on Obama backfire on her in the primaries. When her campaign pointed out that Obama was lifting entire sentences and segments of speeches from Massachusetts governor Deval Patrick, her claims were mostly ignored, downplayed, or even met with derision by the mainstream press, despite their absolute accuracy. When Clinton tried to bring it up in a debate, uttering the phrase "change you can Xerox," she was booed by Democrats in the crowd. The booing was what the media reported.[30]

Although "plagiarism" was probably not the right word for it, the stolen speech lines should have at least prompted serious reflection about where Obama's famously inspiring rhetoric comes from.[31] The two are friends going some ways back—Patrick sent a donation to Obama's 2000 campaign for Congress. But is it just a coincidence that both Obama and Deval Patrick employed the shrewd David Axelrod, and that their rhetoric is identical? Given the manifest importance of rhetoric to Obama's campaign, it would seem appropriate to give attention to such a "man-behind-the-curtain" moment.

A month earlier, Clinton had been booed for criticizing Obama's failure to give a straight answer about a vote on which he and Hillary ended up on opposite sides—he had voted against a measure that would have capped at 30 percent interest rates charged to consumers.[32] "You know, Senator Obama, it is very difficult having a straight-up debate with you," she said, "because you never take responsibility for any vote, and that has been a pattern."[33]

After the crowd's boos subsided, Obama gave the kind of riposte that has become typical of his campaign, asserting that Clinton was engaging in the "old politics" that he alone transcends. "I think that part of what people are looking for right now is someone who is going to solve problems and not resort to the same typical politics that we've seen in Washington," he said.

Barack Obama is not to be criticized. He is above that sort of thing. He is *immune* to criticism.

"SMEARING" OBAMA

Robert Novak, perhaps Washington's most-read political reporter (and my former boss), documented this phenomenon in a column that appeared May 22:

> When one of the Democratic Party's most astute strategists this week criticized John McCain for attacking Barack Obama's desire to engage Iran's President Mahmoud Ahmadinejad, I asked what the Republican presidential candidate ought to talk about in this campaign. "Health care and the economy," he replied...Obama embraced that formula once it became clear that he would best Hillary Clinton for the Democratic nomination. He began pounding McCain for seeking the third term of George W. Bush. At the same time, Obama implores McCain in the interest of "one nation" and "one people" not to attack him. The shorthand, widely repeated by the news media, is that the Republican candidate must not "Swift boat" Obama. That amounts to unilateral political disarmament by McCain.[34]

The claim of immunity from all criticism was also what underlies many of the blog and web reactions to the news of this book: any criticism of Obama is a "smear," *ipso facto.*

As he pursues this immunity, the spurious and genuinely false claims about Obama play right into his hands. All presidential candidates suffer from such smears. Remember the 2004 rumor, spread by MTV among others, that Bush would reinstate the draft if reelected?

As I write this, e-mails are circulating the claim that Obama wants to replace the National Anthem with a Coca-Cola jingle about teaching the world to sing in harmony (completely false, obviously). Another claims that his birth in the Territory of Hawaii means he is not a natural-born U.S. citizen and cannot become president. The fact that Obama briefly attended an Islamic school in Indonesia has been falsely spun to suggest that he went to a terrorist-training school. (*Madrassa*, despite its connotation these days, is simply the Arabic word for *school*.) And, of course, there are the yarns about his being sworn in on a Koran and his alleged refusal to salute the flag—all of them lies, of course.

These rumors help his campaign. They give credence to the idea that any attack is a smear.

One consequence of Obama's immunity claim is that even serious issues are out of bounds, as *National Review*'s Rich Lowry (my current boss) noted in a column in spring 2008. He quoted from segments of an Obama speech delivered after his blowout victory in the North Carolina primary to describe exactly what is and is not allowed in a campaign against him:

> Here are the Obama rules in detail: He can't be called a "liberal" ("the same names and labels they pin on everyone," as Obama puts it); his toughness on the war on terror can't be questioned ("attempts to play on our fears"); his extreme positions on social issues can't be exposed ("the same efforts to distract us from the issues that affect our lives" and "turn us against each other"); and his Chicago background too is off-limits ("pouncing on every gaffe and association and fake controversy"). Besides that, it should be a freewheeling and spirited campaign.[35]

This year, Obama cannot win as he has won in the past. He can neither knock McCain off the ballot nor count on his divorce filings to destroy his candidacy. But if the press fails to hold Obama to the usual standard, perhaps he can get a free pass that exempts him from debates about issues like abortion, foreign policy, and his level of experience. He minimizes these legitimate issues by deriding them as "old politics" and "politics of division." Have these really become irrelevant distractions from the issues that really matter to Americans?

Obama's campaign is trying to prevent the "intelligent dialog that this country needs to have." It might just work.

OBAMACONS

As the 2008 presidential campaign turns from the intra-party contests toward the general election, it is also worth asking how conservatives are affected by Obama. A handful of genuine, devoted conservatives have embraced Obama, despite disagreeing with all or nearly all of his ideas. When Doug Kmiec, chair of constitutional law at Pepperdine University and formerly an advisor to Mitt Romney, embraced Barack Obama, it was a really big deal.

Kmiec is no flake, either in the intellectual sense or the ideological sense. He is a serious legal scholar and a conservative. I have known him for several years and interviewed him in the past.

In a February 13 piece in *Slate,* shortly after his candidate exited the race for president, Kmiec focused on the role of his Catholic faith in choosing a candidate:

> [N]ow that Romney's out, whom might Catholics turn to? Since I served at one time as Reagan's constitutional lawyer, it would be natural for me to fall in line behind John McCain. Don't worry about his conservative lapses, says President Bush, the foremost expert on lapsed conservativism. There is no gainsaying that McCain is a military hero deserving of salute. But

McCain seems fixated on just taking the next hill in Iraq. His
Iraqi military objective is laudable, but it assumes good reasons
to be there in the first place.[36]

That piece was the beginning of Kmiec's public path toward endorsing
Barack Obama over a month later. I chose to reproduce the paragraph
above because it captures many aspects of the funk that many conservatives are in right now. President Bush has proven a big disappointment. When the Republicans lost their congressional majority in 2006,
it was hard to feel sad—they seemed to have forgotten why they were
sent to Washington in the first place. Despite more than a year in the
minority, they often seem like they still have not remembered.

John McCain, who disagrees with conservatives on a wide variety of
issues, has won the Republican nomination. He could well win in
November, staving off a far worse outcome, but even this brings with it
little satisfaction. The conservative movement faces deep problems today
and cannot be saved by a McCain victory alone.

There seems to be little light up ahead. The only hope for a resur-
gence of conservative ideas in mid-2008 seems to be the Democrats'
total and willful blindness on the question of energy prices—their
intransigent resistance to solving a problem they actually hope continues for environmental reasons.[37]

In this environment, what's a conservative to do when confronted
with this message of hope and change? Should he forsake everything he
believes and jump into Obama's lanky, open arms? The idea of Obama
winning over conservatives' guts, if not their minds, is not as absurd as
it may first seem. As Kmiec notes in his endorsement of Obama:

I am convinced, based upon his public pronouncements and
his personal writing, that on each of these questions he is not

closed to understanding opposing points of view and, as best as it is humanly possible, he will respect and accommodate them.

Obama really does give that impression at times. It's worked before. He became president of the *Harvard Law Review* precisely by convincing the minority bloc of conservative students at the publication that he would give them a fair deal—after several ballots, they threw their support behind him and put him over the top.[38]

But of course, it's one thing to be president of the *Law Review*, and quite another to be given the White House. In the former position, one has every reason to be fair-minded and all of the means to do it—all kinds of articles can be published with which one does not agree. In the latter position, the president sets policy. He can create only one policy per issue—he cannot conduct two opposite policies at the same time.

And as we will see in the coming chapters, Obama the legislator and Obama the author are not necessarily the same man. And neither even remotely resembles Obama the orator. For a conservative:

- Obama the orator is cotton candy. You might even enjoy watching him speak sometimes, but you know there's nothing to any of it.
- Obama the author is deeply reflective, if at times short-sighted. He is a committed liberal, but the kind with whom you would really enjoy sipping scotch and having a conversation about almost anything.
- Obama the legislator is the kind of man who looks right through you while you speak. You can tell he is not really paying attention. He thanks you when you are done, and then proceeds to ignore everything you said. He votes with

his contributors, his Machine bosses, or the left-wing groups he knows he owes. Which one it is depends in each case on the issue at hand.

David Mendell, Obama's biographer, noticed that during his Senate campaign Obama presented his liberal positions in such a "passive, two-pronged way" that even conservatives thought they were listening to someone with whom they agreed.[39] It just wasn't the case.

The Right must understand Obama's appeal and recognize his significant downside. There are real dangers to an Obama presidency toward which conservatives currently appear complacent in their justifiable depression. Although happy to pour scorn upon liberals with records and ideologies just like Obama's—Michael Dukakis, John Kerry, George McGovern—conservatives have been a bit shy about attacking Obama on the issues.

If Obama succeeds in convincing the mainstream media that he should be spared criticism, he will have shut down the legitimate channels of public discourse. This is no more an example of "new politics" than the tactic of having all of one's opponents thrown off a ballot.

In part, it may be that conservatives have still not overcome their glee at his defeating the Clintons. But another crucial element in this equation is that Obama has done so little to generate ill feeling. He has never tried and failed to implement controversial policies—think of former First Lady Clinton's attempt at health care reform. Nor again has Obama had to campaign against any serious Republican candidate until this election. Most of the elbows Obama has thrown have been aimed at Hillary—if anything, that has made conservatives more fond of him.[40]

But as we have seen, many in the press already demonstrated their deference toward Obama in his race against Clinton. If they did not take Clinton's legitimate criticisms of him seriously, will they be any more generous toward a Republican candidate? If conservatives do not hold him accountable, who will?

One respected journal began as early as May the task of immunizing Obama before the general election campaign had even begun. On May 19, 2008, *Newsweek* published a long and extraordinary piece that could have been written by Obama's press shop:

> The Republican Party has been successfully scaring voters since 1968, when Richard Nixon built a Silent Majority out of lower- and middle-class folks frightened or disturbed by hippies and student radicals and blacks rioting in the inner cities. The 2008 race may turn on which party will win the lower- and middle-class whites in industrial and border states—the Democrats' base from the New Deal to the 1960s, but "Reagan Democrats" in most presidential elections since then. It is a sure bet that the GOP will try to paint Obama as "the other"—as a haughty black intellectual who has Muslim roots (Obama is a Christian) and hangs around with America-haters...Sen. John McCain himself has explicitly disavowed playing the race card or taking the low road generally. But he may not be able to resist casting doubt on Obama's patriotism.[41]

This article embraces and accepts Obama's immunity claim uncritically. It equates legitimate criticisms of Obama with illegitimate smears, suggesting that all are equally unjust.

What is it about Barack Obama that gives him not only his supernatural power over so many hearts and minds, but also turns the political instincts of experienced reporters like Richard Wolffe and Evan Thomas into the gooey, mushy mess quoted above? Moreover, how is it that so many Americans have such unrealistic hopes and dreams wrapped up in a man who in any other context would be considered just another inexperienced freshman senator whose time to run for president is eight to twelve years hence?

The Bible on which Barack Obama took his Senate oath is still warm. His followers want to have him added to its pages, and the media seem willing to do the writing for them.

CHAPTER FIVE

OBAMA IN WASHINGTON: STILL NOT A REFORMER

B arack Obama is a good writer, and he knows how to tell a good story.

In *The Audacity of Hope*, he relates his 2005 visit to Thornton Township High School, in a predominantly black suburb south of Chicago, to conduct a "youth town hall meeting."

The students must have been excited to have this opportunity—a chance to question their state's newly elected and highly popular United States senator. To prepare for Obama's visit, they were surveyed about the quality of their education, with the idea that they could present their concerns.

Obama writes:

At the meeting they talked about violence in the neighborhoods and a shortage of computers in their classrooms. But their number one issue was this: Because the school district couldn't

afford to keep teachers for a full school day, Thornton let out
every day at 1:30 in the afternoon. With the abbreviated sched-
ule, there was no time for students to take science lab or foreign language classes.

How come we're getting shortchanged? they asked me.
Seems like nobody even expects us to go to college, they said.

They wanted more school.[1]

While reading about his visit to Thornton, I wondered whether maybe
Obama missed the tension that must have gripped that room as those
students, mostly black and disproportionately poor, pleaded with him
for more school. I wondered in particular how the teachers who stood
in attendance felt as it all transpired. For they knew something of
which Obama was probably unaware: the average teacher in Thornton
Township District was earning $83,000 that year, short days notwith-
standing (the figure does not include the administrators, who make
more).[2]

That was just the average. Some of the teachers in attendance that
day were probably making more than $100,000—over one-quarter of
Thornton Township District's teachers did in 2005.

Did the teachers worry that Obama might realize the real cause of
the short day? With teachers that expensive, how could *any* such school
district "afford to keep teachers for a full school day"?

The elementary school day in Chicago proper is even shorter, at five
hours and forty-five minutes. Until 2003, it was only five and a half
hours long. This is not for lack of funds: Chicago public schools already
spend $10,550 per pupil[3]—20 percent above the national average—and
they have the shortest school day of any major city in Illinois.[4]

The Chicago Teachers Union (CTU), an early endorser of Barack
Obama for president, has vigorously resisted attempts to increase
instruction time. In 2007, CTU demonstrated its might by taking on

Mayor Daley, thwarting his attempts to force full days upon teachers. Their new contract contained no extra hours, but significant pay raises for the next four years.[5] Deborah Lynch, the previous CTU president, had agreed in 2003 to a fifteen-minute increase in the school day in exchange for a seven-day reduction in the school year and large annual raises. This minor concession—a net five hours of extra teaching per year—was used against her in the next teachers' union election, which she narrowly lost.[6]

For teaching less than six hours a day, nine months out of the year, even the lowliest twenty-two-year-old teacher in Chicago straight out of college will earn $43,702 this year, plus $3,059 in employer pension contributions[7]—modest, but more than the city's median income.[8] If he spends his summers on the beach (without taking any graduate classes) and stays for four years, he will be making $57,333 in 2012, with a $3,992 pension contribution. He has a secure job and a guaranteed raise every year, regardless of economic conditions. He finishes the school day when other people are headed back to the office after lunch. If he makes his summers more productive, he can move into a higher salary "track" by going to school over the summer. The salaries of the most educated, skilled, and experienced teachers in Chicago will almost certainly be above $100,000 by the time he gets there.

For the money they spend, the Chicago public schools provide very little in the way of results at the high school level. The four-year graduation rate, depending on how you measure it, is as low as 54 percent.[9] According to one recent study, only 6 percent of entering freshmen in Chicago public high schools will obtain college degrees by age 25.[10] Only 31 percent of Chicago high school juniors meet or exceed state standards on the Prairie State Achievement Examination.[11]

Education is one of Senator Obama's favorite issues. His writing demonstrates a genuine appreciation for the fact that he could never have gotten as far as he has without the top-quality education he received—an elite private school in Honolulu and undergraduate and law degrees from two of America's most prestigious academic institutions. And in his book and his speeches, he acknowledges that there are serious problems with American education.

In his Senate stump speech of 2004, Obama brought up education constantly:

> When I see my five-year-old and my two-year-old, it makes me weep because I see children who are just as smart and just as beautiful as they are, who just don't get a shot...It's unacceptable in a country as wealthy as ours that children every bit as special as my own children are not getting a decent shot at life.[12]

As a U.S. senator and as a state legislator, Barack Obama has had an opportunity to do something concrete about these children who are not being given "a decent shot" by the system. And he highlighted the problem of shortened school days in his own book. But in real life, this issue hits too close to home for him. He cannot criticize CTU for depriving Chicago schoolchildren of a full day and a full year of school. The union is his ally, his endorser, his donor, his supporter. He is committed to *the union*, not necessarily to the issue of education. Obama's description of his relationship with CTU and other unions is revealing:

> I owe those unions. When their leaders call, I do my best to call them back right away. I don't consider this corrupting in any way; I don't mind feeling obligated...toward teachers in some of the toughest schools in the country, many of whom have to dip into their own pockets at the beginning of every school year to buy crayons and books for their students...[13]

That certainly sounds better than saying that he "does not mind feeling obligated" toward Chicago unions who demand short work days and short work years. The CTU rewarded Obama for his loyalty in October 2007 by endorsing him for president, providing a counterweight on the same day that its parent union, the American Federation of Teachers, endorsed Hillary Clinton.[14]

Obama has acquired an undeserved reputation for reform in education because he offers mild rhetoric about a merit-pay program for teachers. But he takes all of the teeth out of the idea by promising his allies that the measure of "merit" will not be determined by student achievement—"arbitrary tests"—but by some yet undiscovered measure to be chosen by teachers' unions.[15] Obama's merit pay also comes only in exchange for six-figure teacher salaries.[16]

In addition, Obama has not supported even obvious reforms, such as those pertaining to classroom discipline, a huge problem in urban schools. The state legislature rarely becomes involved in such an issue, but when it did in 2001, Obama twice voted "no" on a bill that let school districts require unruly students to complete suspensions before they could be shunted into new school districts.[17]

Many Americans watched Obama's March 18 Philadelphia speech[18] on race and focused in on his refusal to disown his eccentric pastor. But his former state Senate colleague Republican Steve Rauschenberger winced when he heard Obama describe how politicians have failed inner-city schools—"we still haven't fixed them"—which especially harms black children, who make up 47 percent of Chicago's school population.[19]

"What set me off personally," says Rauschenberger, "was to see him tell us that we've failed urban school kids. Sure we have, but it wasn't without his help. He was a defender of the status quo in the city of Chicago for eight years. And as a national rock star, he could be turning his guns back at the education system in Chicago. He doesn't."

Before he became a politician, Obama had not been so deeply committed to placating teachers' unions and avoiding fundamental reform issues. He noticed in the 1980s, and later lamented in his 1995 book, that no one had the guts to be frank with educators about the poor product they were providing in public schools on Chicago's South Side. The church pastors, Obama wrote in *Dreams from My Father*, were hesitant to address education reform because of

> . . .the uncomfortable fact that every one of our churches was filled with teachers, principals, and district superintendents. Few of these educators sent their own children to public schools; they knew too much for that. But they would defend the status quo with the same skill and vigor as their white counterparts of two decades before... Efforts at reform—decentralization, say, or cutbacks in the bureaucracy—were part of a white effort to wrest back control... As for the students, well, they were impossible.[20]

Somewhere along the line, as he entered politics and aligned himself squarely with the CTU, Obama seems to have lost track of this lesson. Today, when he discusses education reform, he tinkers around the edges. He talks about some important educational questions—funding, teacher training techniques, etc.—but not fundamental questions, such as what to do with failing teachers and administrators, a serious merit-pay system with truly objective standards, and whether Chicago teachers should work full days and full years for the fair wage they receive. As David Brooks put it:

> [W]hen you look at the actual proposals Obama offers, he doesn't really address the core issues... He proposes dozens of

programs to build on top of the current system, but it's not clear that he would challenge it. He's all carrot, no stick. He's politically astute—giving everybody the impression he's on their side—but substantively vague. Change just isn't that easy.[21]

On the issue of education, as with his endorsements of Machine politicians, Obama saves up his political capital for advancement—he doesn't squander it by fighting messy battles for reform that might put him at odds with his political allies. For Obama, reform is something to discuss during election campaigns, not to be implemented or followed, especially when it could cause him to forfeit a political advantage. This does not separate him from most politicians in either party. It means he is like all of the others.

WHO BROKE THE SYSTEM?

These days, BarackObama.com isn't asking for donations—it's asking for citizens to "declare their independence from a broken system by supporting the first presidential election truly funded by the people."[22]

Obama had originally challenged everyone else in the presidential race to take public financing, but then he had to opt out of it himself on June 19, 2008.

He had no choice—the only way he could bring about Hope and Change was to become the first presidential candidate in history not to take matching funds for the general election.

There was no other way. John McCain and the Republican National Committee were rolling in dough with contributions from Washington lobbyists and political action committees.[23]

The current system was "broken." He explained it in a video email to his supporters, which script he also turned into a USA Today op-ed:

> The decision not to participate in the public financing system
> wasn't an easy one—especially because I support a robust sys-
> tem of public financing of elections. But the public financing of
> presidential elections, as it exists today, is broken—and the
> Republican Party apparatus has mastered the art of gaming this
> broken system.[24]

A few months earlier, Obama had supported the system. He had
praised it repeatedly. He had promised to stick to it. Unfortunately, it
wasn't possible, because the system broke.

Public financing of presidential elections began in the wake of the
Watergate scandal. In order to clean up elections, Congress chose to
have the government provide matching funds to candidates who agree
to follow preset spending limits. The idea here is a pretty typical liberal
one: if the government is financing a candidate's campaign, that means
he's not begging businesses and rich people for cash, which lessens the
likelihood he's being bought off. Many liberal Democrats push for
complete public financing of all presidential and congressional campaigns.

These days, for the presidential run, the amount of money available
in any given campaign is based on how many American taxpayers check
a box on their income tax forms—this year candidates can receive up to
$84 million. John McCain will still be taking the $84 million.

Obama has long been a supporter of public election financing. He
has backed a system much more robust than what exists today. In 2006
at a constituent breakfast, Obama stated that he "strongly support[s]
public financing. . . . you can change the rules on lobbying here in Washington, but if we're still getting financed primarily from individual contributions, then those with the most money are still going to have the
most influence."[25]

In February 2007, Obama was bold enough to challenge the Republicans in the presidential race to promise they would take public financing in the general election.[26] John McCain took him up on that challenge one month later.[27]

Obama wrote on a November 2007 questionnaire from the Midwest Democracy Network: "If I am the Democratic nominee, I will aggressively pursue an agreement with the Republican nominee to preserve a publicly financed general election."[28] On the same questionnaire, he wrote, "I have been a long-time advocate for public financing of campaigns combined with free television and radio time as a way to reduce the influence of moneyed special interests."[29]

In February of this year, he wrote an op-ed stating that he would "aggressively pursue" an agreement with McCain that would set "real spending limits."[30] As recently as April 27, 2008, Obama told FOX News that he would be "very interested in pursuing public financing, because I think not every candidate is going to be able to do what I've done in this campaign"—to raise so much money—"and I think it's important to think about future campaigns."[31]

Obama's fundraising efforts, meanwhile, were shattering all records. He had raised over $265 million by the end of April (of which $10 million was for the general election). McCain, who had raised only $115 million by then, had agreed to accept the $84 million available in public matching funds for the general election.[32] But it was becoming clear to Obama that, at this pace, he could raise a whole lot of money.

Perhaps as much as half a billion dollars.

Just then, someone noticed that the public campaign financing system was broken. Now that it was broken, public financing was no longer the "way to reduce the influence of moneyed special interests." So Obama didn't do it. There was no longer any need for "aggressively pursuing an agreement" with the Republican nominee. So Obama didn't pursue it.

"There was no aggressive pursuit of negotiations with the McCain campaign, there was no pursuit, period, of negotiations with the McCain campaign," McCain legal counsel Trevor Potter told reporters.[33]

Obama explained that if he took public financing, it might be hard to compete with the outside "527 groups" who will mercilessly smear him. Of McCain, he said: "[W]e've already seen that he's not going to stop the smears and attacks from his allies running so-called 527 groups, who will spend millions and millions of dollars in unlimited donations."[34]

"No conservative 527 groups have materialized," the *Washington Post* noted.[35] But what if they do? And the groups more favorable to Obama—MoveOn.org and the labor unions, for example—might lack the resources to compete with those conservative groups, should they materialize. It should be noted that in 2004, the pro-Democrat 527s outspent the pro-Republican 527s $282 million to $111 million, according to the Center for Responsive Politics.[36] As of mid-year 2008, the Democratic 527s had slightly outraised their GOP counterparts, but then when you throw in the labor unions and pro-choice groups, Obama's 527 army is already better funded than McCain's.[37]

But Obama has eschewed federal financing so that he can raise more money than anyone ever has. That will fix the broken system.

In January 2007, Obama told CNN's Larry King, "I'm a big believer in public financing of campaigns. And I think that for a time, the presidential public financing system works."[38]

We know, then, that sometime between January 2007 and mid-June 2008, somebody went and broke the public campaign financing system.

Who did it?

Unfortunately, we may never find out.

But in order to fix it, Barack Obama must first break it some more. He needs your contribution to help. You can donate through his website. All proceeds go toward reform.

DREAMS FROM MY FARMER

As in Chicago, conservatives and liberals in Washington often find common ground on issues of good government.

As in Chicago, Barack Obama is not usually part of that agreement when it happens.

In less than four years as a United States senator, he has voted for some of the worst bipartisan special-interest legislation to move through the chamber. At times—as with the question of ethanol—he has positively championed corrupt systemic arrangements.

The media have uncritically applied to him the "reformer" label because of his promises to change Washington. It seems unimportant that he has done virtually nothing while in Washington to change it.

In *The Audacity of Hope,* Obama worries about the ugly image that Americans project to the world in the area of trade. We demand, he writes, that "developing countries eliminate trade barriers that protect them from competition, even as we steadfastly protect our own constituencies from exports that could help lift poor countries out of poverty."[39]

This laudable concern did not prevent him from voting for a farm bill this year whose purpose was largely to "protect our own constituencies from exports that could help lift poor countries out of poverty." By supporting the farm bill, Obama voted to increase subsidies for American crops[40]—the majority of the money goes to commercial farms with an average net worth of nearly $2 million.[41] He voted to keep in place tariffs and import limits against crops from developing countries, especially against sugar from developing countries like Brazil and the Caribbean nations. The bill that Obama voted for even bars the U.S. government from providing food aid by purchasing crops from the developing countries we try to feed. When the Bush administration vetoed the bill, demanding at least that this last provision be changed, Obama voted to override the veto.[42]

While taking this vote, Obama had at his side several Republican and Democratic senators from farm states, who are equally obeisant to big agribusiness. When it comes to corporate plunder of the federal government, Obama's record reflects his ideas of unity and "post-partisanship."

This is even truer on the question of federal ethanol subsidies. It is a rare policy on which you'll find National Review's editors agreeing with Paul Krugman, the liberal columnist at the New York Times. But then again, it's a rare policy that is so nakedly wasteful with such a negative net public benefit.

Krugman wrote about ethanol on his Times blog in February 2008: "Bad for the economy, bad for consumers, bad for the planet—what's not to love?"[43]

But Obama loves ethanol. He loves it so much that his energy plan would outlaw new cars that can't run on high-ethanol blends (that includes most cars sold today).[44] He brags about how he inserted a new ethanol subsidy into a 2006 tax bill.[45] He gushes over ethanol in The Audacity of Hope:

> The bottom line is that fuel-efficient cars and alternative fuels like E85, a fuel formulated with 85 percent ethanol, represent the future of the auto industry. It is a future American car companies can attain if we start making some tough choices now...[46]

In 2008, ethanol's ravages started to make headlines—this "green fuel" was contributing to record-high food prices[47] and causing food riots in the developing world. It was exhausting water supplies,[48] driving up gasoline prices,[49] and exacerbating smog.[50] Environmentalists, who almost universally oppose ethanol, complained that its production process is driving up emissions from coal.[51] Consumers were suffering and the impact on the environment was a net negative.

Worst of all, ethanol makes no substantive contribution to American energy independence. Consider these statistics, and I will do the math for you below.

- A gallon of ethanol contains 75,700 British Thermal Units of energy.[52]
- A gallon of gasoline contains 115,000 British Thermal Units of energy.[53]
- American firms produced 6.5 billion gallons of ethanol in 2007.[54]
- Americans use 388.6 million gallons of gasoline per day.[55]
- To produce five gallons of ethanol from corn, one must spend the energy equivalent of roughly four gallons of ethanol for farming, shipping, and processing. (In other words, ethanol has a 25 percent net energy yield.)[56]

Run the numbers, and the answer is that America's entire 6.5 billion gallon ethanol production created the net energy equivalent of 2.2 *days' worth* of American gasoline consumption. If you want a more generous estimate, call it *three* days' gasoline consumption. But do not call it "energy independence."

That's the physics of ethanol.

Here are the economics of ethanol: In exchange for that minuscule output, federal and state governments provide between $6.3 billion and $8.7 billion in annual direct and indirect subsidies—that includes direct payments as well as estimates of the economic distortions caused by mandates (high food prices, for example).[57] When government subsidized corn ethanol production in 2007, it was like spending $9.00 to create a gallon of gasoline, and doing it 853 million times. If you are still unsure about ethanol, think of it this way: If you could turn gold into lead, would you do it?

Senator Obama apparently would.

Without government subsidies, no one would make corn ethanol. Without government mandates, no one would buy corn ethanol. The ethanol industry receives more in subsidies each year than it spends buying corn.[58] It plunders government with an efficiency that no political Machine will ever match. And Barack Obama is an even bigger supporter of ethanol than he was of the Stroger Machine.

Obama's Illinois colleague in the Senate, Dick Durbin—long a champion of federal support for ethanol—is finally starting to feel uncomfortable about it.

"I've supported ethanol from the beginning," Durbin said in April. "But we have to understand it's had an impact on food prices. Even in the Corn Belt, we'd better be honest about it."[59]

When Obama came to Washington in January 2005, ethanol already enjoyed a special income tax credit, protective tariffs, occasional *ad hoc* federal subsidies, and a bevy of statewide subsidies for production, processing, and dispensing. Since then, the subsidies have ballooned, and Obama is pushing for more.

Weeks after being sworn in, Obama traveled back to Illinois for a stop at the ethanol plant of Aventine Renewable Energy, where he endorsed the federal ethanol mandate that has since gone into effect. Current law requires the use of 15 billion gallons of ethanol by 2015.

According to an Associated Press account of the event, "Obama said boosting the nation's ethanol output is a 'no-brainer' ... "[60]

Indeed, it is a "no-brainer," but not in the sense Obama meant it.

Three months later, when the mandate was debated on the Senate floor, a coalition of liberal and conservative senators rose up against it. Liberal New York senator Charles Schumer, who argued his constituents were being robbed, offered the following arguments, which are worth reading in light of Senator Obama's "reform" image:

It hurts drivers and it hurts the free market. It is a boondoggle because it takes money out of the pockets of drivers and puts it into the pockets of the big ethanol producers...It is so unfair to do this. It is wrong to do this. If you come from Iowa or Illinois, and ethanol is good for your gasoline and it is the best way to make it cleaner, that is fine. But if there are other ways to do this...to put a few pennies—and that is all it will be—in the pocket of the family farmer, we charge drivers around the country billions of dollars.

Make no mistake about it, most of those billions will not go to the family farmer, they will go to the Archer Daniels Midlands of the world—a company that was once accused of price fixing. There will be no free market here at all.[61]

Schumer is here attacking Obama's policy. Of course Obama *voted* for ethanol—he voted for it twice that day.[62] In 2007, Congress upped the ante again, nearly doubling the ethanol mandate, Obama, again, backed it. He wants to be president, and that road goes through Iowa, twice. Obama does not stand with the reformers. He is part of the bipartisan consensus in favor of government waste.

OBAMA AND PORK

Obama's reform record is not a complete wash. His most notable accomplishment in Washington was the bill he co-sponsored with Republican senator Tom Coburn, the conservative junior senator from Oklahoma. The Federal Funding Accountability and Transparency Act of 2006—also known as "Google for Government"—helped expose to the sunlight the congressional practice of "earmarking," in which members of Congress direct federal spending to parochial projects—swimming pools, bridges to nowhere—that often have no national importance or congressional authorization.[63] Coburn and Obama's bill, approved over the objection of some of Capitol Hill's worst porkers, really was a small victory for open government and bipartisanship.

This was a real accomplishment for Obama in the name of reform—the second such accomplishment of his career after the Illinois ethics law.[64]

On the more significant question of these spending items themselves, Obama scores better than the dismal standard his colleagues have set, but he still bats below .500. He deserves credit for not always voting against reform.

Of the six earmark-related votes for which he was present in 2007 (he missed nine such votes), he voted against wasteful earmarks on two occasions—one of these votes was unanimous, coming at a time when the Senate was under great political pressure to cut a spinach subsidy out of an emergency spending bill.[65]

Coburn, a real thorn in his colleagues' side, has fought a bipartisan ground war against earmarks, and some Democrats—in particular Russ Feingold of Wisconsin and Claire McCaskill of Missouri—have sided with Coburn against wasteful earmarks. Coburn has forced scores of votes to strip earmarks out of bills and direct the spending toward areas with real need. After Hurricane Katrina, Coburn twice proposed measures that would have pulled money from legislators' pet projects—for example, a baseball stadium in Montana and a visitor's center in Morgan City, Louisiana—in order to redirect the cash toward shoring up levees in New Orleans and rebuilding the city. Obama voted against the reform position on both of those occasions, and in favor of the pet projects.[66]

When Coburn proposed an amendment redirecting funds from the infamous "Bridge to Nowhere" in Alaska to reconstruction of the Twin Spans bridge in New Orleans, Democratic senators Mary Landrieu of

Louisiana, Evan Bayh of Indiana, and Feingold were all willing to stand with him against the pork-barrellers. You should understand how radical this is. Voting to strip a colleague's earmark violates the enshrined rules of that old boys' club. Obama voted with eighty-one of his Senate colleagues against New Orleans and in favor of the Bridge to Nowhere.[67]

After the I-35W bridge collapsed over the Mississippi River in Minnesota in August 2007, Coburn sponsored an amendment to take all federal transportation spending on bike trails and redirect it to bridge safety and maintenance. Obama voted for the bike paths.[68]

In 2006, Obama voted for three of Coburn's pork-busting amendments on one spending bill (nixing, among other things, seafood subsidies).[69] On the other hand, he also voted against two anti-earmark amendments proposed by Senator John McCain, which would have erased several agricultural special-interest spending, including sugar subsidies in Hawaii.[70] In 2005, when he voted to preserve the "Bridge to Nowhere" and two other wasteful projects,[71] he also voted to eliminate an earmark.[72] He voted for one earmark transparency measure[73] and against another.[74]

Obama was familiar with the earmark process before coming to Washington, from his work in the Illinois Senate. He liked to bring home the bacon. In 2001, he steered $75,000 to a South Side charity called FORUM Inc., whose mission was to wire churches and community groups to the Internet. Five FORUM employees, including one who had declared bankruptcy, had donated $1,000 each to Obama's state Senate campaign—their investment clearly paid off. Unfortunately, the group was sued by the state for an unrelated kickback scheme. When the fraudulent scheme was reported, Obama returned the $5,000.[75]

Like nearly every other senator in Washington, Obama has secured his own earmarks, although he has decided to forgo them for fiscal year

2009, now that he is a presidential candidate. According to an earmark database built by Taxpayers for Common Sense, he was the sole Senate sponsor of twenty-nine earmarks in spending bills for fiscal year 2008, amounting to $10.7 million. The *Seattle Times* noted that Obama's pork recipients on the 2008 defense appropriations bill returned the favor with $16,000 in campaign contributions.[76]

For 2007, Obama earmarked $1 million for the University of Chicago Medical Center. The vice president of this center is his wife, Michelle Obama, who had received a pay raise of nearly $200,000 at just the time when Obama became a senator.[77] When the *Chicago Tribune* editorial board asked him about the potential conflict of interest here, he said that supporting the earmark was perfectly appropriate, although it was "probably something that we should have passed on to [Illinois Senior Senator Dick] Durbin."[78]

In other words, when your earmark creates an appearance of impropriety, the solution is to hide it by having someone else sponsor it.

Earmarking is standard practice that is not inherently corrupt. But it is often wasteful, and it has been at the heart of real corruption scandals, such as the one that sent Republican congressman Duke Cunningham to prison. Cunningham had agreed to obtain specific defense earmarks in exchange for bribes. Most members of Congress, like Obama, simply "trade" earmarked cash for campaign funds. Although it is illegal to make such a trade explicitly by agreement, it is done legally and informally by almost everyone.

Obama typically secures less in earmarks than do many lawmakers—he only requested $740 million in his first three years in Congress, compared to Hillary Clinton's $2.3 billion for this year alone.[79] But generally Obama plays nice and votes for other people's earmarks. He does not lead on the issue, but it takes quite a reformer to vote against bridges and bike paths to nowhere.

POST-PARTISANSHIP

Obama's work on ethics reform in the Senate received particular attention two years ago because it threw him into a testy exchange with his current opponent for the presidency, John McCain. In a February 2006 meeting, Obama convinced McCain of his reform credentials by promising to work with him seriously on a bipartisan lobbying and ethics reform package.

It was one of those tough moments in the Senate where everyone digs in. The leadership in both parties had reached partisan gridlock. Most Republicans lacked the will to pass serious reforms, but they were desperate to pass *something* after a series of high-profile ethics scandals in their ranks. Democratic leaders, whose commitment to ethics reform was only slightly less cosmetic, wanted to block all reforms until the following Congress. This would heighten the value of Republican scandals as a political issue for the 2006 election.

This was long before all of the presidential politicking had begun. McCain, Obama, Republican senator Susan Collins (Maine), and Democratic senator Joe Lieberman (Connecticut)[80]—the chairwoman and ranking member of the committee of jurisdiction—met to discuss how they could work together and pass something. A McCain advisor said that Obama gave him "private assurances" that he would consider supporting a bipartisan task force and develop a package that same month, before the legislation went to Lieberman and Collins's committee. Both senators' staffs agree that McCain and Obama chatted amicably after the meeting.[81]

Apparently, McCain thought they had an agreement.

Then Obama's party leaders took him aside and set him straight. They had an election plan, and they weren't about to have him ruin that by working on both sides of the aisle to accomplish something substantive in 2006.

Obama then wrote a letter to McCain in Washington-speak. I have set the key terms off in bold to make the meaning clearer.

> I know you have expressed an interest in creating a task force to further study and discuss these matters, but **I and others in the Democratic Caucus** believe the more effective and **timely** course is to allow the committees of jurisdiction to roll up their sleeves and get to work on writing ethics and lobbying reform legislation that a majority of the Senate can support. **Committee consideration of these matters through the normal course** will ensure that these issues are discussed in a public forum and that those within Congress, as well as those on the outside, can express their views, ensuring a thorough review of this matter.

Here is what he's really saying:

- "I and others...": "My party is closing ranks. I cannot help you."
- "Timely": "You are delaying ethics reform."
- "...normal course": "You are trying to bypass the committee over which Lieberman and Collins preside, even though they were with us when we talked about your plan."

Unfortunately, this really is how people write letters and talk in Washington. It is about as dumb as it gets.

But don't take my word for it—*National Journal's* Marc Ambinder wrote:

> "Next thing we know," a McCain adviser said, "[Obama] releases the letter to the press before sending it to McCain,

insinuating McCain and others wanted to slow-go lobbying reform."... A McCain aide said that press calls alerted them to the letter early [February 3], as McCain was on his way to [a] security conference in Munich. [82]

Three aides said McCain was astonished when he read the letter. His task force would be pressed to recommend solutions by the end of [February 2006], probably before any legislation would emerge from the several Senate committees... A McCain aide explained the senator was offended by what he saw as Obama's insinuation that McCain was trying to bypass the traditional committee process in a partisan manner. Another McCain adviser retorted: "Don't blame your decision to stick with your leadership on those who are trying to do something in a bipartisan way."[83]

McCain, whose crusade for campaign finance reform had enraged members of his own party four years earlier, was not so diplomatic in his response. He accused Obama of "partisan posturing" and questioned his commitment to the issue at hand, writing: "I concluded your professed concern for the institution and the public interest was genuine and admirable...thank you for disabusing me of such notions." [84]

Obama was clearly wounded in his response. He called McCain's charges "bizarre" and "regrettable," and wrote that he had "no idea" what prompted McCain to strike out like that.

"The fact that you have now questioned my sincerity...is regrettable but does not in any way diminish my deep respect for you nor my willingness to find a bipartisan solution to this problem."[85]

For someone who has only been in Washington for three years, Obama is *really* good.

CHAPTER SIX

THE STEALTH
LIBERAL

P olitical conventions are timed strategically to give a party and
a presidential candidate a boost ahead of Election Day. They
are euphoric events for the party faithful in attendance. They
hearten the depressed and bolster their belief in the cause. They give the
faithful a chance to mingle with fellow-travelers and true-believers.

What's more, millions tune in to watch the most important speeches.
A convention represents an opportunity for a party to reach out to
independents, to pitch their most popular ideas to the voting public and
to form first impressions with millions of viewers who are perhaps less
involved in the political process.

Having by good fortune avoided both a serious primary and a serious
general election in 2004, Barack Obama approached the Democratic
National Convention as his party's new hot commodity. As we saw in
Chapter 3, it did not hurt that he had helped other Democratic candidates—campaigning and raising money for the Democratic Senate effort.

Also working in his favor, of course, was his easy election in Illinois. There was no risk of embarrassment, that he might give the speech and then lose. He might as well have been a Senator already.

There were other important party figures, though, who could have stolen the show. Former Vermont governor Howard Dean had been the insurgent candidate of that year, at one point the frontrunner for the nomination. His message had inspired millions of liberals to give him $40 million—much of it over the Internet. But once Dean's famous "scream" following his disappointing loss in the Iowa caucuses made him the butt of many unkind jokes, he was relegated to a brief speaking slot. His seven-hundred-word speech was low-key and underwhelming, lacking in emotion or empathy.

How was Barack Obama chosen to give the keynote speech in Boston? He professes modestly that he does not know why he was chosen.[1] But this was a task for which neither his youth nor his inexperience would be impediments—in fact, both were assets in this context. Obama was a fresh and handsome face for the cameras, sure to be a winner.

The right doors had opened once again.

Obama is an unquestionably good orator, in addition to being an excellent writer. In *Dreams from My Father*, he offers a hint of how he acquired his strong command of the English language. During his childhood in Jakarta, Indonesia, his mother, Stanley Ann Dunham, had suddenly learned of her second husband's treatment at the hands of the Suharto government—something he had hidden from her. Whereas she had previously supported the acculturation of young "Barry" in Indonesia, she changed her attitude completely at this point, deciding that his opportunities as an American would be much greater than anything he could enjoy in that foreign land. She put Barry on a grueling regime with the American English correspondence course she had ordered for him.

"Five days a week," he writes, "she came into my room at four in the morning, force-fed me breakfast, and proceeded to teach me English lessons for three hours before I left for school and she went to work."[2] His mother would surely have been proud of his delivery at the Democratic convention on July 27, 2004. He even made his wife cry.[3]

Yet today, few remember the speech's curious ideological content. A euphoric national media, already hostile to President Bush, asked few questions about why this young state senator appeared to have shown up at the wrong convention to give his speech.

Simply remove the references to John Kerry, and Obama could almost have delivered that speech at the *Republican* National Convention. He made a strong appeal to cultural and even fiscal conservatives that would have been surprising had it come from any other Democrat.

> The people I meet in small towns and big cities and diners and office parks—they don't expect government to solve all of their problems. They know they have to work hard to get ahead, and they want to. Go into the collar counties around Chicago, and they'll tell you that they don't want their tax money wasted, by a welfare agency or by the Pentagon. Go into any inner-city neighborhood, and folks will tell you that government alone can't teach kids to learn.[4]

Obama urged inner-city parents to "turn off the television sets and eradicate the slander that says a black youth with a book is acting white."[5] In what appeared to be a direct rejection of the "Two Americas" speech—the class-warfare rhetoric espoused that year by vice-presidential nominee John Edwards—Obama said there was just *one* America, which he praised as the only place where he could have

succeeded as he had: "I stand here knowing that...in no other country on earth is my story even possible."[6]

He quoted the Declaration of Independence passage mentioning "the
unalienable right to life" in a convention packed with supporters of
abortion on demand.

The speech contained no red meat for the party faithful, no direct
criticism of Republicans, of President Bush, or even of the Iraq War. He
preached the virtues of American business and political participation.
"Fellow Americans, Democrats and Republicans, Independents—I say
to you tonight, we have more work to do."[7] His speech moved from
one emotional moment to another—sentence after sentence with which
no reasonable human being could disagree. He spoke of the problem
of workers losing jobs, of parents who can't afford to send their children to college, of families struggling to make ends meet. He criticized
the media and professional political campaigners—two easy targets, to
be sure—and placed himself in opposition to them, as a figure seeking
unity.

> Even as we speak, there are those that are preparing to divide
> us—the spin-meisters, the negative ad peddlers, who embrace the
> politics of "anything-goes." I say to them tonight, there is not a
> liberal America and a conservative America, there is the United
> States of America. There is not a Black America and a White
> America, a Latino America and an Asian America. There is the
> United States of America!...There are patriots who opposed the
> war in Iraq, and there are patriots who supported the war in
> Iraq. We are one people, all of us pledging allegiance to the Stars
> and Stripes, all of us defending the United States of America![8]

The speech was full of empathy and passion, but it also may have been
the least substantive address of the convention. That Obama could be

so widely praised for a speech so free of content is a tribute to his oratorical skill, his good looks, and to the good feeling he creates.

Ann Richards's keynote address at the 1988 convention was not so memorable, even though she said almost exactly the same thing:

> We've been told that the interests of the South and Southwest are not the same interests as the North and the Northeast. They pit one group against the other. They've divided this country. And in our isolation we think government isn't going to help us, and we're alone in our feelings—we feel forgotten.
>
> Well the fact is, we're not an isolated piece of their puzzle. We are one nation, we are the United States of America![9]

If the similarity is striking, it is probably because Obama had been given a copy of Richards's speech as well as the 1984 speech by Mario Cuomo when he began writing his own first draft.[10] His speech combined the time-tested and focus-group-tested wisdom of the past with his own Illinois stump speech—his Senate campaign had used focus-groups to test messages as well.[11] Obama's speeches are so good, his biographer writes, also in part because he and advisor David Axelrod parse every single word in Obama's speeches, analyzing and repeating the delivery in a process that Axelrod compares to guitarists in a jam session.[12]

Neither Hillary Clinton nor John Kerry could have given that speech and received such praise. They lacked the story, the oratory, and the raw appeal that Obama brought. He could afford to spare the red meat without being offensive to liberal stalwarts.

Did his conciliatory speech mean that Obama was a moderate Democrat—perhaps even slightly conservative? Was he, as a *Newsweek* cover would proclaim, "Seeing Purple"?[13] Was this the new young leader trying to take the Democratic Party in an entirely new direction?

Not really. Or at least, Obama's record contains no such indications of moderation. The more accurate explanation seems to be that, four years before his run at the presidency, Obama and his speech-writers (whose role was to smooth out material he provided for them) had mastered the art of making people feel good about political speeches lacking in content about politics, policy, or governance.

It was all cotton candy.

Obama did not *have* to talk like a liberal. He would prove his *bona fides* to his party's left wing just a few months later. He would join the United States Senate and proceed to vote exactly like every other liberal Democrat, without deviation or imagination. He would remain so faithful to his left-wing principles that he was named by the respected *National Journal* as the most liberal member of the United States Senate in 2007.[14] By *National Journal's* reckoning, Obama voted to the left of Barbara Boxer, of Liberal Lion Ted Kennedy, and of his presidential rival, Hillary Clinton.

Obama speaks of "Change," but his conduct in office is basically the same as previous Democratic nominees such as Michael Dukakis, John Kerry, and George McGovern. He is certainly to the left of Bill Clinton. Even if he is not a reformer in any real sense of the word, he definitely *is* a liberal.

DOCTRINAIRE

You've probably never read *Black Commentator*. It's a small, far-left publication with editorial offices in New Jersey. You may have noticed the paper in the fall of 2003 during the confirmation hearing of Janice Rogers Brown, a conservative black justice on California's supreme court—they're the ones who created and distributed the cartoon of her in an exaggerated afro wig and huge lips, being greeted to the federal judiciary by President Bush, who accidentally calls her "Ms. Clarence."

To give you an idea of the tone and the slant of this publication, their lead editorial on January 23, 2003 was titled, "Condoleezza Rice: The Devil's Handmaiden." The thesis of this piece: "Condoleezza Rice is the purest expression of the race traitor. No polite description is possible." The publication, you might guess, is not terribly relevant outside of certain radical black circles, but it is relevant to understanding Barack Obama. This publication successfully pressured him to repudiate an endorsement by Democratic moderates at the beginning of his run for the U.S. Senate.

In its June 5, 2003 issue, the *Commentator's* Bruce Dixon called out Obama for the fact that his name had appeared on the Democratic Leadership Council's list of 100 rising stars. (Dixon refers to the DLC as "the corporate money apparatus of the Democratic Party.")[15] Dixon also pointed out that at the very same time Obama's name showed up on the DLC list, the text of his 2002 speech against the Iraq War was abruptly removed from his campaign website without explanation.

Was Obama selling out? Was he a "summer soldier?" After all, a May 2003 Gallup poll had suggested that 79 percent of Americans still believed the Iraq War was going well.[16]

On June 13, 2003, Obama responded to this criticism with a letter in which he denied any direct contact between his office and the DLC:

> I don't know who nominated me for the DLC list of 100 rising stars, nor did I expend any effort to be included on the list beyond filling out a three line questionnaire asking me to describe my current political office, my proudest accomplishment, and my cardinal rules of politics. Since my mother taught me not to reject a compliment when it's offered, I didn't object to the DLC's inclusion of my name on their list. I certainly did not view such inclusion as an endorsement on my part of the DLC platform.[17]

Obama put the speech back up on his website, and explained that it had been removed in the first place only because his staff was trying to keep it stocked with fresh material.

Black Commentator was not so easily placated. On June 19, 2003, they responded: "Although you minimize the weight of your decision to be listed in the New Democrat Directory... we give you credit for knowing better than that."[18] They challenged him to repudiate the DLC altogether because of its support for free trade and the Iraq war, and because of the DLC's purported opposition to a single-payer government health system.[19]

Obama responded again in the following issue, on June 26, 2003. The *Black Commentator* cover story was headlined: "Obama to Have Name Removed from List." Obama wrote: "I am not currently, nor have I ever been, a member of the DLC."[20]

He noted that the DLC included him in their "New Democrat" directory "without my knowledge... Because I agree that such a directory implies membership, I will be calling the DLC to have my name removed, and appreciate your having brought this fact to my attention."

This happened when the DLC's support might have actually meant something—not much, but at least a few extra donations. The Democratic primary field in the Senate election was still very much wide open at that point. Yet before even arriving in the United States Senate, Obama had repudiated his party's moderates rather than disappoint a tiny website run by socialists in New Jersey.

This incident reveals far more about Obama's political thinking than did the words of his conciliatory keynote convention speech.

THE ISSUES

Obama is not a different kind of Democrat. He is not more moderate or more sympathetic to any fresh ideas, let alone to conservative ones. His record and his writings suggest that if he is more moderate than the average Democrat it is in style rather than substance. As he puts it: "I won't deny my preference for the story the Democrats tell, nor my belief that the arguments of liberals are more often grounded in reason and fact."[21]

In *The Audacity of Hope*, Obama offers numerous insights into his policy positions, all of which should be taken seriously. Some of them are written in the code of Washington-speak. Some are clear and unmistakable. Others become clearer when compared to his voting record. In many cases, Author Obama is not as shy about his liberalism as is Orator Obama. And even on the occasions when Author Obama seems open to new ideas, the facts on the ground never seem to intrude on Legislator Obama's thought process.

There is no need to agree with the conservative take I will offer on Obama's issues. The point is simply that his liberal take is unmistakable. In fact, if you're a liberal, reading the following might make you support Obama even more—but if you're honest, I think you'll agree he's no centrist. Many of the measures I discuss below are complex, and space constraints require me to give simple summaries. I admit, Obama would describe the bills differently, but my descriptions are accurate, in any event.

During his campaign for Senate, Obama "backed federal legislation that would ban citizens from carrying weapons, except for law enforcement," as *Tribune* reporter David Mendell reported it.[22] "National legislation will prevent other states' flawed concealed-weapons laws from threatening the safety of Illinois residents," Obama said.[23]

While he has no constitutional problem with laws affecting the right to bear arms, he cites constitutional grounds for his votes against tougher punishments against gang members who use guns to kill people.[24] In 2001, he voted against a bill that added extra penalties for crimes committed in furtherance of gang activities, contending that it discriminates against minorities.[25] He voted against another bill making

it a criminal offense for accused gang members, free on bond or on probation, to associate with other known gang members.[26]

Through affirmative action, Obama writes, the federal government
should be allowed to discriminate on the basis of race when awarding
college scholarships.[27] Although he sends his own children to an elite
private school, Obama opposes school choice through vouchers or tax
credits that can be used toward education. Such programs may be the
only hope for many poor inner-city black children—particularly in
cities with intractably bad school systems, like Chicago—to get the
good primary and secondary education that would render affirmative
action programs in education unnecessary.

Obama is a union man, dedicated to carrying water for organized
labor even in most extreme circumstances. His fealty to unions explains
why, even as expenses mounted for rebuilding New Orleans, he was
defending federal regulations that increased the costs and slowed the
pace of reconstruction—the Davis-Bacon requirement that government
contractors pay an inflated union wage on every job, whether or not
they hire union workers.[28] The idea behind this law is to make union
labor more competitive at its higher price.

Obama wants—and has voted[29]—to effectively abolish secret-ballot
elections in the workplace when employees determine whether to
unionize. This is a gift long sought by union organizers who have
watched their ranks deplete over the years as private sector unions
become less relevant to workers. The provision Obama seeks, critics
charge, would allow them to intimidate and harass workers until they
sign cards in support of the union, which the employer would then be
required to recognize.[30]

Obama's writings on free trade are mixed and include some rhetoric
in favor of free trade. But he votes quite consistently against free trade
using a variety of pretexts that partisan congressional Democrats have
almost universally adopted in recent years, at the urging of the unions

that spent $58 million to elect them just in 2006.[31] Without rejecting free trade *in principle*, they simply reject it in almost every particular instance.

Sometimes Obama argues against free trade by insisting on labor and environmental regulations that are unrealistic in developing countries. Sometimes he argues that American workers might be displaced if we make it possible for poorer countries to export their crops or livestock or textiles or manufactured goods to America. Either way, he finds a way to vote no. He has voted for exactly one free trade agreement—with the tiny Sultanate of Oman—and he opposes agreements with Colombia, Panama, and South Korea.

On the Central American Free Trade Agreement, he writes that he voted "No" because "it was the only way to register a protest against what I considered to be the White House's inattention to the losers from free trade."[32] He even says that he took no joy in this vote. In fact, he was simply voting the party line—the union line. There is nothing wrong with this, but it is not a "post-partisan" position.

Obama sometimes tries to transcend partisanship in his writings—this transcendence almost never translates into action. In *The Audacity of Hope*, he acknowledges that "if you have a conversation with ... liberals about the potential costs of regulation to a small-business owner, you will often draw a blank stare."[33] He goes on later in his book to offer the literary equivalent of the liberal's "blank stare" when he writes that "government policies can boost workers' wages without hurting the competitiveness of U.S. firms."[34] He shows the same "blank stare" when he proposes "a new tax on small businesses that do not provide health care to their employees"—many of them because they cannot afford to.[35]

This new "non-insurance tax," an unspecified, flat percentage of a company's payroll, is designed to cover the high cost of his government health care proposal. Obama's plan contains five methods for "reining in medical costs," but none will realistically produce large enough savings to pay for the program—hence the need for the new tax. Obama's program would insure those who lack coverage but make too much money to qualify for such existing entitlement programs as Medicaid and SCHIP. His new government program would have "affordable premiums, co-pays and deductibles," and subsidies for those who need them. Parents' insurers would be forced to cover children until they reach the age of 25. He includes multi-billion dollar federal expenditures on medical technology and "health promotion."

Like most liberal programs that seek a public good through central planning, Obama's health plan creates what economists call "moral hazard." Unless the "non-insurance tax" is very, very high—which has its own drawbacks, obviously—it gives employers an incentive to kick workers off the insurance rolls and into the arms of the government program. Moreover, state and federal government agencies (which already pay nearly half of American medical costs) do not have a good record of saving money except through dramatic cuts in services, or by simply not paying for them. In Obama's state, Medicaid owed doctors some $1.5 billion as of 2006.[36]

In January 2000, Obama gave a speech advocating price-controls for prescription drugs.[37] He followed up with a concrete proposal to resurrect this failed, Nixon-era idea with a January 2001 bill[38] that would have established a government "review board" to set maximum prices for drugs in Illinois. Had his bill passed, it would have given the governor power to appoint five board members who could set the prices. Obama has a long history with such ideas. He proposed a study panel in 1998 to recommend whether Illinois should similarly regulate auto insurance prices.[39]

In his book, Obama worries about the creation of tax-exempt Health Savings Accounts (HSAs), which 6.1 million Americans have signed up for since their creation four years ago.[40] "[W]hat if you work for an employer who doesn't offer a health-care plan?" he asks.[41]

This is precisely the person an HSA can help most. An HSA lets you save money, tax-free, to pay deductibles and out-of-pocket health costs. Your employer can contribute to it and even provide the accompanying insurance plan (or you can buy a plan yourself), but you get to keep the money in it if you lose your job or change jobs. You can even pass that money along when you die. It makes you less dependent on your employer for your health insurance. It's a win-win if you own one.

Obama calls this market-based solution, which makes people less dependent on employers for health care, "shredding the employer-based system" of health insurance.[42]

Obama does not feel that you should be similarly dependent on your employee for day-care. He supports additional tax subsidies for commercial day care, even if such subsidies effectively penalize stay-at-home parents, both by freezing them out and by driving up their cost of living.[43]

On energy, Obama opposes further drilling for oil on American soil and in American waters because there might not be enough to cover our entire demand:

> This approach might make economic sense if America harbored plentiful and untapped oil supplies that could meet its needs (and if oil companies weren't experiencing record profits). But such supplies don't exist. The United States has 3 percent of the world's oil reserves. We use 25 percent of the world's oil. We can't drill our way out of the problem.[44]

His figures do not lie, but they were obviously chosen for their conclusion rather than to illuminate the issue—something else that does not separate Obama from other politicians. America was the world's third-largest oil producer in 2006, and we currently produce about 40 percent of the oil we use, despite our small share of the world's "proven" supply.[45] Considering that Americans are now sending $140 abroad for each barrel of imported oil, only strict ideology can sustain the idea that more domestic production would not help at all—especially in a politician like Obama who, for parochial and political reasons, supports a far less practical solution like ethanol.

"MAKING LEMONADE OUT OF LEMONS"

Like almost every presidential nominee before him, Obama has tacked to the center rhetorically since securing the nomination.

In late June 2008, Obama's campaign claimed in a television advertisement that he "passed" a 1997 welfare reform law that "slashed the rolls by 80 percent." It is an audacious claim, considering that Obama *opposed* welfare reform at the time and tried to weaken it. He proposed exceptions to welfare-to-work requirements[46] and to the law's five-year limit on benefits.[47]

Obama didn't draft the welfare-reform bill his ad claims he "passed" in Illinois. Rather he added himself as a co-sponsor two months after it was proposed by Republican senator Dave Syverson. It was a bill that the Senate had to pass in order to conform to the federal welfare-reform laws. It passed with only one senator voting against.

Obama participated in several hours of negotiations with Syverson on some parts of the welfare reform bill. Two years later, he would brag to a Chicago neighborhood publication of these negotiations, stating, "I made sure our new welfare system didn't punish people by kicking them off the rolls."[49] Just before voting for the bill, he said on the Senate floor, "I probably would not have supported the federal [welfare reform] legislation," and added that he was voting for this bill because "I'm a strong believer in making lemonade out of lemons."[50] He said around that time that he found it "disturbing" that President Clinton would sign it, and—more importantly—Obama refused twice on the campaign trail in 2007 to answer whether he would have signed welfare reform as president.[51]

Obama's liberalism extends beyond his positions on issues to other aspects of his world-view. The reason civility has declined in America, he suggests, is that today we lack a nice, liberal television anchor whom we all trust to tell us the way things are: "We have no authoritative figure, no Walter Cronkite or Edward R. Murrow whom we all listen to and trust to sort out contradictory claims."[52] Most conservatives would view this as a positive development.

If you are a Christian, Jew, or Muslim who has objections to the mainstreaming of homosexuality in American culture, Obama believes that your opinion is hurtful and you should not express it. For "no matter how much Christians who oppose homosexuality may claim that they hate the sin but love the sinner, such a judgment inflicts pain on good people—people who are made in the image of God, and who are often truer to Christ's message than those who condemn them."[53]

Obama is a New Deal liberal who looks back to President Franklin D. Roosevelt for inspiration. In a speech at the National Press Club, he said: "President Roosevelt believed deeply in the American idea. He understood that the freedom to pursue our own individual dreams is made possible by the promise that, if fate causes us to stumble or fall, our larger American family will be there to lift us up."[54]

He is a Great Society liberal, whose wife once noted, with an admirable forthrightness liberal politicians don't display: "The truth is, in order to get things like universal health care and [a] revamped education system then someone is going to have to give up a piece of their pie so someone else can have more."[55]

"PRESENT"

If Obama cast many controversial votes in Springfield, he also *avoided* many controversial votes. An interesting aspect of his career in the state Senate was his habit of voting "present" on controversial legislation instead of voting "yea" or "nay." He did this about 130 times over his eight-year career there, which other Illinois senators say is unusually high.[56] As Nathan Gonzales of the *Rothenberg Political Report* noted, "We aren't talking about a 'present' vote on whether to name a state office building after a deceased state official, but rather about votes that reflect an officeholder's core values."[57]

Unlike in the United States Congress, bills in Illinois have a fixed numerical threshold for passage—in other words, a "present" vote is equivalent to a "no" vote for all practical purposes. But for rhetorical purposes, a "present" vote is different in that critics and journalists must discuss it differently. For example, Barack Obama did not vote *against* a bill to prevent pornographic book and video stores and strip clubs from setting up within 1,000 feet of schools and churches—he just voted "*present.*"[58] Obama voted "present" on an almost-unanimously passed bill to prosecute students as adults if they fire guns on school grounds.[59] He voted "present" on the partial-birth abortion ban and other contentious issues that are discussed in Chapter 10.

This habit of his underlies the bitter joke that adorned the T-shirt of at least one Hillary Clinton supporter at her concession rally in Washington, D.C. in June: "Remember in November: vote present."[60]

OBAMA-NOMICS

"I added it up for the first time," Michelle Obama says to the six working mothers who sit with her around a table in the basement of a Zanesville, Ohio day-care center. "Between the two kids, on extracurriculars outside the classroom, we're spending about $10,000 a year on piano and dance and sports supplements and so on and so forth. And summer programs. That's the other huge cost. Barack is saying, '*Whyyyyyy* are we spending that?' And I'm saying, 'Do you know what summer camp costs?' "[61]

She was out on the campaign trail, discussing her family's financial problems. Byron York, my colleague at *National Review,* watched and took notes as Mrs. Obama commiserated with these mothers and their struggles living in Muskingum County—median household income: $37,192.[62] It's a far cry from the $240,505 the Obamas made (adjusted gross income) in 2000 or the $272,759 they made in 2001.[63] It is even farther from Mrs. Obama's current compensation from the University of Chicago Hospital, where she works in community relations. Her salary went from $121,910 to $316,962 in 2005, the same year her husband was sworn in to the United States Senate from where he would earmark funds for her employer.[64]

A month earlier, in Van Nuys, California, her husband had listened to four voters talk about their fears over mortgage and credit card debt. He told them that he felt their pain. "Five years ago, before I had spoken at the convention, before my book sales took off, *et cetera*, we were in the same situation," he said. "My wife and I borrowed to go to college and law school because we don't come from wealthy families. When I got out of law school and we got married, our combined student loan debt was higher than our mortgage."[65]

Obama was apparently referring to 2002, when he and his wife made a combined $238,327. This was only an average year for Obama—his family was already making five-and-a-half times the median income by 2000.[66] Even if you exclude Barack's modest state senator salary (in the range of $58,000 during his service), their family would have been in the 95th percentile for household income in America that year.[67]

The Obamas have every right to discuss the common man's plight, but they certainly do exaggerate their own poverty. It is a longstanding tradition of America's "old politics"—the politician who was born in a log cabin he built himself.

In 1993, they had bought the three-bedroom condominium in Hyde Park that Obama, while engaging in a typical politician's exaggeration, once mistakenly referred to as "a one-bedroom condo without a garage."[68] The young, struggling Obamas had been able to save up $111,000 in cash, which they used as a down-payment on the $277,500 condo.[69] The resulting $166,500 mortgage could have easily been less than the student debt of two Harvard Law graduates.

Life may have been hard for Obama's family at $240,000 per year, but he just recently voted for a budget that would raise the taxes on single people with a taxable income of more than $32,000 (by increasing the 25% bracket to 28%).[70] Obama voted this way, as he usually does, in step with all of his Democratic colleagues. It was their budget, and Barack Obama, like all partisan Democrats in the Senate, votes for his party's budget.

In his book, Obama bows to all of the liberal nostrums on tax policy. He has no time for the idea that lower marginal tax rates help promote investment and employment, instead stating simply that the government needs more money, and the rich should be happy to contribute. "[L]et's be clear," he writes. "The rich in America have little to complain about."[71] The line is amusing in light of Obama's complaints about his personal finances in 2002.

Obama has pushed for an immediate withdrawal from Iraq, which would save the government well over $100 billion per year. The savings from this peace dividend, however, are not enough to support all of the spending he wants to do. He plans to raise taxes so that the government can take still more from the productive sector of the economy. He has voted repeatedly to return personal income tax rates to where they were in 2000, which would at this point be the largest tax increase in history.[72]

"I consider the Bush tax cuts for the wealthy to be both fiscally irresponsible and morally troubling," he writes.[73] This does not apply just to the Bush tax cuts, but to almost any effort to lower taxes. As a liberal, he supports higher taxes, not lower ones. He voted to preserve Illinois' death tax.[74] Obama today talks about closing "corporate tax loopholes."[75] In Springfield, this meant that he voted in 2003 to squeeze businesses by repealing tax credits for "educational and vocational" employee training and research and development.[76] This bill, which passed narrowly, even raised taxes on fire insurance. In the U.S. Senate, Obama has yet to find a tax increase that he does not support. He has voted dozens of times to raise federal taxes. He stated in a television interview that he wants to raise the top capital gains tax rate from 15 percent (depending on one's income) to somewhere between 20 percent and 28 percent.[77]

Following his $1.9 million book deal of 2005 that made Obama a millionaire, he will be able to pass something along to his daughters. This is a good thing—something that nearly every American would like to do. But Obama opposes the creation of personal accounts in Social Security, which would allow millions of low-income Americans to pass something to the next generation when they die. Instead, he wants their retirement money to be absorbed back into the government when they die. He takes this position on Social Security because he worries that, if given choices about how to invest for retirement, some investors might not be able to beat the average 1.23 percent return[78] that the Social Security program currently promises young workers.[79]

Despite the sophisticated financial world in which we live, where more than 60 percent of Americans are invested in the stock market (and even more own bonds or fixed-income instruments), Barack Obama insists that we are better off pooling our money with the federal government, where it accumulates no interest.

> It makes sense for all of us to chip in to a pool that gives us at least some guaranteed income in our golden years.[80]

He is a liberal who instinctively wants to maintain government control of your retirement.

Obama writes that the Social Security system is not in crisis, because it has been fixed before:

> In 1983, when facing a similar problem, Ronald Reagan and House Speaker Tip O'Neill got together and shaped a bipartisan plan that stabilized the system for the next sixty years. There's no reason we can't do the same today.[81]

He leaves out something important: The 1983 "fix" of Social Security required increasing the retirement age from 65 to 67, cutting benefits, and (for the first time) taxing them. Obama does not plan to do this. His solution to Social Security is to increase the payroll tax, in addition to the income tax, the capital gains tax, and his new health insurance tax on employers.[82] There is no problem in America that Barack Obama cannot solve with a tax increase.

Again, you need not agree with my conservative take on all or any of these issues. You may think that Obama is correct on every single point. But these positions show he is not a *different* kind of politician. He is the *same* kind of politician as the ones we have had rolling around Washington for years. He is a rigid, doctrinaire liberal who votes and thinks along his party line. His moderating rhetoric should not be taken at face value.

CHAPTER SEVEN

THE RADICAL INFLUENCES

Everything was absolutely ideal on the day I bombed the Pentagon. The sky was blue. The birds were singing. And the bastards were finally going to get what was coming to them.[1]

S o begins Chapter 29 of Bill Ayers's 2001 book, *Fugitive Days*, a memoir of his experiences as a left-wing terrorist in the Weatherman movement. Ayers did not plant the bomb in the Pentagon himself, but both his book and Senate testimony on the incident[2] speak to his involvement in the plot. Ayers writes that he and his wife shrieked with delight when they heard the news reports on the radio after the bomb exploded, twenty-five minutes after a telephone warning.

"The Pentagon," he writes, "was ground zero for war and conquest, organizing headquarters of a gang of murdering thieves, a colossal stain on the planet, a hated symbol everywhere around the world... We'd already bombed the Capitol, and we'd cased the White House. The Pentagon was leg two of the trifecta."[3]

This is a man with whom Barack Obama associates. The two have served together on boards, and Ayers has contributed to one of Obama's campaigns. David Axelrod, Obama's strategist, has described their relationship as "friendly."[4]

Without going any further—without overstating the connection between these two—it is a remarkable relationship for a presidential nominee to have.

Obama dismisses concerns about his Ayers connections by condemning the terrorist activities and pointing out that Ayers has moved beyond terrorism. But Bill Ayers has never apologized for setting his bombs. He's never admitted he was a terrorist. He has recently said that he regrets not setting *more* bombs.

Would *you* be "friendly" with this man or anyone like him? Would any of your friends?

Although they should not be overstated, Obama has many radical ties. As a teenager, he had a communist mentor who told him not to trust white people. Later, he would steep himself in the radical philosophy of community organizer Saul Alinsky and train others in his teachings. He would inherit his first elected office from an admirer of the USSR, and seek to placate and even sign pledges for the same kinds of radical groups she did, some of whom identify themselves as socialist and communist. As a candidate for president, he has chosen some extremists as political advisors and he counts some among his fundraisers.

Obama is not a Marxist for his associations and alliances with Marxists, or a radical for his association with radicals. But his ideological influences are decidedly radical, which is an important consideration for voters. I provide the following material on Bill Ayers and on the other radical connections and influences in Obama's life not as a way of suggesting Obama endorses their actions or their far-out beliefs, but as a way of raising some worthwhile questions:

- Why does Obama associate with such people?
- What influence have they had on him?
- What do these relationships tell us about his judgment and the type of people with whom he will entrust executive powers if elected?

WILLIAM AYERS, TERRORIST

In a 2001 interview with the *Chicago Tribune,* Ayers denied that he was a terrorist: "The reason we weren't terrorists is because we did not commit random acts of terror against people," he said.[5] In the spring of 2008 on his blog, he made a similar assertion:

> I've never advocated terrorism, never participated in it, never defended it. The U.S. government, by contrast, does it routinely and defends the use of it in its own cause consistently.

Even if you accept Ayers' definition of terrorism, his claim is contradicted by sworn testimony. According to Senate testimony by an FBI mole within his organization, Ayers was indeed involved in the planning—and his wife, Bernardine Dohrn, in the execution—of a police station bombing in San Francisco in February 1970 that killed one and injured two others.[6] Larry Grathwohl, a Vietnam veteran who had earned the trust of the Weathermen after being recruited by them, testified in a classified session before a 1974 Senate subcommittee that Ayers had discussed the deadly incident after the fact.

[H]e cited as one of the real problems that someone like Bernardine Dohrn had to plan, develop and carry out the bombing of the police station in San Francisco, and he specifically named her as the person that committed that act...He said that the bomb was placed on the window ledge and he described the kind of bomb that was used to the extent of saying what kind of shrapnel was used in it...[I]f he wasn't there to see it, somebody who was there told him about it, because he stated it very emphatically.[7]

Grathwohl also testified about an unsuccessful Weatherman bombing in Detroit, which he said Ayers had planned for a time when the maximum number of people would be present:

The only time that I was ever instructed or we were ever instructed to place a bomb in a building at a time when there would be people in it was during the planning of the bombing at the Detroit Police Officers' Association building and the 13th Precinct in Detroit, Mich., at which time Bill said that we should plan our bombing to coincide with the time when there would be the most people in those buildings.[8]

Grathwohl tipped off police to that plot, and they cleared the area. When they finally found the bomb, it was unexploded[9] at the Police Officers' Association. It contained thirteen sticks of dynamite with an M-80 firecracker to detonate them. All were found unexploded, along with a burnt-out cigarette.

"The only thing Bill didn't take into consideration in making his bomb," Grathwohl testified, "was the fact that these wicks, those fuses on those firecrackers are waterproof with heavy paraffin, and a cigarette burning by itself does not always have enough heat to melt that paraffin and light the powder. And I didn't volunteer any information to the contrary." Grathwohl said he didn't know who actually planted the bomb.

Dohrn is probably most famous for her reaction to the Charles Manson murders, which she romanticized as a revolutionary coup at a Flint, Michigan, Weathermen War Council in December 1969:

> Dig it! First they killed those pigs, then they ate dinner in the same room with them. They even shoved a fork into the victim's stomach! Wild![10]

In his book, Ayers was nearly as colorful in his revolutionary philosophy, although reviewer Timothy Noah notes that he left out of *Fugitive Days* this famous statement he had made: "Kill all the rich people. Break up their cars and apartments. Bring the revolution home. Kill your parents."[11]

Ayers and Dohrn escaped prosecution only because of government misconduct in collecting evidence against them. Ayers was a free man promoting *Fugitive Days* when on the morning of September 11, 2001, a story in the *New York Times* was published, quoting him: "I don't regret setting bombs. I feel we didn't do enough."

You could say that his timing was bad, but Ayers was unaffected by the terrorist attack that day. Five days later, Ayers was quoted in *New York Times Magazine*:

> This society is not a just and fair and decent place... We're living in a country where the election was stolen, and we didn't have a mass uprising. It's incredible. We're all asleep. The pundits all pat themselves on the back: "God, what a great country."... It makes me want to puke.[12]

On April 17, 2008, Mayor Richard Daley warned against attempts to create "guilt by association," or "tarring" his political ally, Barack Obama, "because he happens to know Bill Ayers."[13]

Obama himself has been more defensive about it:

> The notion that somehow as a consequence of me knowing somebody who engaged in detestable acts 40 years ago, when I was 8 years old, somehow reflects on me and my values doesn't make much sense to me.[14]

Obama would obviously never approve of, let alone emulate, what Ayers did. And the fact that Ayers is considered a respected faculty member at a respected university and a respected citizen in Hyde Park says a lot more about the state of academia today than it does about Obama, who made Ayers's acquaintance through state senator Alice Palmer when she first invited him to run for her Senate seat.[15]

But it remains both relevant and interesting that Obama is "friendly" with an unrepentant terrorist who was involved in a movement that killed innocent people, and that he even accepted donations from him to his campaign. How many unrepentant Communist terrorists do you have as friends? How many politicians have such a donor, even if the contribution was just $200?[16]

BILL AYERS AND ERIC RUDOLPH

Obama has worked with Ayers on various projects through the charitable Woods Fund of Chicago, and with members of his family through the Chicago Public Education Fund. He also appeared with Ayers on an academic discussion panel on juvenile justice.[17] If Ayers had apologized, repented, changed his ways and moved on, Obama's defense—

that Ayers' deplorable acts happened decades ago—would make much more sense.

Ayers still believes that bombing police and government buildings was the right thing to do.

At one point, Obama tried to address his acquaintance with Ayers by noting that he counts conservative senator Tom Coburn as a friend without sharing his views—so why not someone of Ayers's radical stripe?[18] Obama recognized quickly that this was a mistake and called Coburn to apologize for the unflattering comparison. Evidently, Coburn was not fully satisfied, for he complained a month later about the incident to radio host Sean Hannity.

"Why answer a question by throwing a friend under a bus?" asked Coburn. "He did not answer the question, and if you're running for the President of this country there is not any question about your associations, your friends, that you should not have to answer. And the fact is that he has never answered the question."[19]

A better comparison than Coburn might have been Eric Rudolph, whose bombings of abortion clinics, a gay nightclub, and the Olympics killed two and wounded hundreds. If Rudolph—whose cause, anti-abortion and anti-gay, was just as political as Ayers'—had gotten away with his crimes due to a technicality, how many politicians would sit on panel discussions with him, even if he had well-articulated and high-minded things to say about justice or education or health care?

Ayers may be the most extreme of Obama's associates, but Obama has been around radicals of a less violent stripe all his life.

Like many Americans, Obama had a dalliance with radicalism in his college days. He writes that in order to "avoid being mistaken for a sellout," he hung out with "the more politically active black students. The foreign students. The Chicanos. The Marxist professors and structural feminists and punk-rock performing poets." He writes, self-mockingly, that "[w]hen we ground out our cigarettes in the hallway carpet or set our stereos so loud that the walls began to shake, we were resisting the bourgeois society's stifling constraints. We weren't indifferent or careless or insecure. We were alienated."[20]

Much of the young Obama's courtship of radicalism had to do with his inner conflict about his racial identity. For answers, he turned to the literature of a communist (Richard Wright, who was expelled from the party), a fellow traveler (W. E. B. DuBois, who eulogized Joseph Stalin as "a great man"[21]), and to other black authors such as Ralph Ellison and James Baldwin. He looked at where each one's racial angst led him as a black man living in a white world. "Each man," Obama writes, "was finally forced to withdraw, one to Africa, one to Europe, one deeper into the bowels of Harlem, but all of them in the same weary flight, all of them exhausted, bitter men, the devil at their heels."[22]

Obama also looked into and flirted with the black nationalism of Malcolm X. He explains over the course of several pages, interspersed with anecdotes, why he rejected nationalism as an unworkable and ineffective approach.[23] But he also rejects what one reviewer of *Dreams* calls "the unrealistic politics of integrationist assimilation—which helps a few upwardly mobile blacks to 'move up, get rich, and move out.'"[24]

THE SHOES HE FILLED

Ten years before she ran for the United States Congress and left her Senate seat to Barack Obama, Alice Palmer was attending a completely different kind of congress.

The year was 1986, and she was attending the 27th Congress of the Communist Party of the Soviet Union. Upon her return, Palmer, a journalist with the Black Press Institute, shared her impressions of what she saw in an interview with the *People's Daily World*. She was very optimistic about the future of the USSR:

> The Soviets plan to provide people with higher wages and better education, health and transportation, while we in our country are hearing that cutbacks are necessary in all of these areas.[25]

Palmer noted that the Party Congress had drawn up a "comprehensive five-year economic plan" whose certain success would demonstrate the nation's might and determination. The Reagan Administration, Palmer told the magazine, was making conditions worse in the United States:

> "We Americans can be misled by the major media. We're being told the Soviets are striving to achieve a comparatively low standard of living compared with ours, but actually they have reached a basic stability in meeting their needs and are now planning to double their production..."
>
> Like the Reagan administration, the Soviets talk of increasing productivity among workers and curbing waste at various enterprises, Palmer noted, "but the Soviets do not link these issues with ruining the living standards of human beings."[26]

Just as that five-year plan was ending (some people say it didn't work out so well), Alice Palmer was winning her state Senate seat. During her fifth year in Springfield, she had groomed Barack Obama to succeed her, even bringing him to a fundraiser at Bill Ayers's house in Hyde Park.[27]

Clearly, she was leaving him with big shoes to fill.

Obama obviously broke with Palmer when he threw her off the ballot in 1996, but he continued to associate with her radical ilk. His close ties to the far Left would persist throughout his career—for example, we saw earlier how he repudiated his party's moderates in 2003 in a long exchange of letters with the radical *Black Commentator*.[28] Obama's ties to the far Left also manifested themselves much earlier, when he first sought the endorsement of the Marxist "New Party" in Chicago.

According to *New Ground*, the newsletter of the Chicago Democratic Socialists of America (DSA), Obama appeared at the New Party's summer 1995 meeting to seek their endorsement in his state Senate race.[29] The New Party, the newsletter states, contained a heavy contingent of DSA members and also members of the Committees of Correspondence for Democracy and Socialism, a splinter group that broke away from the Communist Party USA after the fall of its financial and ideological patron, the Soviet Union.

Obama obtained the New Party endorsement, but as *New Ground* states, it came with a price:

> Once approved, candidates must sign a contract with the NP. The contract mandates that they must have a visible and active relationship with the NP.

That Obama made such public gestures toward the radicals who had supported his predecessor is surely relevant as he seeks the presidency. And they certainly liked him. Palmer's radical friends did not long lament her departure from the political world. After Obama had Palmer's name taken off the ballot, *New Ground* endorsed him without so much as mentioning her demise:

> Luckily, Mr. Obama does not have any opposition in the primary. His opponents have all dropped out or were ruled off the ballot. [30]

Alice *who*?

It was as if a purge had taken place.

"THE AMERICAN WAY AND ALL THAT SH-T"

Beyond his reading of Marxist authors during college (not outside the norm for most students), Obama cites among his youthful influences "a poet named Frank" who was a friend of his grandfather. Frank served as a mentor to Obama even as a boy, when he and his grandfather would visit the old black poet and the two adults would drink whiskey and while away the hours.

"I was intrigued by old Frank," writes Obama, "with his books and whiskey breath and the hint of hard-earned knowledge behind the hooded eyes."[31] Obama would help Frank and his grandfather compose dirty limericks.

This "Frank" is an intriguing character whose advice to young Barack is eye-catching and provocative. The advice ranges from words of wisdom about women ("They'll drive you to drink, boy... And if you let 'em, they'll drive you into your grave") to far more radical counsel about racial identity.

For example, Obama recalls that when he was a teenager, his grandmother had become afraid of an aggressive panhandler who was black. Her attitude toward the beggar's race deeply upset Obama's grandfather.

"It *is* a big deal," Obama's grandfather had told him. "It's a big deal to me. She's been bothered by men before. You know why she's so scared this time? I'll tell you why. Before you came in, she told me the fella was *black*."

Obama was disturbed by what had happened. He drove to old Frank's house to talk it over, and Frank imparted another bit of counsel to him: You can *never fully trust white people*. Speaking of Obama's grandfather, Frank said:

> He *can't* know me, not the way I know him. Maybe some of these Hawaiians can, or the Indians on the reservation. They've seen their fathers humiliated. Their mothers desecrated. But your grandfather will never know what that feels like. That's why he can come over here and drink my whiskey and fall asleep in that chair you're sitting in right now. Sleep like a baby. See, that's something I can never do in his house. *Never.* Doesn't matter how tired I get, I sill have to watch myself. I have to be vigilant, for my own survival... What I'm trying to tell you is, your grandma's right to be scared. She's at least as right as Stanley is. She understands black people have a reason to hate. That's just how it is. For your sake, I wish it were otherwise. But it's not. So you might as well get used to it.[32]

Later in Obama's book, Frank urges him to be careful in college, lest he become a traitor to his race. The young Obama takes Frank seriously when he warns that he risks...

> ...leaving your race at the door...leaving your people behind... Understand something, boy. You're not going to college to get educated. You're going there to get *trained*. They'll train you to want what you don't need. They'll train you to manipulate words so they don't mean anything anymore. They'll train you to forget what it is that you already know. They'll train you so good, you'll start believing what they tell you about equal opportunity and the American way and all that sh-t... Until you want to actually start running things, and then they'll yank on your

chain and let you know that you may be a well-trained, well-paid
n——r, but you're a n——r just the same.[33]

Obama doesn't give us the full identity of this man who influenced
him as a kid. Such half-disclosure is in keeping with the tone of
Obama's story-telling memoir—he creates pseudonyms and compos-
ites for many real-life characters. But if you follow the clues that
Obama provides—that Frank is a poet living in Hawaii who used to
run with Langston Hughes—he can be only one man: Frank Marshall
Davis. Davis was reportedly a Communist who worked on behalf of
the Soviet Union.

The earliest source I can find saying that "Frank" is in fact Frank
Marshall Davis is a March 2007 article on the website *Political Affairs*,
a self-described Marxist magazine. The article was adapted from a
speech by Gerald Horne "at the reception of the Communist Party USA
archives at the Tamiment Library at New York University."[34]

Davis never admitted to being a member of the Party during his lifetime, but there's solid evidence he was. A 1951 commission in Hawaii
reported to the territory's legislature that Davis was a member of the
Communist Party USA. This did not merely mean he believed in Marxist ideology, but rather he was a member of the Soviet-backed and
funded organ within the U.S.

Davis-friendly editor John Edgar Tidwell also identifies Davis as a
member of the Communist Party in the introduction to a collection of
Davis poetry: "Sometime during the middle of the war, he joined the
Communist party."[35] When Davis testified before a Senate subcommittee in 1956, he took the Fifth Amendment when asked if he was a
member of the Party.[36]

Members of CPUSA acted in the interests of their sponsor, the Soviet
Union, and all but the covert members adhered publicly to the Soviet—

at that time Stalinist—line. A July 7, 1935 communiqué from Moscow, coming long before Davis went to Hawaii, illustrates the seriousness of this development and gives some historical background. It urged Communists in Honolulu to agitate for the withdrawal of American military forces from the islands, in line with Soviet objectives in Asia:

> The growing discontent of the masses of the population in the Hawaiian Islands with the regime of colonial oppression and the exploitation of American imperialism with its policy of militarisation of the Hawaiian Islands makes it essential for the CP USA to give every possible assistance to the development of the mass revolutionary movement in Hawaii . . . [I]t is the first and foremost task of the American Party to assist this process and raise the slogan of "Right of self-determination for the Peoples of Hawaii, up to the Point of Separation", to demand the withdrawal of the U.S. Armed Forces, and to expose the policy of the militarisation of Hawaii as part of the war plans of American imperialism.[37]

CPUSA's activities, as Davis's life demonstrates, changed over time along with the interests of the USSR. Tidwell writes that Davis—involved with Communists but not yet a member in the pre-war period—had been especially uncomfortable with the Party's activism against U.S. involvement in World War II. (The Soviet Union had signed the Molotov-Ribbentrop non-aggression pact with Nazi Germany.[38]) But Davis collaborated in those efforts all the same, appearing in November 1940 as a sponsor and speaker at an anti-war conference sponsored by a Communist Party front group.[39] This is not to imply that Davis was sympathetic to Hitler—quite the opposite—but even before the war, he went along with the Soviet-controlled CPUSA enough to co-sponsor the event.

When Davis moved to Hawaii, he caused a stir among anti-communist liberals with his activism. Ed Berman, a white member of the executive committee of the NAACP's Honolulu branch, wrote the national NAACP to warn leaders that Davis had come from Chicago in 1948 as part of a Soviet effort to take over their branch:

> I was at one of the election meetings at which one Frank Marshall Davis, formerly of Chicago...suddenly appeared on the scene to propagandize the membership about our "racial problems in Hawaii. He had just sneaked in here on a boat, and presto, was an 'expert' on racial problems in Hawaii. Comrade Davis was supported by others who recently 'sneaked' into the organization with the avowed intent and purpose of converting it into a front for the Stalinist line.[40]

The national NAACP, under the staunchly anti-Communist leadership of Roy Wilkins, revoked the charter of the Honolulu branch rather than allow this takeover.[41]

Davis had not been alone among black intellectuals in embracing Soviet Communism in the struggle to end racism, but he was firmly in the minority. He certainly operated outside of the tradition from which Martin Luther King Jr. and the Civil Rights Era would later emerge. The NAACP and other anti-racist organizations at the time viewed the Communists as exploiters of the race issue with an entirely different agenda:

> In refusing to cooperate with Communists, NAACP representatives insisted that the Communists did not honestly care about the plight of African Americans but merely sought to exploit the race issue. The party was denounced as depending completely on political and ideological directives from Moscow

and of sacrificing the interests of black people to the foreign policy concerns of the Soviet Union.[42]

The experiences of Richard Wright, whose books Obama had read as a teenager, confirmed such suspicions. Wright, who was ostracized from the Party against his will in 1944, had become disillusioned, among other things, by blatant racial discrimination from Communists who wanted to hold him up as a symbol but refused even to welcome him into their own homes.[43]

In Davis, Obama had a mentor—a father figure on racial issues—who had lived his life far outside the political mainstream of black America. Davis wrote that "the Soviet Union held the same position internationally that blacks were in domestically. Russians were looked upon as the n——rs of the globe...I considered Red Russia our friend."[44]

In his poems, Davis praised the Red Army and at times went far beyond what his Communist comrades were willing to tolerate.[45] His poem, "War Quiz for America," reads, in part:

> If it works in lands I never saw before
> Against strangers with faces new to me
> Then it must be the right thing to use
> Against all foes of freedom
> Against all apostles of fascism
> Against some people I know
> Right here in America
> ...Say, Uncle Sam,
> Are you sure you want me to have a gun?[46]

Today, some conservatives on the Internet write as though Obama is a Manchurian candidate who will bring about a socialist revolution once in the White House—this is simple paranoia. To be sure, Obama is probably more liberal than any previous presidential nominee, but that obviously does not make him a communist.

The influence on Obama of a man like Frank Marshall Davis is important mostly in understanding how his view of the world was formed—he has embraced some ideas while obviously rejecting others. Davis's influence did not turn Obama into a communist or a habitual stoker of racial grievance. To his credit, Obama generally avoids such rhetoric. Even so, for a post-partisan politician promoting a "new politics," Obama can be quick to attribute bad faith to his opponents in the area of race:

> We know what kind of campaign they're going to run... They're going to try to make you afraid of me. He's young and inexperienced and he's got a funny name. And did I mention he's black?[47]

RADICAL ADVISORS STILL

It would be foolish to fear Barack Obama just because he had a communist father-figure when he was young. But it is significant that he continues to surrounded himself with radicals as a presidential candidate.

On June 18, 2008, Obama's campaign announced its "senior working group on national security." Among the foreign policy advisors was Anthony Lake, whom President Clinton nominated in 1996 to head the Central Intelligence Agency. The appointment had to be withdrawn for a number of reasons,[48] among them a 1996 appearance on Tim Russert's *Meet the Press*, in which Lake had said that the recently deceased Alger Hiss may not have been guilty of spying for the Soviet Union. "I've read a couple of books that have certainly offered a lot of evidence that he may have been," said Lake. "I don't think it's conclusive."[49] (He later claimed he had simply been caught off-guard by the question.[50])

The Obama campaign's black advisory council includes Cornel West,[51] an African-American studies professor at Princeton University who calls himself a "progressive socialist."[52] West has written that Marxist thought is "an indispensable tradition for freedom fighters," which "becomes even more relevant after the collapse of Communism in the Soviet Union and Eastern Europe than it was before." West paid a visit in early 2006 to Venezuela's left-wing strongman Hugo Chavez, who has re-written his nation's constitution to give himself unprecedented executive power and is still attempting to install himself at the ballot box as president for life. "We in the United States have so many lies about President Hugo Chavez and the Bolivarian Revolution," West once said. He would later say that he "went to Venezuela to see the democratic awakening taking place."[53]

Also on the black advisory council is Charles Ogletree, a Harvard law professor who argues in favor of reparations to the descendants of slaves. Ogletree "has advised Obama on reforming the criminal-justice system as well on constitutional issues."[54]

Another foreign policy advisor, Robert Malley, had to resign after it was revealed that he had been meeting with the terrorist group Hamas,[55] which in 2006 called for attacks against the United States.[56] Hamas political adviser Ahmed Yousef stated in April that his group supports Obama's foreign policy ideas. Obama has said he would not meet with the leadership of Hamas, but has said he will meet with the president of Iran, a major Hamas backer and funder.[57]

It would be unreasonable to expect Obama to accept as advisors only those who agree with every single belief he holds. But it would be difficult to find so many radicals in the ranks of any of the other serious presidential campaigns from either party.

Among Obama's fundraisers is Jodie Evans, a co-founder of Code Pink, an anti-war group known for disrupting congressional hearings and organizing controversial demonstrations in front of the Walter Reed Hospital in Washington. In January 2007, Evans led a delegation of former Guantanamo detainees and family members of current detainees to Cuba to protest the prison, scoring a public relations victory for Cuban dictator Fidel Castro.[58] Evans caused a stir in June 2008 when she praised Venezuelan strongman Chavez on a Kansas radio show (she asked, "Why is being a communist anti-American?"). Evans promised to bundle more than $50,000 for Obama's campaign.[59]

COMMUNITY ORGANIZER

If Obama could understand and get along with radicals like Palmer, Ayers, and Dohrn, it is not because he agrees with everything they stand for—it is probably because they share similar ideological influences.

One of them is Saul Alinsky, a left-wing community organizer who fought to bring jobs and government services to Chicago neighborhoods until his death in 1972.[60] Alinsky's disciples—the very organizers who had worked with the man himself—were the ones who hired Obama as a community organizer in Chicago in 1985. Obama has also participated in training hundreds of others in Alinsky's methods. Obama would later say that "his years as an organizer gave him the best education of his life."[61]

The immensity of Alinsky's influence in Democratic politics is demonstrated by his influence in the lives of the two top Democratic candidates for president this year. Hillary Clinton wrote her senior thesis on Alinsky, and he personally offered her a job when she graduated from Wellesley.[62]

Alinsky opens his groundbreaking book, *Rules for Radicals* with this disturbing dedication:

> Lest we forget at least an over-the-shoulder acknowledgment to the very first radical: from all our legends, mythology, and history (and who is to know where mythology leaves off and history begins—or which is which), the first radical known to man who rebelled against the establishment and did it so effectively that he at least won his own kingdom—Lucifer.[63]

This dedication would be purged from some subsequent editions so that Alinsky's ideas could be spread more easily among clergymen.

Alinsky, who founded the Industrial Areas Foundation to train young radicals, endorsed popular education, in which organizers persuade members of the community from different backgrounds (though generally members of the lower classes) to realize common problems and to embrace the organizers' answers to these problems.

Alinsky compares the "community organizer's" role to that of a labor organizer:

> He has taken a group of apathetic workers; he has fanned their resentments and hostilities by a number of means...Most important, he has demonstrated that something can be done, and that there is a concrete way of doing it that has already proven its effectiveness and success...Through action, persuasion, and communication the organizer makes it clear that organization will give them the power, the ability, the strength, the force to be able to do something about these particular problems. It is then that the bad scene begins to break up in to specific issues.[64]

Having stirred up dissatisfaction among the lower class regarding their situation, organizers next manipulate the mutual self-interest of varied and oft-opposed groups in order to put pressure on the authorities and thus change a community's situation. The key is to *Agitate, Aggravate,*

Educate, and then Organize. With a delicate understanding of psychology and human nature, Alinsky discusses at length how to prod members of a community toward the organizer's desired course of action while making them think they came up with the ideas themselves.[65]

Alinsky has a very fluid understanding of ethics that more or less matches that of Ayers and explains his reliance on intimidation and the stirring of discontent as tactics for radical action. He claims that "in war, the ends justify almost any means," and that "in action, one does not always enjoy the luxury of a decision that is consistent both with one's individual conscience and the good of mankind."[66] He writes that "[t]he Radical may resort to the sword but when he does he is not filled with hatred against those individuals whom he attacks. He hates these individuals not as persons but as symbols representing ideas or interests which he believes to be inimical to the welfare of the people."[67]

Morality is merely a "rhetorical rationale for expedient action and self-interest."

Integrity is not necessary to activism, but the *appearance* of integrity is important. "All effective action requires the passport of morality," he wrote. He also insists that "moral rationalization is indispensable at all times of action, whether to justify the selection or the use of means or ends."[69] Indeed, appearance plays a large and important role in Alinsky's work: "Power is not what you have, but what the enemy thinks you have."[70]

Alinsky subscribed to the Chicago School of sociology, which taught that "individual pathologies like delinquency and crime are the result of 'root causes' solvable by progressive, community-based social action."[68]

Obama was a master of Alinsky's tactics and understood his philosophy well. Mike Kruglik, once a fellow organizer, told *The New Republic* last year that Obama was "the undisputed master of agitation.... With probing, sometimes personal questions, he would pinpoint the source of pain in their lives, tearing down their egos just enough before dangling a carrot of hope that they could make things better."[71]

Alinsky urged his followers not to display class *hatred* toward the middle classes—at least not overtly. Instead, he offered a narrative of class *condescension*, which viewed them as lost, confused, aimless, and pitiable. He noted that any attempt to disabuse them of their irrational religious beliefs should be avoided because it would be met with hostility,[72] that their insistence on good manners should be respected by radicals, who tended to eschew such niceties as they employed rudeness and intimidation to solve community problems. He wrote:

> Seeking some meaning in life, they turn to an extreme chauvinism and become defenders of the "American" faith. Now they even develop rationalizations for a life of futility and frustration. "It's the Red menace!" Now they are not only the most vociferous in their espousal of law and order, but ripe victims for such as demagogic George Wallace, the John Birch Society, and the Red-menace perennials.
>
> Insecure in this fast-changing world, they cling to illusory fixed points—which are very real to them. Even conversation is charted toward fixing your position in the world: "I don't want to argue with you, just tell me what our flag means to you?"... They use revealing adjectives such as "outside agitators" or "troublemakers"...
>
> The "silent majority," now, are hurt, bitter, suspicious, feeling rejected and at bay. This sick condition in many ways is as explosive as the current race crisis. Their fears and frustrations at their helplessness are mounting to a point of a political para-

noia which can demonize people to turn to the law of survival in the narrowest sense.[73]

That may sound familiar. Consider the comments that Barack Obama was recorded making about rural, middle-class Christian voters at a cocktail fundraiser with wealthy San Franciscans:

> You go into these small towns in Pennsylvania and, like a lot of small towns in the Midwest, the jobs have been gone now for 25 years and nothing's replaced them. And they fell through the Clinton administration, and the Bush administration, and each successive administration has said that somehow these communities are going to regenerate and they have not.
>
> And it's not surprising then they get bitter, they cling to guns or religion or antipathy to people who aren't like them or anti-immigrant sentiment or anti-trade sentiment as a way to explain their frustrations.[74]

Obama was here paraphrasing Saul Alinsky—displaying this same *radical condescension*.

Alinsky had been organizing in Chicago during the tumultuous days of the late 1950s, when "White Flight" was turning over the demographics of entire neighborhoods from white to black. Unscrupulous realtors were scaring white Chicago homeowners into believing that their home values would plummet as soon as black neighbors moved in. These realtors could then buy up block after block of houses at reduced prices and sell them to blacks on unfavorable terms and at much higher prices—a phenomenon known as "block-busting."

Some Catholic parishes in Chicago were trying to slow or stop this flight of ethnic whites to the suburbs, and Alinsky worked with diocesan officials to preserve racially mixed neighborhoods. At one point, he proposed a "quota" system to prevent the self-segregation that ultimately occurred all across Chicago.

> He thought whites might accept the quota if they were guaran-
> teed that black population would not exceed five percent in a
> neighborhood. Another possibility was contiguous white and
> black neighborhood organizations set up to work together.
> Their mutual leadership could negotiate agreements on such
> issues as housing sales and rentals...[75]

These ideas, which depended on a high degree of central planning, were unworkable and went nowhere. It was just one of many failures that characterized Alinsky's activism both during and after his life. In his 1991 book *The Promised Land*, journalist Nicholas Lemann writes that this kind of activism, which characterized many of the programs established and run on a local level during the time of Lyndon Johnson's Great Society, "presumed a link between political empowerment and individual economic advancement that doesn't exist."[76]

Even once they had established a grudging alliance with Mayor Richard J. Daley (father of the current mayor) to create integrated and functional neighborhoods, Alinsky's allies found themselves powerless in saving neighborhoods such as Woodlawn (on the near South Side) from a loss of private businesses and an increase in crime that drove away residents with steady jobs.[77] As Lemann puts it:

> The history of the Woodlawn organization in Chicago was a
> perfect demonstration of the shortcomings of the empower-
> ment theory in the real world of a late-twentieth-century Amer-
> ican city; no matter how well organized a poor community

was, it could not become stable and not-poor so long as the
people with good jobs kept moving out and the people left
behind had very little income.[78]

Despite their educational value to him, Obama likewise found his days
as an activist to be somewhat futile in terms of results for the community. This is what prompted him to get a law degree so that he could
accomplish more,[79] and then to go into politics. The leaders of the mostly
poor and black communities in which he was "agitating"—Roseland
and West Pullman on the South Side of Chicago—often felt the same
way. He recorded their complaints after one high-profile failure:

> "Ain't nothing gonna change, Mr. Obama," she said. "We just
> gonna concentrate on saving our money so we can move outta
> here as fast as we can."[80]

At first, Obama had worked with his boss, Jerry Kellman (given the
pseudonym "Marty Kaufman" in the book) in a futile attempt to help
area residents get factory jobs that were already disappearing from the
area because of automation and global competition. Obama realized
that not only were the jobs disappearing, but that too many of the people in their neighborhoods lacked the skills and education to hold them
down.[81] Obama writes also of a $500,000 initiative that organizers had
set up for members of the community just before he began his work—
a job bank run out of a university. It had failed miserably and inex-
plicably. The money was spent, but no one in the neighborhood found
a job.[82]

After that, his main goal became to bring government money and
services into these South Side neighborhoods. He writes in *Dreams
from My Father* of the two biggest projects he ever tackled—one was
to bring a branch of the Mayor's Office of Employment and Training

(MET) to the area, to refer unemployed residents to training programs. In this project, he succeeded. His other major project was to have asbestos removed from apartments in the Altgeld Gardens public housing projects. Although Obama successfully got the Altgeld residents to pressure city officials and meet with them—he even got citywide news coverage of the problem—this turned out to be a big disappointment. The coverage became a problem when the meeting with the Chicago Housing Authority broke down in scuffles. The asbestos problem was never fully fixed: some Altgeld residents still have asbestos in their apartments even to this day.[83]

And when he came back from Harvard to the South Side, Obama would notice that these neighborhoods had deteriorated significantly.

> Upon my return to Chicago, I would find the signs of decay accelerated throughout the South Side—the neighborhoods shabbier, the children edgier and less restrained, more middle-class families heading out to the suburbs, the jails bursting with glowering youth, my brothers without prospects.[84]

Obama, like other street organizers in the Alinsky mold, never had much of a chance. He had a narrow range of solutions to offer South Siders that matches with the rigid adherence he has shown in office to liberal ideas.

He pursued manifestly worthy goals; protecting people from asbestos in government housing projects is obviously a good thing and a responsibility of the government that built them.

But after Kellman's attempt to work with the unions failed, the proposed solution to *every* problem on the South Side was a distribution of government funds, the effect of which is necessarily limited and temporary. In the long run, many of the most significant problems that plagued Roseland and West Pullman—family breakdown, dependency, unemployment, and yes, racism—would require major changes in personal habits and attitudes that activism could never bring about.

Obama's experience on Chicago's South Side did not disabuse him of the idea that government spending can serve as the economic keystone of a large, successful community. As a state senator, we saw that he would be suspicious of efforts to reform welfare that would make it a temporary program for those most in need and throw many people off the rolls and into jobs.[85] Of his negotiations on implementing welfare reform in Illinois, he would later say, "I made sure our new welfare system didn't punish people by kicking them off the rolls."[86]

And as we shall see in Chapter 11, his solution to the failure of public housing was to have the government give large government grants to developers who could only produce the same kind of misery in the same kind of large housing complexes, just with different landlords.

Today, Obama views his job as a politician much like the one he was doing as a community organizer:

> What if a politician were to see his job as that of an organizer, as part teacher and part advocate, one who does not sell voters short but who educates them about the real choices before them? As an elected public official, for instance, I could bring church and community leaders together easier than I could as a community organizer or lawyer... We must form grass-roots structures that would hold me and other elected officials more accountable for their actions.[87]

Perhaps a politician can be compared to a community organizer—but can a politician be any more effective than Obama or Alinsky was, applying centrally planned government solutions to problems that go much deeper than politics? Byron York has put it well: "Obama applied his considerable organizational skills to perpetuating the old, failed way of doing things."[88]

FUNDING FATHER

The connection between Obama and Ayers is circular in nature. For when he first came to Chicago, Obama's organizing salary had been paid for by the Woods Fund of Chicago, where he and Ayers would later serve together on the board from 1999 to 2002.[89]

The Woods Fund is today a $72 million foundation. Originally founded to help civil rights groups, it has drifted toward radical causes over the years. Today it gives large grants to left-wing organizations.[90] The fund's stated mission is to break down "structural barriers to job opportunities, job retention and job advancement" for people in neighborhoods like the ones in which Obama was an organizer.

At the Woods Fund, Obama and Ayers together also helped provide Obama's old law firm boss, Allison Davis, a $1 million grant for a community development project.[91]

The Woods Fund gives grants to several organizations, including:

- The Center for Tax and Budget Accountability, a group that lobbies members of the Illinois state legislature for what they call "fair, efficient and progressive tax, spending and economic policies."[92] CTBA's web site urges members to contact their representatives in support of a 67 percent hike in personal and corporate income taxes, and urges a broadening of services subject to the sales tax in order to raise still more tax revenue.[93]

- The Tides Foundation, which, according to the Discover the Networks Project, "receives money from donors and then funnels it to the recipients of their choice. Because many of these recipient groups are quite radical, the donors often prefer not to have their names publicly linked with the donees."[94] The Proteus fund, a similar donation middleman, also receives Woods grants.
- The Midwest Academy, a training camp for radicals founded by disciples of Saul Alinsky.
- The Center for Community Change, another Alinsky activism organization.
- The Arab American Action Network, run by Rashid Khalidi, who in 2000 held a fundraiser for Obama. The group, which received $75,000 in two different grants in 2001 and 2003, is creating an oral history project on "an-Nakba"—the great "catastrophe" of Israel's founding.[95]

The most noteworthy and best-known Woods grant recipient is probably ACORN—the Association of Community Organizations for Reform Now. ACORN is a left-wing group that has historically helped elect Democrats and affected social change through intimidating public officials, in the Alinsky tradition.[96] ACORN uses taxpayer money to conduct these activities—it has received 40 percent of its funding from taxpayers over the last three years.[97] Its other main source of funding is financial settlements with the corporations ACORN fights—indeed, these account for more of the group's money than all donations they receive from foundations and churches combined. "ACORN's business model," a report on the group states, "involves choosing a corporate target, attacking it, reaching a financial settlement, and then beginning the cycle again with a different target."[98]

ACORN has fought to repeal welfare reform and pass laws that drive big box stores such as Wal-Mart (and the jobs they create) away from poorer communities. They have successfully stormed Chicago's City Council and intimidated the mayor of Baltimore.[99]

ACORN also conducts voter registration drives through its Project Vote, and its members boast that they have played a key role in Obama's election campaigns.[100] It was with Project Vote that Obama had assisted in a 1992 registration drive. Obama also represented ACORN in a 1995 lawsuit over Illinois's implementation of the Motor Voter law.

Of course, according to ACORN leader Toni Foulkes, ACORN loves Obama.

"It was natural for many of us to be active volunteers in his first campaign for State Senate and then his failed bid for U.S. Congress... By the time he ran for U.S. Senate, we were old friends."[104]

Barack Obama has many ties to radicals—some violent, some intriguing, and some just odd. Some of these ties came about by accident, others he consciously forged and strengthened. Obama is not a Marxist or a radical. He is certainly not a terrorist-sympathizer. Yet it is clear that radicals have influenced his judgment. He has inherited ideas about "bitter" people who "cling to illusory fixed points;" ideas about central planning; and ideas that sometimes lead him to impute racism to his opponents.

Of greatest significance are the radical advisors with whom Senator Obama surrounds himself even now. Should he become president, will he entrust such men and women with executive power?

CHAPTER EIGHT

REVEREND WRIGHT AND OBAMA'S FAITH

The government lied about the Tuskegee experiment. They purposely infected African American men with syphilis. Governments lie.... The government lied about inventing the HIV virus as a means of genocide against people of color.[1]

N ot one word of the above paragraph is true—not even the part about Tuskegee. In that unforgivable story of government malfeasance, the United States government did not *infect* anyone with syphilis. What really happened is that they *did not treat* their test subjects: black men who already had the disease.[2]

Still less true, and much crazier, is the assertion that follows, that the United States government created the Human Immunodeficiency Virus, which causes AIDS, and that it released it to kill black people. It is bad enough that anyone should say this. It is even worse that it comes from

151

a man with spiritual authority—a man who could convince many cred-
ulous people it is true.

Of course it was the Reverend Jeremiah Wright who held and shared
precisely this uninformed view on April 13, 2003. It was in this sermon
that he made what has become one of the most oft-quoted declarations
of the 2008 presidential race:

> The government gives them the drugs, builds bigger prisons,
> passes a three strikes law, and then wants us to sing "God Bless
> America?" No, no, no! Not "God Bless America!" God damn
> America! That's in the Bible, for killing innocent people![3]

This is the very kind of "Gospel truth" that frequently came from the
pulpit at the church where Barack Obama became a Christian, was married, and attended nearly every week since law school; this is the church
where he brought his children to learn about Jesus Christ. And, of
course, the speaker who uttered those words on April 13, 2003 was the
same man responsible for bringing Barack Obama to Christ.

Rev. Wright was a hard man to get along with. Stanley Kurtz relates
in *National Review* that Wright had arrived by invitation at Trinity in
1972 and that by 1975 "nearly all of the members who had originally
invited him had left. In 1983, a group of particularly active and promi-
nent members uncomfortable with Wright left Trinity and the UCC for
a local Pentecostal Apostolic church."[4]

It is easy to understand. In his many inflammatory sermons, Wright
mocks black Republicans: "They live below the C-level. They live
below the level of Clarence, Colin and Con-damn-esia!"[5]

He explains the September 11, 2001 attacks in this way:

> We have supported state terrorism against the Palestinians and
> the black South Africans, and now we are indignant—because the

stuff we have done overseas is now brought right back into our own front yards! America's chickens are coming home to roost.[6]

Not only would Wright give such sermons, but the church sold the videos. Senator Obama documents in *Dreams from My Father* his first Wright sermon—the one that changed his life forever. Surprisingly, he does not comment on its racial angle, even though the book focuses carefully on the topic of race relations. Wright had said:

> It is this world, a world where cruise ships throw away more food in a day than most residents of Port-au-Prince see in a year, where white folks' greed runs a world in need, apartheid in one hemisphere, apathy in another hemisphere...That's the world! On which hope sits![7]

It certainly does not approach "God Damn America," but even on that first occasion, Obama heard Wright blaming "white folks," in this case for world hunger. This is no accident, as we shall see, but a crucial part of the theology that underpins Wright's christology and his church's worship.

Obama relates that this first sermon caused in him a fundamental revelation. Indeed, the sermon was not merely a tirade against white people—it had spiritual content as well. Obama noticed only at the end of it that he had been crying while listening.[8] After this, he would be baptized by Wright in his church, having led up to that point a life more in line with the secular humanism of his parents.

STAND BY YOUR MAN

As all of the damaging material from Wright's controversial sermons began to hit the Internet in the spring of 2008, Obama did not have the luxury of ignoring it and letting it drag him down. The answer was his famous race speech of March 18 in Philadelphia. He would not disown Wright—a key figure in his life and that of his family—nor would he leave the South Side church that the man had built up.

Perhaps a sudden defection would not have been credible. It might have smacked of opportunism, not only to those in his congregation, but also to those millions of television viewers who had just learned about Wright and found him frightening as the mentor of a potential president. It's one thing to force a campaign aide to resign the second a controversy is revealed—it's quite another to dump your pastor of twenty years the minute his public sermons become public knowledge.

Obama certainly could not claim ignorance about Wright's reputation as a fractious and colorful character, prone to making controversial and at times racist statements. Even before Wright became so controversial, David Mendell wrote that his sermons "more resemble left-wing political rants than religious preaching."[9] Wright had already called Bush voters "stupid" in one sermon.[10]

Oprah Winfrey had bailed out of Wright's congregation, in part out of fear for her public image and her business interests. She had been a full-fledged member beginning in 1984, but her attendance became more sporadic over the years until she stopped attending altogether in the mid-1990s. One reason was Wright's fiery sermons. *Newsweek* quoted an unnamed friend of Oprah in explaining her decision:

> Oprah is a businesswoman, first and foremost. She's always been aware that her audience is very mainstream and doing anything to offend them wouldn't be smart. She's been around black churches all her life, so Reverend Wright's anger-filled message didn't surprise her. But it just wasn't what she was looking for in a church.[11]

That it "didn't surprise her" is, one hopes, an exaggeration. Surely, very few black churches misinform their congregations so blatantly, teaching that AIDS was created by the U.S. government in order to kill black people, or that the government deliberately supplies the inner-city with drugs. The *Newsweek* article notes that Oprah "was eager to bond with the movers and shakers in her new hometown's black community," and that she appreciated the church's work with the poor. But Rev. Wright was just too far out for her.

One of Obama's advisors gave *Newsweek* another explanation for Obama's continued attendance at Trinity, implying that he had stayed at the church because he was not "secure in his blackness."

> "[His] reasons for attending Trinity were totally different [from Oprah's]," said one campaign adviser, who declined to be named discussing the Illinois senator's sentiments. "Early on, he was in search of his identity as an African-American and, more importantly, as an African-American man. Reverend Wright and other male members of the church were instrumental in helping him understand the black experience in America. Winfrey wasn't going for that. She's secure in her blackness, so that didn't have a hold on her."[12]

It is *an* explanation. But if one takes Obama's writings on the topic of faith seriously—and they are reflective, intense passages—this explanation seems very superficial.

Obama often describes his faith experience by reference to the humanistic principles he inherited from a mother wary of religion[13] and a father who was a "confirmed atheist."[14] But he still grew up with guideposts for his moral life.

"There are some things that I'm absolutely sure about," he writes in *The Audacity of Hope*; "the Golden Rule, the need to battle cruelty in all its forms, the value of love and charity, humility and grace."[15]

Obama had revealed in his earlier book his aversion to religion during his youth, in a way that undoubtedly helps explain his attraction to Saul Alinsky's activism (see Chapter 7).

> Issues, action, power, self-interest. I liked these concepts. They bespoke of a certain hardheadedness, a worldly lack of sentiment; politics, not religion.[16]

Yet during those days as a community organizer, Obama recognized that his work was suffering because the pastors in Chicago generally viewed him as an outsider—as someone willing to use their congregations for his own purposes, but whose motivations remained unclear because he did not attend church himself.[17]

Does this make Obama a religious opportunist? Does it mean that he "got religion" for reasons having nothing to do with faith? Was he following Alinsky's advice and simply taking up the manners of those he was trying to convince? Many conservatives and supporters of Hillary Clinton accused him of as much after his patronizing comments about "bitter" people embracing faith—a suggestion that working-class Christians adhere to their faith out of a perhaps naïve credulity in its power to make a miserable life more tolerable. Voters saw this same thing, it appears, considering his 74 percent to 26 percent loss among white Catholics in Pennsylvania's Democratic primary shortly afterward.[18]

But on this topic, Obama has more than earned the benefit of the doubt. It is in the area of faith that he has made his greatest political miscalculations in this campaign, and they are the miscalculations of a believer. For all of his shrewdness as a politician, Obama was willing to pay a steep political price for prolonging his association with Wright and Trinity Church under some very trying circumstances. Would a believer of mere convenience have stood by Wright when he had absolutely nothing to gain politically? Would he have donated so much money to Trinity—$5,000 in 2005 and $22,500 in 2006?[19] He even helped send outside money to Wright. In 2002, when Obama served on the board of the Woods Fund, it approved $6,000 in grants to Trinity.[20]

Obama could have changed his church affiliation earlier without attracting too much attention, particularly after his election to the U.S. Senate. But he did not take that path.

In an article titled "Obama's Faith" in the June 10, 2007 edition of the Trinity Church bulletin (nine months before the Wright explosion), Professor Robert M. Franklin, then of Emory University, applauded Obama for not abandoning his roots among the South Side's working poor for a more affluent church in a wealthier neighborhood.[21] Having chosen Trinity for himself and for his family, Obama remained loyal to Wright, his pastor of two decades, until things became so intensely personal that the price was finally too great to bear.

All of this speaks to Obama's sincerity. But it should also cause some questions about his judgment. It's absurd to believe that Barack Obama hates America or would say anything like what Wright has publicly declared—e.g., that the government deliberately introduced AIDS into the black community in order to exterminate it.[22] Obama's writings on race are, for the most part, very level-headed, even philosophical. Yet he did still attach himself to Wright, knowing what kind of preacher he was. He did so after hearing his first Wright sermon, which blamed the white man for the world's problems.

IT'S NOT JUST WRIGHT'S SERMONS

As with his political associations, Obama's major influences in the realm of faith are undeniably radical. He chose them that way, knowingly. It is not only Wright himself that embodies that radicalism, but also Trinity's newsletter, its guest preachers, and its new pastor, who would himself create new problems before Obama finally disowned Wright and left Trinity.

Of course no one can justly hold Obama responsible for Rev. Wright's words, but what about the stated philosophy of the church he chose to join?

Would you join a church that proclaimed itself to be grounded in the writings of a racist?

"The vision statement of Trinity United Church of Christ," the church's website states, "is based upon the systematized liberation theology that started in 1969 with the publication of Dr. James Cone's seminal book, *Black Power and Black Theology*."[23]

James Cone is a professor at Columbia University's Union Theological Seminary. What is Cone's Black Liberation Theology? Rev. Andrew Greeley, a Catholic priest and professor of religious sociology at the University of Arizona, referred to Cone's "Nazi mentality" and called his work "a theology filled with hatred for white people and the assumption of a moral superiority of black over white."[24]

That may sound like an exaggeration, but Cone's book—the one referred to on Trinity's site—is replete with such embarrassing, racist quotations as these:

> Because white theology has consistently preserved the integrity
> of the community of oppressors, I conclude that it is not Christian theology at all.[25]

And:

> [I]nsofar as this country is seeking to make whiteness the dominating power throughout the world, whiteness is the symbol
> of the antichrist. Whiteness characterizes the activity of

deranged individuals intrigued by their own image of themselves and thus unable to see that they are what is wrong with the world. Black theology seeks to analyze the satanic nature of whiteness and by doing so, prepare all nonwhites for revolutionary action.[26]

And:

[L]iberal whites... want to be white and Christian at the same time; but they fail to realize that this approach is a contradiction in terms—Christianity and whiteness are opposites.[27]

And:

Intrigued by their own expertise in Christian theology, white religionists think they have the moral and intellectual right to determine whether black churches are Christian. They fail to realize that their analysis of Christianity is inseparable from their oppressor mentality which shapes everything they say about God.[28]

That's just for starters—nearly every page is covered with such material. I found and compiled five single-spaced pages of such material literally by opening a 1986 edition of Cone's book at random and looking at the pages I landed on. I had to stop eventually—it was far more than I could ever use.

Bear in mind that Cone wrote this screed in 1970. He wrote it long after the integration of the armed services, long after *Brown v. Board of Education*, after the Civil Rights Act of 1964 and the Voting Rights Act of 1965, and after major advances in black prosperity had begun. Many of these positive developments had been at least partly the result of work by white Christians. But over the following decades, Cone would publish new editions of this book with these passages unaltered. According to the theological father of Trinity Church, white people are hopeless oppressors, incapable of entering the Kingdom of Heaven. As Cone puts it:

> There will be no peace in America until whites begin to hate their whiteness, asking from the depths of their being: "How can we become black?"[29]

In this context, Wright's controversial sermons really appear somewhat mild. But Cone's writings provide the context from within which the founding influences of Obama's former church come. Trinity Church's website still holds Cone up as its inspiration.[30] Also, Cone's book, from which I quote above, is the first selection from its bookstore in the "Africentric Theology" category.[31]

From Cone's book, and from every word of Rev. Wright I've read (admittedly a small sample), we see a pattern in Trinity's brand of Christianity: it is not a religion that asks its adherents to look within, root out sin, live virtuously—and by extension treat their neighbors with the virtue of charity, care for the poor, and fight racism. Cone's and Wright's Christianity appears instead to preach a message that the *self* is the innocent victim, the Christ-figure. The Gospel, instead of being a book from which to learn how to live, is treated as a text that justifies the identification of others as one's own oppressors. One of Wright's sermons, which you can watch on YouTube, offers ample testimony of this:

> Jesus was a poor black man who lived in a country—and who lived in a culture—that was controlled by rich, white people. The Romans were rich, the Romans were Italian, which means they were European, which means they were white, and the Romans ran everything in Jesus' country.

It just came to me within the past few weeks...why so many folk are hating on Barack Obama. He doesn't fit the mold: he ain't white, he ain't rich, and he ain't privileged.

Hillary fits the mold. Europeans fit the mold. Giuliani fits the mold. Rich, white men fit the mold.

Hillary never had a cab whiz past her and not pick her up because her skin was the wrong color. Hillary never had to worry about being pulled over in her car as a black man driving in the wrong [neighborhood].

I am sick of Negroes who just do not get it. Hillary was not a black boy raised in a single-parent home. Barack was...

Oh, I am so glad that I got a God who knows what it is to be a poor black man in a country and a culture that is controlled by and run by rich, white people. He taught me, Jesus did, how to love my enemies. Jesus taught me how to love the hell out of my enemies and not to be reduced to their level of hatred, bigotry, and small-mindedness.

Hillary ain't never had her own people say she wasn't white enough. Jesus had his own people siding with the enemy. That's why I love Jesus, y'all. He never let their hatred dampen his hope.[32]

Very little, if any, of this is really about Jesus. It is about grievance. It is about *bitterness*. Given these sentiments, Obama's remarks in San Francisco make even more sense.

Ironically, black liberation theology might be better embodied by the preaching of Rev. Michael Pfleger, a white Catholic priest, than it is by Wright himself. Most people don't know that Pfleger and Obama have a deeper connection than simply a former mutual friend in Rev. Wright.

Pfleger, who, like Wright, served as an advisor to the Obama campaign,[33] caused additional problems for Trinity Church in May by preaching to Trinity's largely black congregation mocking whites who say: "Don't hold me responsible for what my ancestors did." To this plea, Pfegler responds:

> But you have enjoyed the benefits of what your ancestors did! And unless you are ready to give up the benefits—throw away your 401 fund, throw away your trust fund, throw away all the money they put away and the company you walked into 'cause your daddy and your granddaddy and your great-granddaddy— unless you're willing to give up the benefits, then you must be responsible for what was done in your generation, because you are the beneficiaries of this insurance policy! We must be honest enough to expose white entitlement and supremacy whenever it raises its head...

He then tore into Senator Hillary Clinton, referring to an incident in which she had cried prior to the New Hampshire Democratic primary:

> When Hillary was crying, and people said that was put on, I really don't believe it was put on. I really believe that she just always felt, *This was mine! I'm Bill's wife, I'm white, and this is mine!*...And then out of nowhere came, "Hey, I'm Barack Obama." And she said, *Aw, Damn! Where did you come from? I'm white! I'm entitled! There's a black man stealing my show!* [feigned bawling]. She wasn't the only one crying—there was a whole lot of white people crying.[34]

Father Pfleger's pious sentiments were greeted with hearty applause by the congregation, reinforcing Trinity's radical credentials still more.

Chicago Mayor Richard M. Daley, facing multiple investigations, indictments and convictions of staff for running the city's patronage operation, could still count on the endorsement and support of Barack Obama in 2007. Daley has returned the favor with his support this year.

Illinois Senate president Emil Jones is Obama's political godfather and another patronage-minded machine politician. He worked assiduously in Springfield to "make" Obama a U.S. senator by handing Obama sure-to-pass legislation just before completion and by giving him the prized chairmanship that guaranteed him support from labor unions.

AP PHOTO/RANDY SQUIRES

John Stroger, before suffering a stroke in 2006, was the Boss of Cook County's Democratic Machine. When Stroger faced a strong primary challenge from a liberal, reform-minded Democrat in 2006, Obama refused to clean up the patronage system in Chicago. After his stroke, Stroger's son Todd replaced him on the ballot. Obama endorsed the young Stroger. The Machine still lives.

AP PHOTO/STEPHEN J. CARRERA, FILE

Antoin (Tony) Rezko, convicted in June 2008 on sixteen counts of fraud and money laundering, was a top fundraiser and donor to Barack Obama. Rezko, a developer, benefitted from developer subsidies that Obama sponsored and voted for in the Illinois Senate.

Barack Obama paid $1.65 million for this house—$300,000 below the list price—on the same day Tony Rezko bought the adjoining lot from the same seller. The deal highlights how close the two men were.

Obama was one of few Democratic officeholders to support Alexi Giannoulias for state trea-surer in 2006. Giannoulias's family bank had been loaning money to mafia figures. He had supported Obama's 2004 Senate campaign, and the campaign kept accounts at Giannoulias's family bank.

Sen. Ted Kennedy (D.-Mass.) is known as the "Liberal Lion." But according to *National Jour-nal's* 2007 ratings, Obama's voting record was more liberal than Kennedy's—and that of every other U.S. senator. Winning the support of Senator Kennedy and his family was cru-cial to Obama's primary victory.

Gianna Jessen survived a saline abortion in 1977. In Springfield, Obama voted against—and was the only senator to speak against—a bill requiring hospitals to care for children like Gianna born during failed abortions.

About ethanol, a fuel made from food, liberal columnist Paul Krugman writes, "Bad for the economy, bad for consumers, bad for the planet—what's not to love?" Obama has always been a big booster of ethanol, leading the charge on mandating its use and even proposing to outlaw new cars that cannot run on high-ethanol blends.

AP PHOTO/TRINITY UNITED CHURCH OF CHRIST

ERIK S. LESSER/GETTY IMAGES

(Above) Obama's former pastor, Rev. Jeremiah Wright, said in sermons that the U.S. government had created AIDS and spread drugs as a way of committing "genocide." Obama stood by him until Wright criticized his "new politics."

(Left) Fr. Michael Pfleger, a Catholic priest and friend of Rev. Wright, once threatened a gun shop owner, "We're going to find you and snuff you out." In a 2004 interview, Obama cited Pfleger as an early spiritual influence who helped form Obama's "moral compass."

Michelle Obama's employer, University of Chicago Hospitals, raised her pay from $121,910 in 2004 to $316,962 in 2005, two months after her husband became a U.S. Senator. Barack Obama would later request a $1 million federal earmark for the hospital.

The relationship between Pfleger and Obama goes back twenty years, to Obama's community organizing days on the South Side.[35] In 2004, Obama cited Pfleger as one of the spiritual advisors who help him maintain his "moral compass."[36] In 1995, Pfegler was among the early donors to Obama's first campaign, giving him $500. In 1999, when Obama announced his quixotic run for Congress, he named Pfleger as one of his first supporters.[37]

The two shared a more substantial financial tie as well, in the form of government largess. Obama, as a state senator, had obtained $225,000 in government earmarks for Pfleger's ministries. Pfleger had given him just modest contributions of $1,500 over six years.[38]

Pfleger invited Wright to preach to his Catholic parish in the midst of the controversy with Obama, and Wright was greeted with "a standing ovation."[39] Before delivering his own "hate whitey" sermon, Pfleger had vigorously defended Wright: "I know Jeremiah Wright. ..And I'm not going to allow people to call him a racist, anti-American, or bigot."[40]

An admirer and defender of the Nation of Islam leader Louis Farrakhan,[41] Pfleger had once handed over his church's pulpit to Al Sharpton.[42] This sort of thing is a no-no in Catholic churches, but Pfleger was never a stickler for the rules. He attracted even more attention when he had Harry Belafonte address his congregation and denounce Colin Powell and Condoleeza Rice as the "house slaves" of the Bush administration.[43]

At one public protest, where he appeared along with Jesse Jackson, Pfleger twice promised to "snuff out" the owner of a suburban gun shop, after spelling out his name for everyone in the cheering crowd.

We're going to find you and snuff you out!...You know you've got to hide like a rat! You've got to hide like a rat! We're not going to continue to let you hide. We're going to catch you and pull you out!...We're going to snuff out John Riggio![44]

Pfleger says his remarks were not a death threat. Pfleger's ministerial work was being subsidized by grants from taxpayers, obtained by Senator Barack Obama.

"TOOT" THE RACIST

Obama has never promoted the hatred toward white people or toward America that characterizes the theology of his church and his former pastor. Indeed, when Obama talks about race, his language is usually more than just moderated—he often sounds conservative and conciliatory on this topic.

But why would he bring his family to such a church as Trinity every week? He was not ignorant about what went on there. Even when he ended his friendship with Wright, it was not the racism or conspiracy theorizing that did it, but Wright's personal disrespect toward him and his campaign.

Some of Obama's supporters have tried to deny that Rev. Jeremiah Wright was a significant influence in his life. Obama himself has avoided such denials, knowing them to be untrue. Long before Wright had become radioactive, the left-leaning Rev. James Wallis told *Rolling Stone* magazine about Wright's influence on Obama:

> "If you want to understand where Barack gets his feeling and rhetoric from," says the Rev. Jim Wallis, a leader of the religious left, "just look at Jeremiah Wright."[45]

In a 2004 *Chicago Sun-Times* profile on Obama, religion columnist Cathleen Falsani wrote that Wright had become a "close confidant" of

Obama.[46] Obama even took a break from campaigning to celebrate Wright's impending retirement with him in March 2007.[47]

The same issue of the church newsletter that contained Franklin's piece on Obama's faith also contained a now-infamous "open letter to Oprah Winfrey," accusing the State of Israel of creating a special "ethnic bomb" that kills blacks and Arabs while leaving whites unharmed. Given that this was in the church bulletin, alongside the Scriptures and hymns for the day and the article about Obama himself, it seems reasonable to suppose that Obama was aware of it. There is no evidence that any of this, however, caused tension between Wright and Obama.

The burning of the Wright-Obama bridge took some time. It was a sad process fraught with further errors by Obama that were very damaging to his primary campaign. In his March 18 speech on race in Philadelphia, Obama did criticize the specific bigoted and anti-American statements that Wright had made from the pulpit. But he still refused to disown his pastor, who he said "contains within him the contradictions—the good and the bad—of the community that he has served diligently for so many years."

Obama said: "I can no more disown him than I can disown the black community," and then continued:

> I can no more disown him than I can disown my white grandmother—a woman who helped raise me, a woman who sacrificed again and again for me, a woman who loves me as much as she loves anything in this world, but a woman who once confessed her fear of black men who passed her by on the street, and who on more than one occasion has uttered racial or ethnic stereotypes that made me cringe.[48]

Obama's purpose in these remarks had been simply to assert that there was more to his pastor than the angry man who had been seen on the news—that people are complex and should not be judged based on one or two angry statements of hatred for America or for white people.

But that he should—as several commentators put it—"throw his grandmother under the bus" with such an embarrassing revelation of her supposed racist attitudes seemed completely gratuitous, even cruel. That week, he tried to make up for it by explaining that her offending behavior was so culturally ingrained that it was understandable, but it ended up coming across as if his grandma was just a "typical white person" in her racism.[49] It may have just been rhetorical clumsiness, but it was hardly racial healing.

Obama's grandmother, whom he always knew growing up as "Toot," was now put on the same level as the demagogue Jeremiah Wright. Obama had set her cringe-worthy remarks equivalent to "God damn America."

The irony here is that, aside from an incident in which Obama's grandmother had expressed fear of an aggressive panhandler who happened to be black, Obama's stories about her had made her seem very enlightened in her views about race. She had stood up against racism on two noteworthy occasions during the brief period when she and Obama's grandfather lived in Jim Crow Texas. Obama recounts both incidents in *Dreams from My Father*.

On one occasion, Toot had befriended a black janitor at the bank where she worked—a man she called "Mr. Reed." Obama describes him as "a tall and dignified black World War II vet." She was verbally assaulted by a white co-worker one day while she was talking with Mr. Reed—for showing a black man such respect as to "call a n——r 'Mister.' "[50] She later found him weeping over the incident: "What have we ever done," he asked, "to be treated so mean?" She spoke to her husband about the matter, and decided she would go right on calling him "Mister" anyway.[51]

The other story was even more dramatic. Obama's mother, then eleven or twelve years old, brought a black girl home to play in the yard. White children from the town were standing at the edge of the yard, taunting the two girls and throwing stones at them: "N——r Lover! Dirty Yankee!"[52]

Obama's grandmother had returned home to find this appalling scene. After chasing the other children away, she tried to bring her daughter and the black girl inside, where it would be safer (the black girl ran away). After this incident, she talked to her husband again, and he gave a piece of his mind to the other children's parents and to the school principal. (Unfortunately, they were not very receptive.)

Also, no commentator appears to have noticed that Obama's disparaging comments about his own grandmother effectively undo one of the impressive literary points he makes about race in *Dreams from My Father*. Many years after the incident with his grandmother and the panhandler, Obama is living in Chicago as a community organizer. He goes out on his stoop late at night to yell at a car-full of young black men to turn down their music and move on.

Upon shouting at them, he suddenly considers their situation. He spends a page reflecting on how he could have been sitting in that car just a few years ago.

And then, suddenly, he fears for his own safety:

> I start picturing myself through the eyes of these boys, a figure of random authority, and know the calculations they might now be making, that if one of them can't take me out, the four of them certainly can.... The engine starts, and the car screeches away. I

turn back toward my apartment knowing that I've been both stupid and lucky, knowing that I am afraid after all.[53]

The transformation is striking. Author Obama was a deep thinker who compared his grandmother to himself—who understood that issues of race are complicated and involve much more than race. Politician Obama lacks such nuance. He compares Toot—and "typical white people"—to a racial demagogue who blames white people for his and the world's problems.

As it turned out, Obama was finally able to disown Rev. Wright without "disowning the black community." It happened after the reverend at the National Press Club suggested that Obama's rejection of his extreme rhetoric was mere political posturing.[54]

> Politicians say what they say and do what they do based on electability, based on sound bites, based on polls, Huffington, whoever's doing the polls.

Obama's reaction: "That's a show of disrespect to me. It's—it is also, I think, an insult to what we've been trying to do in this campaign."[55]

When Wright had embraced Cone and black liberation theology, he was simply a bit eccentric. When he had condemned America with crazy conspiracy theories and questioned the integrity of white people in general, Obama described him as "an old uncle who says things I don't always agree with."[56]

But when Wright questioned the "new politics?" That crossed the line.

That ended their friendship.

CHAPTER NINE

OBAMA'S FOREIGN POLICY: INEXPERIENCE AND UNCERTAINTIY

I n a fit of hyperbole, Hillary Clinton once asserted that Barack Obama's only foreign policy experience was "a speech he gave in 2002."[1] This is not true. But Obama is surely more proud of that speech today than he is of an earlier foray into international affairs, at least if the account of state senator Patrick O'Malley is correct.

The date was February 25, 1999. O'Malley, a conservative Republican who would later mount an unsuccessful run for governor, told me the story of what happened in the Illinois Senate Judiciary Committee that day.

O'Malley had proposed a non-binding resolution urging Illinois's Senators to reject American ratification of a treaty President Clinton had signed, which would subject Americans to an International Criminal Court (ICC). Many conservatives like O'Malley worried that such an institution would "diminish America's sovereignty, produce arbitrary and highly politicized 'justice,' and grow into a jurisdictional leviathan."[2] Also of concern was the possibility that U.S. soldiers and diplomats could be tried in a court that did not guarantee them the rights Americans normally enjoy when accused.

It was only a symbolic measure—much like the anti-war resolutions that have been passed by various left-leaning municipalities since 2002—but it was also an affirmation of American civil rights such as trial by jury, the right against self-incrimination, and the presumption of innocence.

"It was a pretty hard bill to vote against," O'Malley tells me.

The resolution consisted of a list of findings about the ICC, followed by the conclusion that Illinois's U.S. senators should not vote to ratify the treaty.

> The International Criminal Court has the potential of violating the rights of Americans, as stated in the United States Constitution and the Bill of Rights...the International Criminal Court does not operate on a presumption of innocence for those accused...the International Criminal Court does not allow for a trial by a jury of one's peers...
>
> RESOLVED...that we respectfully urge the United States Senate to reject the Rome Statute of the International Criminal Court...we instead urge all foreign governments to consider adopting the due process and equal protection guarantees provided by the United States Bill of Rights...

When this resolution came before the judiciary committee, Obama had to make up his mind. On the one hand, he was a civil rights lawyer. Jury trials and presumption of innocence were meaningful concepts to him. On the other hand, the Left had been championing ratification of the ICC; it was all about Internationalism, good faith and good will among nations.

How would Obama vote?

This happened long ago. The available state Senate records show only that the vote that day was 10–0 in favor. There is no roll call vote available, no list of names, and Obama's campaign did not respond to inquiries about his recollections. But by O'Malley's account, Obama was indeed there, and he did not look like he was relishing the opportunity to take this vote. He had been second in line to vote, O'Malley says, and originally did not vote "yes," but "present." After all nine of the other senators had voted "yes," Obama reconsidered with the permission of the committee's chairman.

The vote occurred nearly ten years ago, and the chairman, Carl Hawkinson, told me that he did not remember anything. Either way, O'Malley's version is given credence by Obama's subsequent ambivalence on the issue.

On March 3, 1999, a week after he had voted to condemn the ICC in committee, his liberal conscience might have gotten the better of him. When the resolution came to the floor, he absented himself from the vote (it passed, 52–1, with one present vote).[3] Obama was not actually absent from the Senate that day. He was present to vote for two other unrelated resolutions, one of them sponsored by his political patron, Emil Jones.[4]

Five years later in February 2004, speaking to a small liberal publication, Obama voiced strong support for the ICC, lamenting the "general arrogance" of the Bush administration "that was on display before Iraq... it was true of our unilateral rejection of the International Criminal Court which, had we been a signatory, could have actually dealt with Saddam Hussein in an appropriate setting."[5]

So Obama voted against the ICC in 1999; he was strongly for it in 2004.

In 2008, when he was asked about it on a questionnaire for the American Society of International Law, he appeared to give a qualified "no."

The United States has more troops deployed overseas than any other nation... Maximum protection for our servicemen and women should come with that increased exposure. Therefore, I will consult thoroughly with our military commanders and also examine the track record of the court before reaching a decision on whether the U.S. should become a state party.[6]

In another 2008 questionnaire, for the group Citizens for Global Solutions, Obama appears to be *for* the ICC, but it is not clear. He was asked:

The U.S. has signed, but not ratified many international treaties, including the ICC treaty, Law of the Sea, Kyoto, Women's convention, and the Test Ban treaty. Which treaties, if any, would you support and urge the Senate to ratify?

Obama's response conspicuously omits the ICC treaty, but he writes that he is in favor of "such treaties."

There are a number of meritorious treaties currently pending before the Senate. Some of these are clearly in the national interest, such as the UN Convention on the Law of the Sea, the Comprehensive Nuclear Test Ban Treaty, the International Convention for the Suppression of Acts of Nuclear Terrorism, and the Convention on the Elimination of All Forms of Discrimination Against Women. As president, I will make it my priority to build bipartisan consensus behind ratification of such treaties.[7]

So where does Obama stand on the ICC?

Good question.

GAFFE HEARD 'ROUND THE WORLD

The rap against Obama on foreign policy is not that so much that he's inconsistent but that he doesn't know what he's doing.

Senator Obama was one of fifty-nine state senators in Springfield as recently as November 2004, and so it is understandable if foreign policy is his weakest topic. He characterizes criticism of this weakness as "attempts to play on our fears" but he caused part of his own problem when he decided to base his diplomatic plans on an easily corrected gaffe he made in a July 2007 presidential debate. Since then, he has been very consistent on this: he *will* meet with foreign leaders from Iran, Cuba, and North Korea *without precondition*.

We expect politicians to make minor mistakes. Remember Al Gore, inventor of the Internet? People still like him. George W. Bush frequently has difficulty completing sentences. While running for president in 1999, he did not even know that Pervez Musharraf was the general who had taken control of Pakistan.[8] Bush was still elected president.

Obama, however, stands by his gaffe.

To offer some context, Democrats were criticizing President Bush in 2007 for refusing even to meet with leaders of various states, most of them sponsors of terrorism, in order to conduct diplomacy face-to-face. During a debate, Anderson Cooper showed Obama a question over YouTube from Stephen Sorta of Diamond Bar, California:

> [W]ould you be willing to meet separately, without precondition, during the first year of your administration, in Washington or anywhere else, with the leaders of Iran, Syria, Venezuela, Cuba and North Korea, in order to bridge the gap that divides our countries?[9]

Without hesitation, Obama answered as follows:

> I would. And the reason is this, that the notion that somehow
> not talking to countries is punishment to them—which has
> been the guiding diplomatic principle of this administration—
> is ridiculous.[10]

Hillary Clinton could not wait to get the question herself. Sensing an easy home run, she stung Obama in what would become one of the strongest moments of her entire campaign:

> I will not promise to meet with the leaders of these countries
> during my first year...I don't want to be used for propaganda
> purposes. I don't want to make a situation even worse. But I
> certainly agree that we need to get back to diplomacy... but
> certainly, we're not going to just have our president meet with
> Fidel Castro and Hugo Chavez and, you know, the president of
> North Korea, Iran and Syria until we know better what the
> way forward would be.[11]

For Clinton, there had to be *some* preconditions—how else could such a meeting be in the interest of the United States? There had to an upside. You don't have to take as hard a line as President Bush, she was arguing, but you can't just have a beer with Kim Jong Il after he launched seven missiles in provocation during the summer of 2006.[12] He must first show some cooperation—some substantial sign of good faith—as a precondition. That is how diplomacy works in the real world.

In the months that followed, Democrats ranging from moderate to liberal generally sided with Clinton and against Obama on this point. Former congressman Harold Ford of Tennessee, another young, black superstar in the Democratic Party and chairman of the Democratic Leadership Council, was one of the moderates. "I'll concede you cannot meet with foreign leaders—with terrorists rather—without some conditions."[13]

"This is a fellow who I think shorthanded an answer that in fact was the wrong answer," said Senator Joseph Biden of Delaware, the liberal chairman of the Senate Foreign Relations Committee.[14]

"I would not say that we would meet unconditionally," said former Senate majority leader Tom Daschle, an early and consistent supporter of Obama. "Of course there are conditions."[15]

Obama could just have admitted that he'd shot from the hip— "shorthanded" it—and made a mistake. He could have said that he only meant he'd *meet* with them, and that the part about "no precondition," just didn't register when he heard the question.

And it's not as though Obama has never changed his mind before. It had not been difficult for him to reverse his position on normalizing relations with communist Cuba. On that question, he had written on a questionnaire in 2004 that he wants to do so, and he changed his mind later while running for president.[16]

But this mistake he sticks by. He has embraced it. He has repeated it. And it hasn't been pretty.

As the behavior and rhetoric of Iranian President Mahmoud Ahmadinejad became increasingly hostile, aggressive and strident during 2007, Republicans piled on Obama for promising to meet with him. This prompted Obama's senior foreign policy advisor, Susan Rice, to deny in early 2008 that Obama had ever said he would do so. "He said he'd meet with the appropriate Iranian leaders," she said. "Not necessarily Ahmadinejad."[17]

But Obama *had* said he would meet with Ahmadinejad. In the fall of 2007, when a reporter asked him specifically whether he would meet with Ahmadinejad, Obama answered: "Nothing has changed with respect to my belief that strong countries and strong presidents talk to their enemies and talk to their adversaries."[18]

In May 2008, nearly a year after his gaffe, Obama was still sticking to his language about "no preconditions" in an interview with ABC's Jake Tapper. But he also gave himself a way out:

> What I said was I would meet with our adversaries including Iran, including Venezula, including Cuba, including North Korea, without preconditions but that does not mean without preparation.[19]

Asked to distinguish between those two ideas—preconditions and preparations—Obama stated "There's a huge difference...There are a whole series of steps that need to be taken before you have a presidential meeting but that doesn't mean you expect the other side to agree to every item on your list."[20]

Presumably, though, he was not talking about making sure Kim Jong-il gets the right color M&Ms in his hotel room before the meeting. He's really talking about "preconditions."

As *Oregonian* editor David Reinhard pointed out, Obama's campaign "talks about these nations' leaders having to meet benchmarks before sitting down with him." If that isn't a "precondition," what is?[21]

Obama and his staff seem to be gradually re-defining the two concepts of "precondition" and "preparation" closer and closer to one another so that, by the time Obama walks into the Oval Office, they will be identical. If Obama ever becomes president, it will be good for the country that he does not actually believe what he has been saying now for more than a year about "no preconditions."

But why didn't Obama just admit that he had given a hasty answer? His sensitivity about his foreign policy inexperience may be the source of this painful consistency on his part.

IRAQ

Obama's strongest moment on foreign policy—perhaps his strongest moment ever—came on October 2, 2002. This was the day of his speech against the Iraq War. He deserves full credit for opposing the war at a time when his position was not necessarily popular.

He *takes* full credit for it, too—his website heralds his own courage: "As a candidate for the United States Senate in 2002, Obama put his political career on the line to oppose going to war in Iraq."[22]

He had been asked to speak against the war by one of Chicago's most important left-wing activists, Bettylu Saltzman. She had sought out Obama to address the crowd at Chicago's Federal Plaza on that fall afternoon, eight days before the U.S. House would vote to authorize the invasion of Iraq. At first, Obama had not been sure whether to do it. Biographer David Mendell writes that Obama's top advisor, Dan Shomon, told Obama that he could not turn Saltzman down if he wanted to advance in Chicago politics.[23] (Saltzman disputes Mendell's account.[24])

Obama was taking a risk—the idea of war with Iraq, though deeply unpopular today, was popular enough in 2002 that his principled stand could have cost him dearly.

He gave the speech, and his decision would appear prescient five years later, as it became the single biggest policy point on which he could differentiate himself from Senator Hillary Clinton in the presidential nominating process.

Obama declared that he did not oppose all wars, but that he did oppose this one. Iraq's possession of chemical and biological weapons, he said, did not constitute an imminent threat to America.

> What I am opposed to is the attempt by political hacks like
> Karl Rove to distract us from a rise in the uninsured, a rise in
> the poverty rate, a drop in the median income—to distract us

from corporate scandals and a stock market that has just gone through the worst month since the Great Depression. That's what I'm opposed to. A dumb war. A rash war. A war based not on reason but on passion, not on principle but on politics.

Now let me be clear—I suffer no illusions about Saddam Hussein. He is a brutal man. A ruthless man. A man who butchers his own people to secure his own power. He has repeatedly defied UN resolutions, thwarted UN inspection teams, developed chemical and biological weapons, and coveted nuclear capacity. He's a bad guy. The world—and the Iraqi people—would be better off without him.

But I also know that Saddam poses no imminent and direct threat to the United States, or to his neighbors . . . he can be contained until, in the way of all petty dictators, he falls away into the dustbin of history.

I know that even a successful war against Iraq will require a U.S. occupation of undetermined length, at undetermined cost, with undetermined consequences. I know that an invasion of Iraq without a clear rationale and without strong international support will only fan the flames of the Middle East, and encourage the worst, rather than best, impulses of the Arab world, and strengthen the recruitment arm of Al Qaeda.[25]

Obama's opposition to the war would be crucial to his appeal later on. More immediately, it would differentiate him from Dan Hynes in the 2004 Senate primary.[26]

Obama would later tell David Mendell that this speech was a happy coincidence of good politics and what he considered to be good policy. "Because I thought the politics of [the invasion] were bad, it was liberating—because I said exactly what I truly believed."[27]

Mendell mildly scolds Obama for saying this: "If one parses this statement, Obama is implying that he has given speeches with sentiments that he does not truly believe for the sake of politics."[28]

Prima facie, this criticism appears to be a stretch. But two months after Mendell's book was published, Obama would prove him right.

It all began in 2004 when, without backing away from his opposition to the war in the first place, Obama had muted his criticism of its conduct. He went so far as to identify himself with President Bush's position on its conduct. He told the *Chicago Tribune*: "There's not that much difference between my position and George Bush's position at this stage. The difference, in my mind, is who's in a position to execute."[29]

This statement is not inconsistent with his opposition to the invasion beforehand. But look carefully at Obama's answer when Tim Russert broke down this and other Obama war statements on *Meet the Press* on Nov. 11, 2007:

> **Tim Russert:** In July of '04, Barack Obama: "I'm not privy to Senate intelligence reports. What would I have done? I don't know," in terms of how you would have voted on the war. And then this: "There's not much of a difference between my position on Iraq and George Bush's position at this stage." That was July of '04. And this: "I think" there's "some room for disagreement in that initial decision to vote for authorization of the war." It doesn't seem that you are firmly wedded against the war, and that you left some wiggle room that, if you had been in the Senate, you may have voted for it.
>
> **Barack Obama:** Now, Tim, that first quote was made with an interview with a guy named Tim Russert on *Meet the Press* during the convention when we had a nominee for the

presidency and a vice president, both of whom had voted for the war. And so it, it probably was the wrong time for me to be making a strong case against our party's nominees' decisions when it came to Iraq.[30]

What Obama implied to Mendell, he admitted to Russert explicitly. He *does* sometimes say things he doesn't mean, "for the sake of politics"— in this case to help his party's nominee.

After identifying himself with President Bush's position in 2004, Obama stuck with President Bush's position for some time. In June 2006, Obama—again reiterating how he had opposed the war in the first place—spoke out against setting a withdrawal date from Iraq:

> [H]aving visited Iraq, I'm also acutely aware that a precipitous withdrawal of our troops, driven by Congressional edict rather than the realities on the ground, will not undo the mistakes made by this Administration . . . It could compound them by plunging Iraq into an even deeper and, perhaps, irreparable crisis. We must exit Iraq, but not in a way that leaves behind a security vacuum filled with terrorism, chaos, ethnic cleansing and genocide that could engulf large swaths of the Middle East and endanger America.[31]

Then, in November of that year, with the midterm election finished and the presidential election cycle beginning, Obama suddenly decided it was time to leave: "The time for waiting in Iraq is over. It is time to change our policy."[32]

In January 2007, he proposed legislation to withdraw all combat troops from Iraq within fourteen months, by March 2008. In September 2007, three months before the Iowa Caucuses, he presented a plan to withdraw all troops within sixteen months of his inauguration. His campaign website states:

> Obama will immediately begin to remove our troops from Iraq. He will remove one to two combat brigades each month, and have all of our combat brigades out of Iraq within 16 months. Obama will make it clear that we will not build any permanent bases in Iraq.[33]

Immediately. It had not been so urgent in June of 2006, before the midterm election. But immediate withdrawal is a proven vote-getter in Democratic primaries. After an unpopular six-year occupation, it is not going to hurt him in the general election, either.

Obama accuses the Bush administration of justifying the Iraq invasion based on preconceived ideas and politics instead of reliable information on the ground. Is his plan of withdrawal, adopted so hastily, similarly based on preconceived ideas and politics?

Obama last visited Iraq in January 2006. According to *The Audacity of Hope,* he learned something from his two-day visit. He indicates in the book that there is a lot of reasonable doubt about the question of when and how to leave Iraq—doubt that was reflected in his June 2006 speech against immediate withdrawal.

A tough Marine officer in the field had told Obama's aide that America should pull out of Iraq immediately. A group of foreign correspondents, who had been skeptical of the invasion from the beginning, told Obama that if America leaves Iraq, "the country would collapse into civil war within weeks."[34] In the face of these conflicting opinions from unlikely sources, Obama conceded in his book that "there are no easy answers."[35]

But on the campaign trail, there *are* easy answers for Obama. They became easy right around the time the presidential cycle began.

To be sure, Obama has opposed the war consistently since before it began—as he likes to put it, "I've been against it—2002, 2003, 2004," *et cetera*. But when it comes to the question of what he would do in Iraq *now*, his position appears to be more aligned with the American electoral calendar than with what's actually going on in Iraq.

Probably his followers would not react as positively to this speech:

In 2002, I opposed the war.

In 2004, I was with Bush's plan for Iraq, because I thought it would help John Kerry.

In 2006, I opposed withdrawal by a date certain.

In late 2006, when I started running against Hillary Clinton, I came out for immediate withdrawal.

In 2007, just in time to affect the Iowa caucuses, I released my plan for withdrawal.

OBAMA'S IRAQ INTELLIGENCE

Even if the war was a bad idea, a serious policy-maker must keep informed about whether a sudden withdrawal makes sense today, or whether it instead runs the risk of making a bad situation even worse. Is Obama informed? He has not visited Iraq since January 2006, nor has he spoken to David Petraeus, the commanding general of the Multi-National Force in Iraq, about the situation on the ground there. As of early June 2008, Obama had never even tried to meet with Petraeus, to speak one-on-one, away from the political showmanship of committee hearings and television cameras.[36]

This contrasts sharply with the author of *The Audacity of Hope*, who describes the experience of negotiating a piece of legislation through its final stages:

> It would have been typical of today's politics for each side to draw
> a line in the sand . . . Instead, over the course of several weeks, we
> convened sometimes daily meetings between prosecutors, public
> defenders, police organizations, and death penalty opponents,
> keeping our negotiations as much as possible out of the press.[37]

Those low-key consultations, he notes, reflected greater interest in good policy than in browbeating opponents with an ideological sledgehammer. Since the moment he became a candidate for president, this principle has not applied to Obama's deliberation on Iraq. Finding himself up against Hillary Clinton, he opted for the ideological sledgehammer.

Asked by a reporter recently whether he had even attempted to meet with General Petraeus, Obama snapped back: "I haven't—look, it's just a flippant comment, it's not designed to actually talk about substance. It's a political comment that doesn't get anywhere."[38]

Author Obama considered it an important part of his "new politics" to separate policy from politics when the stakes are high. For Candidate Obama, that's "just politics."

HONESTLY . . .

Part of the appeal of Obama's writing is the frankness with which he approaches most topics. He notes, for example, of the politician:

> He may not lie, but he understands that there is no great
> reward in store for those who speak the truth, particularly
> when the truth may be complicated.[39]

Barack Obama does not need to lie. He has consultants and advisors to do that for him.

For one, he has David Axelrod, Mayor Richard M. Daley's spokesman, on his campaign.

Axelrod's job—like that of any candidate's spokesman—is to say whatever maximizes the probability of getting his candidate elected. It does not matter whether it is true. He skillfully saw Mayor Daley through the hired truck and illegal patronage scandals, insisting at one point, "The so-called 'Machine' doesn't exist anymore."[40]

On the presidential level, he is just as good.

More than a year after the United States added a "Surge" of 21,500 American soldiers into Iraq, there exists a broad consensus that it improved the situation on the ground. In May 2008, there were fewer U.S. servicemen killed there than in any month since the war began.[41] Perhaps this strategy will help end the occupation sooner in an orderly fashion.

Many policy-makers disagreed with the idea when it was hatched. Obama was one of them. In January 2007 when the Surge was being considered. Obama was just beginning his presidential run. Just over a month earlier he had decided it was time to leave Iraq. And so he said:

> We cannot impose a military solution on what has effectively become a civil war. And until we acknowledge that reality, we can send 15,000 more troops, 20,000 more troops, 30,000 more troops. I don't know any expert on the region, or any military officer that I've spoken to, privately, that believes that that is going to make a substantial difference on the situation on the ground.[42]

You wouldn't think he ever said that if you listen to David Axelrod: "He never disputed the fact that if you throw a surge of American soldiers in an area, that you can make a difference," Axelrod had told MSNBC's Joe Scarborough in late May 2008. [43]

If you listen to Susan Rice, Obama's foreign policy advisor, you'd almost think Obama thought up the Surge himself:

> [A]s Barack Obama said when the surge was announced, anytime you put the finest men and women in uniform on the ground in greater numbers, you're going to have a positive security benefit, and, indeed, we have.[44]

There's nothing wrong with Obama's position—he could not have seen the future in early 2007. But can his spokesmen deny that he said what he said?

We've seen the same factual inaccuracy in Obama's critique of his opponent's foreign policy:

> We are bogged down in a war that John McCain now suggests might go on for another 100 years.[45]

And:

> [McCain] says that he is willing to send our troops into another hundred years of war in Iraq.[46]

McCain hadn't said that—he had said that we might still have bases there for a long time (even a hundred years), like we have in Japan and South Korea.

The media watchdog website FactCheck.org replied about the first Obama claim: "Actually, McCain suggested no such thing."[47] Liberal columnist Frank Rich accused Obama of "libeling" John McCain.[48] Media critic Zachary Roth at the *Columbia Journalism Review*, wrote "Obama is seriously misleading voters—if not outright lying to them—about exactly what McCain said."[49]

Axelrod rushed to Obama's defense: "He is not saying that Senator McCain said we'd be at war for a hundred years."

But he *did* say it.

UNANIMITY

Hillary Clinton once called Obama "naïve" about foreign policy, and this charge goes beyond the question of whom he would or would not meet with as president "without precondition," or whether he can make up his mind about the International Criminal Court. His otherwise studied and nuanced account of recent political history, offered up over several pages in *The Audacity of Hope*, has a glaring blind spot.

Writing of the period that spanned from the end of World War II through the Reagan administration, Obama writes:

> I realized, too, that a set of unique circumstances had underwritten the stability of the governing consensus [of previous years]...not just the shared experiences of the war, but also the near unanimity forged by the Cold War and the Soviet threat...[50]

Near unanimity? This reflects a misunderstanding that also appears elsewhere in the book, and which colors Obama's view of foreign policy today. He writes that in the old days, "[p]olitics usually ended at the water's edge...Moreover, that consensus extended to the public at large."[51]

This is not true, though. "Unanimity" was very much lacking in foreign policy during the Cold War, particularly at its end, when President Reagan was trying to do the necessary work of taking apart the Soviet Union.

Obama seems wholly unaware of liberal Democrats' opposition to the policies that helped destroy the Soviet Union, and even certain legislators' collaboration with the Soviets. This lack of awareness shades his view of the run-up to the Iraq War as well.

Obama is referring to the Democrats' bad reputation on national security issues when he writes: "In reaction to a war that is ill conceived, we appear suspicious of all military action."[52]

In fact, the Left's failure to convince the public in 2002 that the Iraq War was a bad idea stemmed in large part from the Left's historical lack of credibility on foreign policy. That, in turn, goes back to its reflexive opposition to almost all anti-Soviet American military activity—hot or cold—from the Nixon era until the fall of the Soviet Union.

During the Reagan administration, a significant number of Democrats mechanically opposed the very policies that undid the USSR—an aggressive and hostile foreign power which posed a greater long-term danger even than today's Islamic terrorists.[53] The reaction of liberals and Democratic lawmakers to Reagan's famous "Evil Empire" speech of March 8, 1983[54] and his call for a space-based strategic defense initiative provides a small glimpse of how many Democrats did not see the Soviets as an enemy the way Reagan did. They did not even view "victory" as an attainable goal, preferring instead coexistence with a power that had no intention of coexisting with the United States of America.

They ridiculed Reagan on the House floor: Democratic congressman Ed Markey of Massachusetts mocked: "The force of evil is the Soviet Union and they are Darth Vader. We are Luke Skywalker and we are the force of good."[55]

New York congressman Tom Downey, also a Democrat, said, "Mr. Speaker, the only thing the President didn't tell us last night was that

188 THE CASE AGAINST BARACK OBAMA

the evil empire was about to launch the Death Star against the United States."[56]

Even House Speaker Tip O'Neill, supposedly friendly with Reagan, got into the act. At the Democratic convention a little more than a year later, O'Neill riffed off of this. "The evil," he explained, "is in the White House at the present time, and that evil is a man who has no care and no concern for the working class of America and the future generations of America, and who likes to ride a horse. He's cold. He's mean. He's got ice water for blood."[57] O'Neill exploded with rage upon learning that American forces had wrested Grenada from the Soviet-backed junta: "He is wrong in his policy. He's caused us continuous harm," adding, "It's sinful that this man is President of the United States."[58]

Such mockery and disdain was the tip of the iceberg. Decoded files from the Soviet Union show that at least two Democratic Senators—Ted Kennedy and John Tunney—were so fearful of Reagan's foreign policy vision that they sought KGB advice in 1983 on how to argue against the president's anti-Soviet policies.[59] There have since been books and articles written on this subject, but there has been no explanation or accountability for what we now know happened.

Before that, in 1975, two years after all American combat troops had left Vietnam, Democrats in Congress had cut off funding for the indigenous war efforts in Saigon, leading to Communist victory and massacres throughout Indochina.[60]

These words, actions, and causes of the Left—ranging from U.S. Senators and a House Speaker to left-wing protestors—hardly convey a "near unanimity" on the Cold War.

Nor do Obama's writings. Despite a professed admiration for what Reagan accomplished, Obama relates in *Audacity* his continued opposition to each discrete step that Reagan took to end Soviet domination.[61] He decries our resistance to Soviet influence in Latin America using the old 1980s terms of art: "funding death squads," "the invasion of tiny, hapless Grenada." He is especially disdainful of the so-called "Star Wars" program, which was crucial to bankrupting the Soviets then and which has today evolved into a working missile defense system that passes test after test.[62] He has even recorded a YouTube campaign video[63] promising to "cut investments in unproven missile-defense systems," and he has voted to cut $50 million from missile defense.[64]

This is why no one listened to the Left's warnings about Iraq in 2002. It explains, in turn, why elected Democrats went out of their way to distance themselves from the peace movement. Fully twenty-nine Democratic senators and eighty-one Democratic congressmen voted in favor of war in October 2002, including Hillary Clinton and John Kerry. What choice did they have? There was an election approaching, and as far as congressional Democrats are concerned, their historical reputation on national security did not afford them the option of standing on principle against war. Not only did Clinton and Kerry vote for war, but each one publicly supported the precise course of diplomatic and military action that President Bush took over the next six months—ill-conceived or no.[65]

That is the "old politics" of foreign policy. Barack Obama is right in the thick of it.

CHAPTER TEN

ABORTION: BARACK OBAMA'S AMERICA

The tiny newborn baby made very little noise as he struggled to breathe. He could not cry—he lacked the strength. He had been born four months premature.

"At that age," says nurse Jill Stanek, "their lungs haven't matured."

Stanek is the nurse who found herself cradling this tiny human being in her hands for all of his forty-five-minute lifetime. He was close to ten inches long. He weighted perhaps half a pound. It's just a guess—no one had weighed or measured him at birth. No happy family had been there to welcome him into the world. No one was trying to save his life now, to put him into an incubator, to give him oxygen or nourishment.

He had just been left to die.

She had seen it all happen. That family had wanted a baby, but when they learned that theirs would be born with Down syndrome, they wanted an abortion. They went to Christ Hospital, in the southwestern suburbs of Chicago. It was a typical second-trimester procedure that Christ performed maybe ten to twenty times a year,[1] commonly known as "induced labor abortion" or "prostaglandin abortion." The doctor administered drugs that would dilate the mother's cervix and induce contractions, forcing a small baby out of the mother's uterus. Most of the time, the baby dies *in utero* during such an abortion—killed by the force of the mother's contractions. But some of these abortions result in a premature baby being born alive.

Stanek was holding one of the survivors. Sometimes these babies would live for just a few minutes after birth. Sometimes they would live for several hours. No one tried to save or treat them. That would defeat the purpose of the procedure. But something had to be done with them while they lived and struggled for air.

The aborting mother had not wanted to hold this baby or even to look at him. A nurse, Stanek's friend, had helped in the abortion. She had been told to take this baby and leave him in a soiled utility closet. (The hospital would later deny that such things happened, stating that they had already set up "comfort rooms" in which to leave the babies to die.[2])

Stanek offered to take the baby instead.

"I couldn't let him die alone," she says. "And so I held him for the forty-five minutes that he lived. He moved a little bit. Of course he didn't cry."

Stanek was horrified by what she had seen. When the hospital first hired her in 1993, she was unaware that abortions were performed there. She had only been in the labor and delivery section for a year when this incident happened.

"I went to work at Christ Hospital thinking that I would be safe from abortion because of its name," she tells me. Prior to that incident, she had learned that Christ is aligned with two Christian denominations that support legal abortion—as it happens, one of them is Barack Obama's former denomination, the United Church of Christ.[3] She already knew they did abortions before she held that baby in her hands. But this was the first time she had seen it happen.

He was very premature, and he had a disability. But he was also a human baby, already born and breathing. He was just left to die.

This was not an abortion—it was something much worse. Even if the medical profession had long ago abandoned the Hippocratic exhortation against participating in abortion, should doctors and nurses be denying medical attention to living babies who were already born and breathing?

Could it even be legal to take a living person of any size, already outside his mother's womb, and leave him to die—to die amid medical waste?

Stanek began by talking to hospital officials, who were dismissive of her concerns. She then sought out help from a pro-life group, the Concerned Women for America, and approached the Republican attorney general of Illinois, Jim Ryan. Ryan made inquiries with the state Department of Public Health, to determine whether this practice was legal.

Meanwhile, Stanek also went to the press. One Chicago columnist, Dennis Byrne, called Christ Hospital after hearing her story and was shocked to learn that it was true—this was in fact done routinely. He called it "a new low in heartlessness" and wrote:

> The argument that abortion doesn't kill a "person" centers on the assertion that a fetus isn't a person until it is born. So what do you call an abortion procedure in which the fetus is born alive, then is left to die without medical care? Infanticide? Murder?[4]

On July 17, 2000, Attorney General Ryan reported back on the investigation of Christ Hospital by the Illinois Department of Public Health
(IDPH):

> On December 6, IDPH provided this office with its investiga-
> tive report and advised us that IDPH's internal review did not
> include a violation of the Hospital Licensing Act or the Vital
> Records Act. No other allegations or medical evidence to sup-
> port any statutory violation (including the Abused and
> Neglected Child Reporting Act about which you inquired)
> were referred to our office by the Department for prosecu-
> tion...While we are deeply respectful of your serious concerns
> about the practices and methods of abortions at this hospital,
> we have concluded that there is no basis for legal action by this
> office against the Hospital or its employees, agents or staff at
> this time.[5]

In leaving born babies to die without treatment, Christ Hospital was
doing nothing illegal under the laws of Illinois. Doctors had no ethical
obligation to treat them. Under the law, they were non-persons.

Stanek had found a cause—a real injustice she wanted to right. She
was going to fight for the rights of these most vulnerable humans.

But this put her on a collision course with state senator Barack
Obama. He would be the one willing to fight her on the Senate floor.
And he would win.

THE "BORN-ALIVE" BILL

Stanek turned to her own state senator, who happened to be the same
Patrick O'Malley we met earlier. In February 2001, O'Malley introduced three bills on this topic—the Senate voted on all three on March

30. The only important one here is Senate Bill 1095, whose scope was carefully limited and whose language was completely unambiguous. Before I summarize it, let me reproduce its text in full so the reader will have no doubt about its intent:

(a) In determining the meaning of any statute or of any rule, regulation, or interpretation of the various administrative agencies of this State, the words "person", "human being", "child", and "individual" include every infant member of the species *homo sapiens* who is born alive at any stage of development.

(b) As used in this Section, the term "born alive", with respect to a member of the species *homo sapiens*, means the complete expulsion or extraction from its mother of that member, at any stage of development, who after that expulsion or extraction breathes or has a beating heart, pulsation of the umbilical cord, or definite movement of voluntary muscles, regardless of whether the umbilical cord has been cut and regardless of whether the expulsion or extraction occurs as a result of natural or induced labor, cesarean section, or induced abortion.

(c) A live child born as a result of an abortion shall be fully recognized as a human person and accorded immediate protection under the law.

Sections (a) and (c) define babies born alive as "persons." Both sections were clearly limited to infants who are both "born" and "alive" or "live." The two sections were redundant, but emphatic. Section (b) provided a clear definition of "birth" and "life" to which no doctor or scientist could object.

That is the whole bill, its meaning unadulterated and undistorted. It clearly does not apply to those *not born*.

Under this bill, babies born alive during an abortion would have to be treated just like every other baby that is born alive and prematurely—not left to die as at Christ Hospital, but given treatment according to the acting physician's medical judgment as to what is necessary and what is possible. The same laws and the same rules of medical ethics would apply to these born, living babies as to any other born, living human being.

This bill was not an abortion law. It did not confer any right or legal status upon any baby not yet born. This bill had no legal conflicts with *Roe v. Wade* decision, which in 1973 had established what effectively became a national, unalienable right to abortion. Born and living survivors of abortion would be unambiguously considered "persons." Medically, scientifically, empirically, they were no different from the many premature babies who are born in American hospitals each year.

There are several survivors of late-term abortions living among us today—such as Gianna Gessen, who survived a saline abortion in 1977 and testified about it before Congress in 1996.[6] She and others like her are obviously just as human as others who were born prematurely.

There was no legal conflict between O'Malley's bill and the right to legal abortion, but Barack Obama nonetheless had problems with it. He was a liberal, a proponent of legalized abortion. This may not have been an abortion law, but when he spoke against it on the Senate floor—he was the only senator to do so—he spoke as though it was. He said that this bill would not pass "constitutional muster."

> There was some suggestion that we might be able to craft something that might meet constitutional muster with respect to caring for fetuses or children who were delivered in this fashion. Unfortunately, this bill goes a little bit further, and so ... this is probably not going to survive constitutional scrutiny. Number

one, whenever we define a pre-viable fetus as a person that is pro-
tected by the equal protection clause or other elements in the
Constitution, what we're really saying is, in fact, that they are persons that are entitled to the kinds of protections that would be
provided to a—a child, a nine-month-old—child that was delivered to term. That determination, then, essentially, if it was
accepted by a court, would forbid abortions to take place. I mean,
it—it would essentially bar abortions, because the equal protection clause does not allow somebody to kill a child, and if this is
a child, then this would be an antiabortion statute. For that purpose, I think it would probably be found unconstitutional.[7]

We will examine Obama's argument more closely in a moment. But for
now, it is enough that he implies that babies born prematurely without
abortions might not be "persons." They might have to be "nine months
old" before they count.

But we saw already that the bill language applies only to babies that
have *already been born*. Birth has been the law's bright line, at least
since *Roe v. Wade*.

Apparently, not for Obama. He voted "present" on this bill. In a
strategy he would say was worked out in conjunction with lobbyists
from Planned Parenthood,[8] twelve other senators voted "present" as
well. It passed the Senate, but later died in a House committee. In
2002, O'Malley would reintroduce the legislation, in three separate
bills. Obama voted against the two bills that received a vote, and once
again, spoke against it on the Senate floor.[9]

In June 2001, three months after Obama's first speech against the
Illinois bill, the United States Senate voted on the language of the Born
Alive Infants Protection Act. Everything was the same as the Illinois
law except for section (c), which stated:

(c) Nothing in this section shall be construed to affirm, deny, expand, or contract any legal status or legal right applicable to any member of the species homo sapiens at any point prior to being born alive as defined in this section.[10]

This did not change the meaning, but it clarified that the bill did not apply to babies not yet born. On June 29, 2001, liberal senator Barbara Boxer of California spoke in favor of this bill:

Of course, we believe everyone born should deserve the protections of this bill...Who could be more vulnerable than a newborn baby? So, of course, we agree with that...We join with an "aye" vote on this. I hope it will, in fact, be unanimous.[11]

It was unanimous, 98–0.

This same bill that Boxer was praising came before Barack Obama's health committee two years later, in 2003. As chairman, he bottled it up in committee and killed it.[12] The *Chicago Tribune* reported during his Senate race that "Obama said that had he been in the U.S. Senate two years ago, he would have voted for" the bill.[13]

Three years later, he would offer this explanation for his opposition to the Illinois legislation in *The Audacity of Hope*:

It mandated lifesaving measures for premature babies (the bill didn't mention that such measures were already the law)—but also extended "personhood" to pre-viable fetuses, thereby effectively overturning *Roe v. Wade*.[14]

This is not true. Such measures were *not* already the law in Illinois. Not according to the Department of Public Health. Not according to Attorney General Ryan. They had said Christ Hospital was doing nothing illegal.

At the time Barbara Boxer spoke in favor of the Born-Alive Infants Protection Act, she was the most avid supporter of legal abortion in the United States Senate. Not only did she have a 100 percent lifetime voting score from the National Abortion Rights Action League,[15] and a 100 percent score from the Planned Parenthood Action Fund,[16] but she was a leader on the issue who regularly proposed amendments to expand access to abortion and government spending on abortion. She has never voted for any legal restriction on abortion.

Boxer was the greatest ally any legalized-abortion advocate had ever had in the United States Senate.

Or at least she was until 2005. That is the year Barack Obama was sworn in.

RADICAL ENOUGH

Hillary Clinton was not radical enough on abortion. She had "failed" the pro-choice movement. That is why abortion rights activist Frances Kissling endorsed Barack Obama.[17]

When the National Abortion Rights Action League endorsed Obama, the vote on their political board was unanimous.[18] It did not matter to the largely feminist organization that Clinton had the chance to become the first woman president. Abortion is their issue, and Obama is their man.

Why do they think this way? Because Barack Obama has a record to prove it. Conservative columnist Terence P. Jeffrey put it aptly: "Barack Obama is the most pro-abortion presidential candidate ever."[19]

That may sound like hyperbole, but here is the proof: When Barack Obama spoke on the Illinois Senate floor in 2001 against Illinois's born-alive protection bill, he did not say that a pre-viable baby *is not* a "person." He argued, rather, that even though the state should perhaps provide care for these babies, any recognition of their personhood would create unacceptable consequences. Again, his words, at length, so there's no uncertainty about context:

> [T]here was some suggestion that we might be able to craft something that might meet constitutional muster with respect to caring for fetuses or children who were delivered in this fashion. Unfortunately, this bill goes a little bit further, and so I just want to suggest, not that I think it'll make too much difference with respect to how we vote, that this is probably not going to survive constitutional scrutiny. Number one, whenever we define a previable fetus as a person that is protected by the equal protection clause or the other elements in the Constitution, what we're really saying is, in fact, that they are persons that are entitled to the kinds of protections that would be provided to a—a child, a nine-month-old—child that was delivered to term. That determination then, essentially, if it was accepted by a court, would forbid abortions to take place. [20]

Consider his words carefully. Obama is open to passing a bill that does something to *care* for these babies who have already been born alive. He does not necessarily want to make them suffer or even die—one might even conclude from this that he actually *does* think they are persons. But, he argues, we cannot legally *recognize* them as "persons." Because if we do, then somewhere down the road it might threaten someone's right to an abortion.

Most people, whatever their view on abortion, agree that the Constitution exists at least to guarantee the rights of born and living human beings. Barack Obama's actions indicate he thinks that before any other rights are granted to "persons," the Constitution exists in order to guarantee abortion rights.

Most pro-choice activists do not take the issue anywhere near that far. Barbara Boxer does not take the issue that far. Hillary Clinton, who voted for the born-alive bill, does not take the issue that far.

Only Barack Obama does. This is why NARAL loves him. It's why Planned Parenthood loves him. The right to abortion comes before all other human rights, including the right to urgent medical care. He is radical enough on abortion.

It goes without saying that Obama votes pro-choice on abortion without exception. He has a 100 percent score from every abortion group. In Illinois, he voted against minor restrictions and major ones. He voted "present" (again, effectively a "no" vote) on requiring parental notification (not parental *consent*) when minor children obtain abortions.[21] He has voted to preserve government funding for abortions.[22]

RALLYING AROUND PARTIAL-BIRTH ABORTION

Obama does much more than just *vote for* abortion. He uses the issue to excite his base and raise money. He makes big promises to lead the abortion-legalization movement forward, to sign their legislation, and to appoint their judges.

On February 17, 2004, Michelle Obama sent a fundraising e-mail to supporters on behalf of her husband, one month in advance of his Senate primary. Such fundraising e-mails have a hook—they try to excite their recipients with some issue, some new outrage by the other party. What was hers? The partial-birth abortion ban Congress passed in 2003. Keep in mind, the late Democratic pro-choice senator Daniel

Patrick Moynihan of New York once said of the procedure: "It is as close to infanticide as anything I have come upon in our judiciary."[23]

Mrs. Obama describes this law as a "ban on a legitimate medical procedure" that "is clearly unconstitutional and must be overturned.... On March 16th, we have a chance to nominate a candidate who will be tireless in the fight to protect women."[24]

Her husband, who voted either "present" or "no" whenever such a ban arose in Illinois,[25] offered this lengthy response to the 2007 Supreme Court ruling on *Gonzales v. Carhart* upholding the same law:

> I strongly disagree with today's Supreme Court ruling, which dramatically departs from previous precedents safeguarding the health of pregnant women. As Justice Ginsburg emphasized in her dissenting opinion, this ruling signals an alarming willingness on the part of the conservative majority to disregard its prior rulings respecting a woman's medical concerns and the very personal decisions between a doctor and patient. I am extremely concerned that this ruling will embolden state legislatures to enact further measures to restrict a woman's right to choose, and that the conservative Supreme Court justices will look for other opportunities to erode Roe v. Wade, which is established federal law and a matter of equal rights for women.[26]

He is not talking not just about abortion, but partial-birth abortion. For Barack Obama, women cannot be equal under the law without partial-birth abortion. Full human rights are not possible without partial-birth abortion.

In Springfield in 1997, two different partial-birth abortion bans came to the floor.[27] Obama had voted against one of them in the Senate Judiciary Committee,[28] but he voted "present" both times on the floor. One of the bans passed, 44 to 5, and became law. Obama's mentor, Emil Jones, voted "yes" on both bills.

In *Audacity of Hope,* Obama explains that the bill contained no exception for the health of the mother.[29] Is partial-birth abortion ever necessary a mother's health? The Physicians Ad Hoc Coalition for Truth, a group of over 600 doctors, wrote: "Never is the partial-birth procedure medically indicated."[30] "Health-of-the-mother" exceptions are plenary exceptions, nullifying the ban entirely, many pro-lifers argue, because of the broadness of the term "health." Indeed, abortionist Warren Hern once wrote, "I will certify that any pregnancy is a threat to a woman's life and could cause grievous injury to her physical health."[31]

Obama appears to be talking about partial-birth abortion in *The Audacity of Hope* when he offers up this reasonable-sounding statement:

> The willingness of even the most ardent prochoice advocates to accept some restrictions on late-term abortion marks a recognition that a fetus is more than a body part and that society has some interest in its development.[32]

But Obama is one of the very few pro-choice advocates who accepts *no restrictions* on late-term abortions, or any kind of abortions. I could find no instance in his entire career in which he voted for any regulation or restriction on the practice of abortion.

THE FREEDOM OF CHOICE ACT

Just as important as what Obama has done and written is what he promises to do if elected president. Speaking before the Planned Parenthood Action Fund on July 17, 2007, Obama said, "The first thing I'd do as President is sign the Freedom of Choice Act."[33]

This bill would effectively cancel every state, federal, and local regulation of abortion, no matter how modest or reasonable. It would even, according to the National Organization of Women, abolish all state restrictions on government funding for abortions.[34] If Obama becomes president and lives up to this promise, then everyone who pays income tax will be paying an abortionist to perform an abortion.

In promising to sign this bill, Obama is promising to abolish state laws that protect doctors and nurses from losing their jobs if they refuse to participate in abortions. He is promising to abolish requirements for parental notification and informed consent for mothers who consider the procedure. Some pro-life groups argue that, as written, the Freedom of Choice Act would abolish even the requirement that only licensed physicians perform abortions.[35]

Politicians' promises are often empty, but this one deserves to be taken seriously. Obama has a real record of "accomplishment" to back it up.

"RADICALS IN ROBES"

The presidency derives part of its particular importance from the power of appointing judges and Supreme Court justices. What sort of judges would a President Obama appoint?

It should not come as a big surprise that he likes liberal judges, not conservative ones. As president, he will appoint judges who strike down any restriction on abortion—like the four who tried to strike down the ban on partial-birth abortion in April 2007.[36] Obama mentioned three of them when asked by CNN's Wolf Blitzer whom he would appoint:

> Blitzer: So, what would be your criteria?
> Obama: Well, I think that my first criteria is to make sure that these are people who are capable and competent, and that

they are interpreting the law. And, 95 percent of the time, the law is so clear, that it's just a matter of applying the law. I'm not somebody who believes in a bunch of judicial lawmaking. I think...

Blitzer: Are there members, justices right now upon who you would model, you would look at? Who do you like?

Obama: Well, you know, I think actually Justice Breyer, Justice Ginsburg are very sensible judges. I think that Justice Souter, who was a Republican appointee, is a sensible judge.

Justices Ruth Bader Ginsburg and David Souter were recently on the short end of a 7–2 ruling on criminal penalties for the promotion of child pornography.[37] They opposed the penalties.

In *Kelo v. New London,* Justice Stephen Breyer joined Souter and Ginsburg to rule that local governments can take away people's homes in order to give them to private developers under the principle of eminent domain.[38]

In *Boy Scouts of America v. Dale,* Obama's favorite justices rejected the argument that a private organization like the Boy Scouts of America should be allowed to set its own standards of conduct for the leaders who influence their scouts by barring openly gay scoutmasters.[39] In this case, it was not gay rights but the First Amendment freedom of association that was hanging in the balance. It had to hang on a five-to-four majority because of Obama's favorite three justices.

As a Harvard-educated lawyer who once served as a lecturer at the University of Chicago law school, Obama knows a lot about law. He has quite a bit to say on the topic of the Constitution and its interpretation in *The Audacity of Hope.*

Justice Antonin Scalia, Obama writes, believes "that the original understanding [of the Constitution] must be followed, and that if we strictly obey this rule, then democracy is respected."[40] He considers that notion absurd: "[I]t is unrealistic to believe that a judge, two hundred years later, can somehow discern the original intent of the Founders or ratifiers."[41]

On the other hand, he likes the way liberal judges approach the constitution. He particularly holds up Justice Stephen Breyer as an example. "Ultimately," he writes, "I have to side with Justice Breyer's view of the Constitution—that it is not a static but rather a living document, and must be read in the context of an ever-changing world."[42]

"GANG OF FOURTEEN"

Shortly after entering the United States Senate, Obama opposed the circuit court appointments of several highly qualified individuals whose real sin appeared to be that President Bush had nominated them. Recall that between 2002 and 2004, the judicial battles had become an enormous election issue that harmed Democrats in the last presidential election.

During the confirmation process, Senate Democratic staff had prepared memos about these controversial nominees in which they made it clear that Hispanic conservative nominees were "particularly dangerous," presumably because it would be tougher to oppose them in more high-profile nomination battles. The memos (leaked to the press by Republican staff after Democrats failed to protect their network folders from outsiders) revealed that Democratic senators on the Judiciary Committee were basically letting highly partisan groups call the shots. Perhaps the most notorious memo stated flatly that "most of Bush's nominees are nazis."[43]

The Senate had reached a real nadir in comity. Democrats, in an unprecedented exertion of minority power, were blocking votes on nominees who had cleared the Judiciary Committee and had majority support in the full Senate. Republicans, meanwhile, were discussing the so-called "nuclear option" that would alter the way things were done in the Senate—they would rule that forty-one-vote filibusters could not be used against a President's nominees, so that a majority of Senators could confirm a judge.

It was just the sort of bitter and extreme partisan gridlock that Obama decries in politics.

In 2005, to avert a crisis between the competing principles of the Senate minority's rights and a President's ability to receive an up-or-down vote on his nominees, seven of Obama's fellow Democratic senators decided to reach across the aisle and find common ground with seven like-minded Republicans. The so-called "Gang of Fourteen" was an exercise in precisely the sort of bipartisanship that Obama extols as the antidote to extreme partisanship. The Democrats in the group included both moderates such as Ben Nelson of Nebraska and liberals such as Daniel Inouye of Hawaii. They promised not to filibuster qualified judges except under "exceptional circumstances." The Republicans promised they would prevent the use of the so-called "nuclear option" which would simply eliminate the filibuster as an option against judicial nominees. Together, they formed a large enough bloc to achieve both goals.

Obama declined to join this bipartisan group. It was Obama's choice not to participate in the bipartisan group. He usually makes that choice. On the other side, many conservatives made and regularly make the same choice—to dig in and insist on their way.

Obama is just like them—he is not a post-partisan healer, but a partisan who uses high-stakes issues to prove their *bona fides* to his party's extreme elements.

He writes that "given the profiles of some of the judges involved, it was hard to see what judicial nominee might be so much worse as to constitute an "extraordinary circumstance worthy of filibuster."[44] These judges, he adds, "showed a pattern of hostility toward civil rights, privacy, and checks on executive power that put them to the right of even most Republican judges."[45]

The seven Democrats in the Gang of Fourteen disagreed with him. In the cases of Priscilla Owen, Bill Pryor, Janice Rogers-Brown, and others, the Gang of Fourteen found no "extraordinary circumstances." They were confirmed.

A DIVIDER, NOT A UNITER

Obama begins one chapter of *The Audacity of Hope* exhorting everyone to respect others for their positions on abortion. He mentions a letter he received from a pro-life doctor, who asked him to take some incendiary abortion rhetoric down from his website. In the end, he does. He finishes the passage thus:

> And that night, before I went to bed, I said a prayer of my own—that I might extend the same presumption of good faith to others that the doctor had extended to me.[46]

It is a wonderful moment, filled with goodwill. Obama's book also includes, without any examples or citations, this assertion:

> Most antiabortion activists, for example, have openly discouraged legislative allies from even pursuing those compromise measures that would have significantly reduced the incidence of the procedure popularly known as partial-birth abortion, because the image the procedure evokes in the mind of the public has helped them win converts to their position.[47]

This questions not only the sincerity of pro-lifers but also their dedication to their own cause. And he is accusing "most" of them. Has there really been a big movement in pro-life circles to prevent action on partial-birth abortion, just because partial-birth abortions make more people oppose abortion?

"I'm pro-life, and I've never heard of anything like that," said Steve Rauschenberger, a former state Senate colleague of Obama.

"No, absolutely not," said Stanek, whose experience at Christ has led her to a career of local activism. She had been unaware of this quotation from Obama's book and was extremely surprised to hear it. "Not at a state level, not at a federal level. That someone would promote a partial-birth abortion ban on the surface, but underneath try to undermine it? No—no way."

To be sure, the pro-life movement is not necessarily of one mind on this issue. I have written that such bans are nice, but ineffective.[48] Some pro-lifers have argued against such bills in the past because, through some sort of legislative compromise, they contained language affirming *Roe v. Wade* that they did not feel they could support in good conscience. There is even a handful of absolutists who want it all at once, rejecting an incremental approach that allows the injustice of abortion to continue with state sanction.[49]

But in my time among conservatives in Washington, I have never met a single pro-life activist—let alone "a majority of pro-life activists"— who cynically hopes that partial-birth abortions keep happening just so that more people will get upset about abortion and become pro-life.

Not one. And certainly not "most."

Obama creates a very mixed impression by calling for respect on the abortion issue on the one hand, and smearing pro-lifers on the other, all in the same book. But we need not rely only on these contradictory quotations to get an idea of Senator Obama's take on politically active conservatives in general, and Christians in particular. Here is what he said about them while running for state Senate:

> The right wing, the Christian right, has done a good job of building these organizations of accountability, much better than the left or progressive forces have. But it's always easier to organize around intolerance, narrow-mindedness, and false nostalgia. And they also have hijacked the higher moral ground with this language of family values and moral responsibility.[50]

"Family values and moral responsibility." Conservatives use these concepts to mask and to propagate "intolerance, narrow-mindedness, false nostalgia."

Is that really what makes conservatives tick? When they talk about cultural issues, are they just clinging to the "illusory fixed points" to which Saul Alinsky referred?[51] Or are they resisting values that they see as truly harmful to society—their perception of Barack Obama's voting record?

Cultural issues get a rap for being *divisive*. This is not true at all. In fact, they are often great unifiers. That partial-birth abortion should be banned is a popular idea. That babies born alive are persons—and should be recognized as such—is an uncontroversial position.

The dividing line on these issues hardly runs through the center of the country. If partial-birth abortion and protection of abortion survivors are "divisive," they are dividing a vast majority of Americans from a small fringe on the Left. Obama's record has made it clear on which side of that line he stands.

CHAPTER ELEVEN

PINSTRIPE PATRONAGE: OBAMA TAKES CARE OF HIS FRIENDS

Antoin Rezko is in the Big House. Barack Obama could be headed to the White House. It will be ironic if the two men serve their disparate terms at the same time, because Obama could never have gotten where he is today without Rezko.

That's not to say Obama hasn't helped Tony Rezko, too—Obama was a champion in Illinois's legislature for pushing subsidies for developers, like Rezko. He also used his position of power to push for government aid targeted directly at Rezko's businesses. His campaign denies that Obama's work benefitting Rezko had anything to do with Rezko's enthusiastic (and, in at least one case, allegedly illegal) fundraising for Obama.

The relationship between Rezko and Obama is much reported and little understood. Who is this guy, anyway? What did he do? How was Obama involved? Didn't the two build a house together, or something like that?

Well, no. They did not. They did purchase adjoining pieces of land. But their complicated, seventeen-year relationship goes far beyond that. Rezko is one of Obama's many connections to the world of subsidized land development. He was a big fundraiser, for Obama and others. He was also a crook with a huge gambling problem.

Rezko was a genius of corporate welfare who used his political connections to rake in millions of dollars. He enriched himself at the expense of the taxpayer using means both legal and illegal. For both kinds of deals, he needed politicians' help.

When it came to illegal transactions, Rezko did not go to Barack Obama. He went to a Republican friend, Stuart Levine, a trustee of the state Teachers' Retirement System. Levine used his official position to steer the money—we're talking about huge amounts, like $50 million—to certain investment firms. Rezko would arrange for the firms' agents to pay a kickback. Levine also sat on another state board, so there were many opportunities for this kind of arrangement.

That was the *illegal* kind of deal. When Rezko wanted to get his hands on state money *legally*, sometimes Barack Obama helped him.

Obama would famously tell the *Chicago Tribune* that it was "boneheaded" to get involved in a land deal with Rezko, one of his largest campaign donors and fundraisers. Rezko's conviction on sixteen counts of fraud, money laundering, and aiding and abetting bribery came down on June 4, 2008. It could be called an exclamation point— or a question mark—to follow the final Democratic primaries.

Obama and Rezko had really been quite close. They were personal friends, dining together now and then with their wives. The Obamas once spent a day at Rezko's Lake Geneva retreat.[1] When asked about the land transaction by the *Chicago Tribune*, Obama said it was precisely his *intimacy* with Rezko that made him feel secure that the deal was on the up-and-up.

"I've known [Rezko] for a long time," he said. "I assumed I would have seen a pattern [of corrupt behavior] over the past 15 years." Obama might have detected this pattern as early as June 30, 2004, had he read the *Chicago Sun-Times* that day. The paper reported on potential kick-back scheme involving Illinois's hospital planning board, and it named Rezko as a contributor to Governor Blagojevich, and reported that Rezko had placed friends on the hospital's board.[2]

The deal was at least "boneheaded" for that reason, if for no other.

The details of the transaction itself are already well covered, if still confusing: In June 2005, Obama and Rezko purchased adjoining pieces of land in Hyde Park—the seller, Frederic Wondisford, split a single parcel in two so he could sell them separately. On the one side was the beautiful dream home sought by Senator Obama, newly wealthy from his $1.9 million book deal. On the other was an empty but green and attractive 9,000-square-foot lot.

Several months before the nationwide real estate bust would begin, Obama purchased the house for $1.65 million—$300,000 below the list price. Rezko's wife purchased the adjoining empty lot for the list price, $625,000.

After Rezko's indictment in September 2006,[3] this deal came to light. The press began to ask some of the relevant questions:

1. Was Rezko buying Obama a bigger yard?
2. Was this purchase possible only because Rezko had become involved?
3. Did Obama get a sweetheart deal?
4. Did Rezko get something in return?

You could argue that Rezko was *effectively* buying Obama a bigger yard, because if someone else had bought the lot, they might have taken steps to build on it. But Obama says that he had always expected Rezko would build on it.[4] Rezko was, after all, a developer.

The other questions, by their nature, cannot really be "proven in the negative." It is futile—perhaps even unfair—to demand that Obama *prove* his innocence.

All parties involved in the deal deny any impropriety. Wondisford, who has refused to speak to the press except through the Obama campaign, says he did not drop the price as a special consideration for Obama or Rezko.[5] Obama says he simply called Rezko, a developer who knew the neighborhood, for advice about buying a house. Rezko told Obama that he knew Wondisford, and then he became interested in the same piece of land. They toured the property together.[6] Rezko later told Obama that he planned to buy the empty lot.[7] The seller says that Obama got a good deal on the house just because no one else made a higher offer.

What of the subsequent transaction, in which Obama paid twice the tax-assessed price for a ten-foot-wide strip of Rezko's lot? It is extremely strange, but who benefits? In the worst case, perhaps Rezko needed some cash to pay his extensive gambling and legal debts.[8] Politicians are supposed to get in trouble for *taking* personal gifts, not for giving them. How could Obama be crooked for paying too much? It is his money, isn't it?

For all of the justifiable speculation, there is no clear evidence that this deal was crooked. This line of inquiry, however, misses the most important point.

WHAT OBAMA REALLY DID FOR REZKO

Far more important than the details of this particular transaction is the deeper question no one is asking: Why would Senator Obama *ever* engage in a transaction with a man like Rezko? Why does Barack

Obama count as a friend and longtime ally a man who has made his entire living filling his bank account with government money and corrupting public officials like Barack Obama?

And then there is one other question: has Barack Obama ever done anything for Tony Rezko?

When asked in 2006, before he became a candidate for president, Obama was unequivocal: "I've never done any favors for him."[9]

But he *has*. Obama performed official acts while in office that benefited Tony Rezko. It is impossible to know Obama's motives, but we can observe the consequences of his actions in office. And he has done quite a bit for Rezko.

In June, *Chicago Sun-Times* reporter Tim Novak reported that Obama "wrote letters to city and state officials supporting his political patron Tony Rezko's successful bid to get more than $14 million from taxpayers to build apartments for senior citizens."[10] The project, Cottage View Terrace, includes ninety-seven apartments. It is a few blocks outside of Obama's state Senate district.

The deal for which Obama helped Rezko get this money also included Obama's old law-firm boss, Allison Davis. He is also a major Obama fundraiser and a developer who has built or renovated 1,500 apartment units in Chicago.[11] From the $14.6 million in state funds that Obama requested, the two men would already be expected to profit through their housing business. But Davis and Rezko were also to collect $855,000 of it in "development fees."

Obama's spokesman and Rezko's lawyer say it is simply a coincidence that the senator wrote these letters to help two longtime friends, Davis and Rezko, get millions of dollars.[12]

Rezko...Davis...and then there are other developers around Obama. Two of them are: Obama advisor, donor and fundraiser, Valerie Jarrett; and Cecil Butler, a donor.

Obama is surrounded by developers. Why?

As a lawyer, Obama had Rezko and other low-income housing developers as clients at his law firm. But the Chicago developers remained very close to Obama long after that and still do. Why is this? What have they done for him? And what has he ever done for them?

Again, we can't ascribe motive from the available evidence, but the paper trail suggests an interesting answer: the developers financed his political career. He wrote letters to get them government money and supported legislation that helped their business.

An important thing to understand about all developers, and especially developers of subsidized housing, is that they are inextricably tied to government. At the very minimum, they need permits to demolish, build, and renovate. Sometimes environmental analyses are required as well. But many developers, having already made the friends needed to get the permits, leverage their political ties for much more: special "empowerment zone" tax breaks, eminent domain takings to acquire coveted lots, discounted land from the city, and, most importantly, subsidies for low-income housing.

Developers need friends in government. In state senator Obama, the developers had a friend. In Springfield, he was a reliable backer and at times even a champion of the subsidy system that made Rezko and other Chicago slum developers wealthy building low-income housing.

In 1998, five months before he wrote the letters to help the project by Rezko and Davis, Obama had been the chief Senate sponsor of a bill that would help their cause. It was not controversial—it passed 58–0. The City of Chicago supported it. But of the many bills in which Obama had a hand that year, it is one of only six that became law for which he was the chief Senate sponsor. He was very interested in this issue.

The bill changed property tax laws, creating an abatement for low-income housing. The argument for it was almost conservative. As

Obama explained to his colleagues on May 13, 1998, this would reduce transaction costs, facilitating the conversion from government-owned public housing projects to tenements built by private developers like Rezko, Davis, and the rest:

> [O]ver the last several years, there's been a movement to reform public housing and to break up some of the large public housing developments that exist and to create more mixed-income affordable housing... Essentially what this bill does is it helps to enhance the potential for privatization of public housing by providing a tax abatement for the construction of multifamily units that will house not only public housing residents, but also market-rate units... [T]he Chicago Housing Authority would like to contract out with private developers to build mixed-income housing. That land is currently not on the tax rolls at all in Chicago, and... if, in fact, this land is leased to a private developer, then those units that are being set aside for affordable housing will receive a tax abatement...[13]

This was one of many housing-related initiatives on whose behalf Obama would work and speak in Springfield.

- Obama co-sponsored a bill in 1997[14] that required certain municipalities to create affordable housing funds using revenues from bonds. Among other things, the funds were to be used to preserve existing buildings and to subsidize construction of new ones.
- In 2001, Obama co-sponsored and passed legislation[15] that increased such developers' state subsidies by creating an "affordable housing tax credit." In other words, if you

donated land or money to a state-approved affordable housing project, you got half of the value back in tax credits,
which could be carried forward to future tax years.[16]

- Obama co-sponsored the Illinois Housing Initiative Act of
  2003,[17] which required the governor to develop a plan for
  more low-income housing. The bill also would have "provide[d] for funding for housing construction and rehabilita-
  tion and supportive services."[18] The governor vetoed it but
  set up essentially the same housing initiative by executive
  order.

- In 2003, the Illinois General Assembly passed, and Governor Rod Blagojevich signed, the Affordable Housing Planning and Appeal Act, whose effect was to require forty-six
  communities in Will, Cook, DuPage, and Lake Counties—
  just outside of Chicago—to increase their stock of "affordable housing" to 10 percent. Included in the definition of
  "affordable housing" is "any housing that is subsidized by
  the federal or State government." It also provided loopholes
  in any local regulations that got in developers' way. The bill
  synopsis said the measure would "allow builders to seek
  relief from local ordinances and regulations that may inhibit
  the construction of affordable housing."[19]

  Overnight, this bill created a demand for more than seven
  thousand new units, based on a document from the Illinois
  Housing Development Authority published in August
  2004.[20] Obama voted for the original law (it passed,
  31–25),[21] and then co-sponsored a bill that moved up all of
  its deadlines by more than a year.[22]

- Obama co-sponsored another 2004 bill[23] that authorized subsidies to developers to cover discounted rents for low-income

tenants—70 percent of the money was earmarked for the Chicago area. As the bill's language puts it, it authorized "grants...directly to developers of new affordable rental housing for long-term operating support to enable the rent on such units to be affordable." Obama was the chief co-sponsor of the same bill in 2002.[24]

Obama sponsored many bills that benefited developers. Some of this legislation passed, and some didn't. Some passed after Obama had moved on to Washington.

In April 1997, Obama was profiled discussing private developer subsidies in the *Chicago Daily Law Bulletin*. The piece notes that as a lawyer, Obama had had as clients "private organizations that built affordable housing for low-income people."

> He said he was impressed that these community development corporations achieved socially beneficial goals without the aid of governmental bureaucracy. But he said their success was based on a federal program providing tax credits for investment in low-income housing.
>
> "That's an example of a smart policy," Obama said. "The developers were thinking in market terms and operating under the rules of the marketplace; but at the same time, we had government supporting and subsidizing those efforts."

Obama was committed to the idea of private developers building low-income housing. From his public office, he helped provide Rezko, Davis, and other such developers with subsidies to develop low-income housing units. He worked to provide them with a rent-subsidy fund that guaranteed them a steady income stream.

And then these friends and supporters of Obama proceeded to neglect their buildings and let their tenants live in squalor or shiver in unheated buildings.

THE SLUM LORDS

Davis, who has developed more than 1,500 apartment units in Chicago, helped develop the now-mostly uninhabitable Grove Parc Plaza project in Obama's old state Senate district.[25] The *Boston Globe*'s Binyamin Appelbaum exposed conditions at Grove Parc Plaza in a lengthy, detailed June article illustrating the failures of developer subsidies:

> Mice scamper through the halls. Battered mailboxes hang open. Sewage backs up into kitchen sinks. In 2006, federal inspectors graded the condition of the complex an 11 on a 100-point scale—a score so bad the buildings now face demolition.[26]

Sewage backups seem to be a common problem in Davis's low-income slums—Appelbaum writes that another of Davis's buildings was cited in 2007 "after chronic plumbing failures resulted in raw sewage spilling into several apartments."[27]

Valerie Jarrett, Obama's advisor, was the chief executive of the company that managed that Grove Parc slum until just recently. Her company also managed another housing complex until its condition became so poor that it was seized by the federal government in 2006.[28] Incidentally, she is the granddaughter of Robert Taylor, after whom the Robert Taylor housing projects, which once stood along the Dan Ryan Expressway, had been named.[29]

Cecil Butler had his Lawndale Restoration complex confiscated by the government in 2006 "after city inspectors found more than 1,800 code violations."[30] He contributed $4,000 to Obama's various federal campaigns.

Tony Rezko began his slum-lord career six days after Mayor Richard M. Daley's election in 1989, when Rezko and partner Daniel Mahru applied for and received a $629,000 loan from the city to rehabilitate an apartment building on 46th and Drexel on the South Side of Chicago. Neither had any experience in the construction business.

Within the first six years of Daley's reign, Rezmar (as they named their company) would receive $24 million in government loans and $8.5 million in federal tax credits. Over the next decade, it would rake in more than $100 million in loans from the city, state and federal government, as well as private bank loans to fix up thirty Chicago buildings for low-income public housing.[31]

Despite all of the cheap money provided by taxpayers, all of Rezmar's thirty buildings have run into financial difficulties. As of 2007, seventeen had gone into foreclosure. Six were boarded up and abandoned.

The City of Chicago has sued Rezmar at least a dozen times for failing to heat its properties. "Their buildings were falling apart," one former city official told the *Chicago Sun-Times*. 'They just didn't pay attention to the condition of these buildings." Rezmar architect Phillip Kupritz admits that "every one of these properties has failed."[32]

During the winter of 1997, Rezmar claimed it lacked the funds to turn the heat on in a thirty-one-unit building in Englewood on the South Side of Chicago—one of eleven Rezmar buildings in Obama's state Senate district. Tenants there went without heat from late December 1996 through mid-February 1997. Despite Rezmar's financial hardship, Rezko still managed to sign a check for $1,000 to the political campaign fund of newly elected state Senator Obama on January 14, 1997.[33]

There is no reason to believe that Obama approved of such outrageous neglect. His staff has told reporters that he was simply unaware of the condition of the eleven buildings his friend owned in his state Senate district.[34]

Obama may also have been acting with the best of intentions when he pushed the developers' legislation, and when he wrote the letters to help his friends get subsidies. But whatever intentions he had, we know for sure that Obama helped cut Rezko and other developers in on millions in taxpayer funds, only to have them cash out and literally leave their tenants in the cold. The outrageous condition of Rezko's buildings does not appear to have caused tension in their relationship. We also know that the developers returned the favor by giving Obama hundreds of thousands in campaign donations. According to the *Boston Globe*:

> Campaign finance records show that six prominent developers—including Jarrett, Davis, and Rezko—collectively contributed more than $175,000 to Obama's campaigns over the last decade and raised hundreds of thousands more from other donors.[35]

Rezko, who raised and contributed a total of $250,000 to Obama throughout his career, was in the political contribution business. He gave to politicians in both parties—like a businessman, not a partisan. He gave to President Bush and to Senator Kerry (D); to Mayor Daley (D) and to Congressman Ray LaHood (R); to Congressman Mark Kirk (R) and to Governor Rod Blagojevich (D). He even once served as campaign finance chairman for Cook County Board president John Stroger.

Rezko's housing development business depended on subsidies from every level of government. He completed the favor-circle by becoming a major political contributor and fundraiser, effectively passing a portion of those subsidies back up the chain. This is the rich man's version of the Stroger Machine, often referred to in Chicago as "pinstripe patronage." The dime-store Machine pol employs the classic technique of lining his client's pockets with a government salary. At the high end, though, the players deal in large government grants, subsidized loans and other big-ticket items.

Obama was one of Rezko's larger investments—in line with Rezko's gambling habit, you could say he "doubled down." In 1995, Obama, who had turned down a Rezko job offer in 1990, already knew that Rezko was the man to approach when he launched his first bid for the Illinois Senate. Rezko raised some $10,000 to $15,000 of the $100,000 Obama collected before winning the race uncontested.[36] Obama originally suggested that Rezko had been responsible for some $60,000 of the money he collected for his campaigns over the years, but reporters discovered that the true number had to be at least triple that amount.[37] After his campaign searched its records this winter, Obama would acknowledge that Rezko had actually raised and contributed about $250,000 to his state Senate races, his unsuccessful run for Congress in 2000, and his 2004 U.S. Senate run.[38] Rezko allegedly used at least one "straw donor" to funnel money to an unnamed "political candidate," and bypass federal contribution limits—the *Chicago Sun-Times* reported, "a source familiar with the case confirmed that Obama is the unnamed 'political candidate.'" Obama's campaign returned the money "for other reasons."[39]

In Chapter Three, we saw the story of how a fortunate Barack Obama won his U.S. Senate primary when the frontrunner exploded in scandal late in the race. Without the financial help he got from developers like Rezko, Obama would never have been in a position to surge ahead. The big money that people like Rezko raise for Obama also makes him seem a viable candidate, so that small donors feel justified in contributing.

Rezko helped Obama get to where he is today. Whatever Obama's intentions, it is a matter of public record that he helped his benefactor through his legislative work on developers' subsidies and through his letter-writing on behalf of a major development project by Rezko and Davis.

Back to the Rezko-Obama real estate deal: Why did it ever happen? Simple.

With such a close working relationship, is it any surprise that the two would become personal friends?

"SUB-PRIME" DONORS

Barack Obama promised supporters early on that his presidential campaign would not take money from lobbyists. As he put it in a fundraising email:

> We're not going to play that game. We're not taking any contributions from Washington lobbyists or political action committees. We're going to transform the political process by bringing together hundreds of thousands of ordinary Americans to build a campaign [40]

This promise he has kept—sort of. He does take money from lobbyists who have recently quit the business, and he has lobbyists raising money from others on his behalf. Alex Bolton, writing in *The Hill* last year,[41] identified three lobbyists who had each raised more than $50,000 for him so far, as well as three others who had recently quit lobbying and were contributing and raising money on his behalf. He also identified by name five executives who serve as Obama bundlers, whose companies were spending millions on lobbying efforts in Washington—some of them had lobbyists working on matters related to Obama's committee work.

You cannot blame Obama for raising money the usual way—for "playing that game."

My colleague Mark Hemingway wrote more recently in *National Review Online* that Peter Bynoe, a former Boeing lobbyist in Illinois, has pledged to raise between $100,000 and $200,000 for Obama.[42] Mike Bauer, another Illinois state lobbyist, has pledged to raise between $50,000 and $100,000. Bauer was suspended from practicing law for improperly taking $300,000 from a family trust fund. Precisely when he took that money, he donated $300,000 to national and local political candidates.[43]

Part of Obama's story is that he is a man of the people. He has impressed everyone with his ability to raise money in small amounts from dedicated fans. On March 29, 2005, the newly elected Senator Obama sent out a fundraising email through MoveOn.org on behalf of his friend and Senate mentor, Robert Byrd of West Virginia. Within 24 hours, more than 15,000 donors had contributed a total of $634,000 to the aging Democrat.[44] Obama has created an impressive army of small donors in this election as well—by mid-2007, he had already raised money from a record-setting 258,000 people.[45]

But Obama also raises big money from bundlers and contributors who "max out." Developers have been a traditional source of his money, as are lobbyist bundlers.

And then there are the bankers—that's where the money is. Obama has three bankers involved in his campaign.

Make that two. Jim Johnson served just briefly as a member of his vice-president vetting committee, but he had to quit. He was the former chairman of mortgage lender Fannie Mae. It was revealed shortly after Obama hired him that Johnson had received loans with favorable rates on three home mortgagees totaling $1.7 million from Countrywide Financial Corp, with the assistance of Angelo Mozilo, his friend and Countrywide's CEO.[46] Obama had previously criticized Countrywide by name. The lender is currently under federal investigation[47] for its role in the current sub-prime loan crisis. Johnson resigned from Obama's campaign on June 10, 2008.

Penny Pritzker is Obama's national finance chairwoman, and a supporter of Obama ever since the beginning of his U.S. Senate campaign.[48] In her family, they don't fight over the remote control. They fight over who took a billion dollars from whose trust fund.[49] Her family owns the Hyatt hotel chain. Aside from the money she raised from others, Pritzker's family contributed at least $39,000 to his 2004 campaign, and they have continued their generosity toward his presidential effort, giving at least $48,000.[50]

Pritzker was chairwoman of the board for her family's bank, Superior Bank FSB, until 1994, when she became director of its holding company. In 1993, she had overseen the fateful decision to adopt a new business strategy of aggressive subprime lending.[51] As the bank neared collapse in May 2001, she wrote a letter promising to "once again restore Superior's leadership position in subprime lending."[52] Superior's collapse that July caused 1,400 account-holders to lose money.

The subprime strategy that Pritzker had endorsed was a major part of the problem leading to the bank's insolvency, according to a release from the federal Office of Thrift Supervision:

> Superior Bank suffered as a result of its former high-risk business strategy, which was focused on the generation of significant volumes of subprime mortgage and automobile loans for securitization and sale in the secondary market.[53]

Even after the large legal settlement that Pritzker's bank was forced to pay out in order to avoid government action against it, these 1,400

account holders came up $10 million short on aggregate.[54] The
Chicago Sun-Times quoted one of the people who lost money, a 63-
year-old woman who had deposited her retirement savings in Superior
just before the collapse: "They still owe me $113,000," she said.[55]

There had been warnings: In 2000, the National Community Rein-
vestment Coalition (NCRC), a financial watchdog group, sent a letter
to federal bank regulators to alert them to Superior's subprime lending
practices, accusing the bank of poor risk management and of targeting
minorities for sub-prime loans at a rate that far exceeded other financial institutions.[56] The warning was not enough to prevent the collapse
the following year.

The Federal Deposit Insurance Corporation (FDIC), which insures
account-holders up to $100,000 against bank collapses, places much of
the responsibility for the collapse on the board and managers at Superior, saying they "ignored sound risk-management principles and failed
to adequately oversee Superior's operations."[57] Superior's collapse cost
the FDIC approximately $750 million.[58] The Pritzkers agreed to pay a
$460 million settlement—$100 million up front, and the rest (without
interest) over a period of 15 years.[59]

In April 2008, Pritzker told *USA Today*: "I regret that Superior Bank
failed." She went on, "My family voluntarily agreed to pay the FDIC
$460 million... without litigation or any allegation by federal regula-
tors of wrongdoing. I am proud of how my family responded to this
situation"[60] (ellipses in the original). According to the Associated Press,
the Pritzkers' 2001 settlement "barred government action against the
owners" who "admitted no liability."[61]

Alexi Giannoulias is another key Obama ally and a banking scion. He
was elected Illinois State Treasurer in 2006, when Obama was one of the
few officeholders backing him. For once, Obama did not back the
favored candidate of the Machine—that was Paul Mangieri, who had

been endorsed by the Illinois Democratic Party, the state party chairman, forty-one state lawmakers, and most statewide officeholders. Instead, Obama endorsed the candidate whose family institution, Broadway Bank, had been loaning money to mafia figures.

"The treasurer's job is a financial job," Obama explained. "He's the candidate who has financial experience."[62] Giannoulias was 29 years old at the time.

Obama kind of owed him. Giannoulias and his family had given more than $10,000 to his 2004 Senate campaign,[63] which in turn kept its accounts at their bank.[64] Giannoulias has pledged to raise $100,000 for Obama's presidential campaign this year.[65]

Broadway had loaned millions of dollars to Michael "Jaws" Giorango, a convicted bookmaker and prostitution ring promoter. When asked about loans the bank had made to Giorango in the 1990s, Giannoulias said he had not been a full-time employee of the bank at that time.[66] Then the *Chicago Tribune* reported that in 2005, when Giannoulias was serving as vice president and senior loan officer at Broadway, the bank had made an $11.8 million loan to Giorango and that Giannoulias had even traveled to Miami to meet with Giorango and inspect a property the bank was financing for him.[67] Of his original explanation, Giannoulias said, "It wasn't an attempt to mislead."[68]

Giorango's co-signer, Demitri Stavropoulos, had been convicted of explosives possession and running a bookmaking operation. In fact, Stavropoulos's wife once had to co-sign a loan on his behalf because he was in prison when the loan was made.[69]

Obama said that he was "concerned" by the revelation and said he would ask Giannoulias about it himself,[70] but it did not change the close political alliance between the two men.

Between 2001 and 2005, the *Sun-Times* reported, the Broadway Bank also loaned more than $10 million to the Stratievsky family, alleged members of the Russian "New Mafiya."[71]

Giannoulias defended the bank's pattern of loaning money to such individuals. "If every time someone got arrested the bank threw them out, I think it would be a problem," he explained. "We look at the commercial viability of loans, and that's where we make our credit decisions."[72]

Mike Madigan, the Democratic Speaker of the Illinois House of Representatives, refused to endorse Giannoulias after he had received the Democratic nomination, refused to take his phone calls, and even refused to put his photograph on the party's campaign website.[73]

"I want some answers. The allegations are there," Madigan said at the time. "My history in politics, if you were alleged to be connected to the mob, you were done. But life seems to go on."[74]

PING-PONG PATRONAGE

Perhaps the most surprising story about Barack Obama and money is one that no one talks about at all. It involves ping-pong. It is the story of how state Senator Obama was paid more than $100,000 for legal work, then helped his client's company get $320,000 in taxpayer grants.

For some reason, only the *Los Angeles Times* has examined the story of Robert Blackwell Jr. and the government grants he received after he invested in Barack Obama.[75]

Obama writes in *The Audacity of Hope* that after his failed congressional run in 2000, he was "more or less broke."[76] His family would make $240,000 that year, but they had large debts, and he had just loaned his losing campaign $9,500 and maxed out his credit card.[77] To keep his family afloat, he writes, he went back after the election to his law firm, Miner, Barnhill & Galland, which he had neglected throughout 2000 (he received no income from the firm that year). He planned to do some legal work to supplement his modest $58,000 salary as a state senator.

In 2001, while serving as a state senator, Obama would earn $98,158 from his law practice. Of that money, $80,000 came from a single client—Electronic Knowledge Interchange (EKI)—which had put him on an $8,000 monthly retainer. This lasted fourteen months and netted Obama $112,000. The company was owned by one Robert Blackwell Jr., a friend of Obama's since about 1995.

Months after Obama received his final payment from EKI, he wrote a request on Illinois Senate letterhead and sent it to state officials for a $50,000 tourism grant to a company named Killerspin. This company was also owned by Blackwell.

Killerspin runs ping-pong tournaments and sells ping-pong gear. After Obama's original request, Killerspin received a $20,000 grant for a ping-pong tournament. Over the next three years, Obama's aide Dan Shomon—who was working for the senator part-time and part-time for Blackwell—would help Killerspin get a $200,000 state grant for its 2003 tournament and a $100,000 state grant for its 2004 tournament, for a total of $320,000.

So Blackwell's company paid Senator Obama a large sum of money. Blackwell's other company received almost three times as much in state grants, with help from Obama and his aide.

The *Times* reports that Obama, in his required legal financial disclosures, buried this six-figure financial conflict of interest amid a list of hundreds of other clients represented by his law firm. He did not mention that the majority of his 2001 income came from EKI—nor was he required to do so under Illinois law. Moreover, the *Times* piece notes:

> The business arrived at an especially fortuitous time because, as the law firm's senior partner, Judson Miner, put it, "it was a very dry period here," meaning that the ebb and flow of cases left little work for Obama and cash was tight.[78]

David Axelrod, the talented spokesman who often defends Mayor Daley, defended Obama thus in the *Times* article: "Any implication that Sen. Obama would risk an ethical breach in order to secure a small grant for a pingpong tournament is nuts."

That *would* be "nuts." But that's not what happened. Would it be "nuts" for a modestly paid public official with personal financial difficulties to risk an ethical breach if there was a six-figure payout involved?

Blackwell and his company's employees made significant campaign contributions to Obama as well. The *Times* reported that on the day after Obama made the original grant request on Blackwell's behalf, Blackwell donated $1,000 to Obama's nascent U.S. Senate campaign.[79]

According to the FEC, in that race Blackwell made six separate donations to Obama, for a total of $15,000—Obama's campaign would return $1,000 of that. In July 2006, he would give $2,100 to Obama's 2010 Senate re-election campaign. In Obama's current presidential race, Blackwell has already donated $11,900, which exceeds FEC limits, and so Obama's campaign has had to return all but $4,600. Other employees of Killerspin have kicked in at least $9,900, and other employees of EKI have contributed at least $8,040.[80] What's more, Blackwell has committed to raise between $100,000 and $200,000 for Obama.[81]

Obama refers often to an ethics bill that he shepherded through the Illinois Senate in its final stages, after state Senate President Emil Jones gave it to him. It banned gifts from government contractors to legislators. Without breaking that law, and at a time when he says he was short of work and short of cash, Obama obtained $112,000, plus campaign contributions, from someone whom he later made into a government grantee through his public office.

In early 2003, after one of Killerspin's tournaments, Obama said of Blackwell:

> I would never bet against Robert on one of his ideas... He's
> extremely good at coming up with moneymaking ideas and
> implementing them[82]

He sure is.

WHAT HOPE?

Hope. Change.

Do you hope that Barack Obama will change politics if he becomes president?

On what grounds?

If Barack Obama is a reformer, he could be the first one ever to become president of the United States having done almost nothing difficult in the name of reform. Consider: What has he really changed? In a positive way?

He did not change politics in Chicago. You can't reform a town like that by becoming a "Soldier for Stroger." By endorsing crooked Machine politicians who reward their campaign donors and door-knockers with a government salary. By backing a mayor whose aides and appointees sell city contracts in exchange for campaign contributions. By endorsing an alderman who pulls a gun on her colleagues. By failing to endorse the rare candidate who has a chance to win and change something in Cook County. By covering up for the excesses of the Chicago Teachers Union, knowing just how abysmal the city's public education is. By earmarking funds for a radical Catholic priest who encourages blacks to hate whites.

Obama did not change politics in Springfield. You can't reform a state like Illinois by voting "present" 130 times to avoid controversial issues. By teaming up with a state Senate Majority Leader whose main concern appears to be placing every member of his family somewhere on the state payroll. By backing for statewide office a financier whose family bank lends money to organized crime. By negotiating to minimize the impact of welfare reform. By writing letters to get state grants for someone who just put $112,000 in your bank account. By co-sponsoring nearly any bill that helps Tony Rezko and his friends make money from the taxpayers for building uninhabitable slums where rodents roam and sewage backs up into the kitchen sinks.

Obama has certainly not changed politics in Congress. You can't reform Washington by earmarking a million dollars for your wife's employer after they double her salary. By voting to throw away money on ethanol, farm subsidies, and the Bridge to Nowhere while much of New Orleans is still underwater. By reaching across the aisle on ethics reform, only to pull your hand back and bury it in your pocket. By earmarking funds for your campaign contributors. By suddenly deciding it's time to leave Iraq only once you start running for president.

It's not that Barack Obama is a bad person. It's just that he's like all the rest of them. Not a reformer. Not a Messiah. Just like all the rest of them in Washington. And just like all the other liberals, too.

That's not entirely true, though—most liberals in Congress know more than Obama does about foreign policy and how diplomacy works. Most of them—nearly all of them—believe that babies have a right to medical care once they have been born alive.

Obama's radical ties don't make him a radical. His ties to Communists don't make him a Communist. His ties to a terrorist don't even remotely make him a terrorist. But his continued relationships with radicals throughout his public life show an important influence in Obama's public career. What ideas are so important to Barack Obama that he desperately seeks the approval of *Black Commentator* and the New Party, but drops the Democratic Leadership Council as if it were a molten porcupine?

These connections do not disqualify Obama from the presidency. But they do raise questions about his judgment. By what criteria does a man choose his friends and end up with the likes of Tony Rezko, Jeremiah Wright, and Bill Ayers? How does he choose his advisors and end up with people who chat with terrorists, advocate reparations for slavery, and praise Hugo Chavez as a champion of democracy?

What sort of nominations does such a man make as president? What kind of diplomacy does he pursue, given that so much of diplomacy consists in reading, understanding, and judging others' intentions and character?

This is why these ties deserve scrutiny. If Barack Obama becomes president, his good judgment, or lack thereof, will affect the entire country.

ACKNOWLEDGMENTS

Without Tim Carney, my dear friend and my editor at Regnery, I would never have started or finished writing this book. The help he provided me went far, far beyond his duties. I owe him and his wife Katie a deep debt of gratitude that I doubt I will ever be able to repay.

Thanks also to Tim's colleagues at Regnery and Eagle Publishing—in particular, Harry Crocker, Marji Ross, Alex Novak, and Jeff Carneal.

I would like to thank Kathryn Jean Lopez, my boss at *National Review Online*, for her support and for giving me leave to write. I thank my other colleagues at *National Review*, particularly Byron York, Rich Lowry, Jim Geraghty, Stanley Kurtz, and others whose work served as an excellent guide.

I thank the members of my family for their help and their understanding as I busied myself writing. I thank my dedicated research staff for their hard work and attention to detail, and Robert Novak, my former boss, for his example and frank advice.

I would especially like to acknowledge the hard-working men and women of the Chicago press, whose considerable contribution to the available corpus of Obama knowledge has been sadly under-examined and under-appreciated by members of the national media. Tim Novak, John Kass, David Jackson, Dave McKinney, and many others at the *Chicago Tribune* and the *Chicago Sun-Times* have become heroes to me in the last few months as I have picked over and plundered the gems from the incredible treasure trove they have produced while covering Chicago and Illinois politics. It goes without saying that more reporters should follow up on the investigative work of Binyamin Appelbaum of the *Boston Globe* on the topic of subsidized low-income housing.

Finally but most of all, I would like to thank God for the many blessings He has bestowed upon me.

OBAMA: TIMELINE OF A (BRIEF) POLITICAL LIFE

Aug. 4, 1961—Obama born in Hawaii.

Feb. 16, 1970—Weatherman terrorist bombing in San Francisco kills one.

Mar. 6, 1970—Unsuccessful Weatherman bombing in Detroit.

Jun. 12, 1972—**Saul Alinsky** dies.

Oct. 18, 1974—**Larry Grothwahl** testifies before a Senate subcommittee on **William Ayers's** involvement in bomb plots.

Apr. 29, 1983—Harold Washington sworn in as first black Chicago Mayor.

May, 1983—Obama graduates from Columbia University.

June, 1985—Obama hired as a community organizer for the Developing Communities Project in Chicago.

Feb. 25–Mar. 6, 1986—**Alice Palmer** attends 27th Congress of the Soviet Union.

1988—Obama hears Rev. **Jeremiah Wright's** "Audacity of Hope" sermon, is baptized.

Fall 1988—Obama starts at Harvard Law School.

Apr. 4, 1989—**Richard M. Daley** elected mayor of Chicago.

Apr. 10, 1989—**Tony Rezko** applies for his first subsidized housing loan from the City of Chicago.

Feb. 1990—Obama elected president of *Harvard Law Review*.

1990—Obama turns down a job offer from **Tony Rezko**.

May, 1991—Obama graduates from Harvard Law School.

November 1991—Ald. **Dorothy Tillman** allegedly pulls a gun during a ward redistricting hearing.

April–October 1992—Obama runs "Project Vote" registration drive in Chicago for ACORN.

Aug. 22, 1992—John "Quarters" Boyle sentenced to three years for stealing $4 million, largely in change, from Chicago toll booths.

Oct. 18, 1992—Obama and Michelle Robinson married by Rev. **Jeremiah Wright.**

January 1993—Obama begins work at the firm of Davis, Miner, Barnhill & Galland.

1993—Obama joins the Board of Directors of the Woods Fund, where he will eventually serve alongside **William Ayers.**

March 1993—Superior Bank securitizes its first subprime mortgage loans for the secondary market.

Jul. 28, 1993—Obamas purchase a three-bedroom condo in Hyde Park with an $111,000 down payment.

Jul. 18, 1995—Publishes *Dreams from My Father.*

May, 1995—State senator **Alice Palmer** already mentioned as planning to run for Congress. Obama is her groomed successor in the State Senate.

July 31, 1995—**Tony Rezko** makes his first political donation to Obama.

July 1995—Obama seeks (and later receives) endorsement of radical New Party.

Nov. 28, 1995—Alice Palmer loses congressional bid.

Jan. 2, 1996—Obama begins process of throwing all of his opponents off the ballot.

Mar. 19, 1996—Obama wins Democratic state Senate primary, unopposed.

Jan. 14, 1997—Tony Rezko, while claiming he cannot afford to turn on the heat in one of his slums, writes a $1,000 check to Barack Obama's campaign.

February 1997—Obama co-sponsors for a bill that creates affordable local housing funds in order to subsidize private developers.

May 31, 1997—Illinois Senate passes Sen. Dave Syverson's (R) welfare reform bill. Obama, who helped negotiate the final version, says he would have voted against federal welfare reform.

September, 1997—John "Quarters" Boyle, despite prison record, hired by City of Chicago.

Nov. 20, 1997—Obama and Bill Ayers appear on academic panel on juvenile justice.

May 13, 1998—Obama sponsors and speaks on bill to facilitate privately built, subsidized low-income tenements. It passes 58–0.

May 22, 1998—At the invitation of senate Democratic Leader Emil Jones, Obama adds himself as co-sponsor of a campaign finance bill that had been proposed over one month earlier. It easily passes.

Oct. 28, 1998—Obama writes state and city officials asking them to give Tony Rezko and Allison Davis $14.6 million for a low-income housing project just outside his Senate district.

Feb. 25, 1999—Votes, in committee, to condemn the International Criminal Court.

Mar. 3, 1999—Skips floor vote on ICC.

Sept. 30, 1999—Announces for Congress and names Father **Michael Pfleger** as a supporter.

January 2000—Proposes price controls for prescription drugs.

Mar. 21, 2000—Loses democratic primary for U.S. Congress to four-term incumbent Bobby Rush.

Aug. 14–17, 2000—Attends Democratic National Convention.

January 2001—Obama announces large state grants for Father Michael Pfleger's ministry.

Spring 2001—Hired on $8,000 monthly retainer by **EKI**, a company owned by **Robert Blackwell Jr.** Makes $112,000 from the arrangement over the course of more than one year.

Mar. 30, 2001—Speaks against recognizing the personhood of premature babies who survive abortions. Votes "present" on the Illinois born-alive act.

May, 2001—**Penny Pritzker** promises to keep Superior Bank solvent through aggressive sub-prime lending.

June 19, 2001—U.S. Senate votes 98–0 in favor of the Born Alive Infants' Protection Act.

July, 2001—Superior Bank placed under conservatorship of the Federal Deposit Insurance Corporation.

Aug. 23, 2001—Bill co-sponsored by Obama, giving special tax credits to donors to private developers of "affordable housing," signed by Gov. **George Ryan.**

Oct. 24, 2001—**Patrick Fitzgerald** confirmed as U.S. Attorney for the Northern District of Illinois.

Apr. 20, 2002—Appears with **Bill Ayers** in a panel discussion on "Intellectuals in Times of Crisis."

Jun. 11, 2002—Altercation with Sen. **Rickey Hendon.**

ca. July, 2002—Obama writes a letter to Illinois officials requesting a $50,000 grant for **Killerspin** for a pingpong tournament—owned by

Robert Blackwell Jr..

Oct. 2, 2002—Speaks out against going to war in Iraq

December 2002—Killerspin's SPINvitational tournament at the University of Illinois, Chicago.

Mar. 14, 2003—Health Committee Chairman Obama bottles up the born-alive infants bill in committee. It is identical to the federal Born Alive Infants Protection Act.

Spring 2003—Obama's speech text against Iraq War disappears from his campaign website.

Apr. 11, 2003—Adds his name as co-sponsor of the Illinois Housing Initiative Act. It subsidizes and creates demand for private low-income housing developers.'

May 21, 2003—Obama votes for the Affordable Housing Planning and Appeal Act, creating demand for at least 7,000 new "affordable housing" units and letting private developers circumvent local ordinances.

June 13, 2003—Re-posts anti-war speech on Internet.

June 26, 2003—Asks to be removed from the DLC New Democrat Directory after being criticized by *Black Commentator*.

Aug. 14, 2003—**Stuart Levine** and **Tony Rezko** steer $50 million in teachers' retirement money to an investment firm and receive a $250,000 kickback from the "finder."

December 2003—Killerspin SPINvitational takes place at UIC.

Mid 2004-2005—**Alexi Giannoulias** of Broadway Bank travels to Miami to meet **Michael "Jaws" Giorango** and inspect a property the bank is financing.

Feb. 27, 2004—Blair Hull's divorce file unsealed.

March 4, 2004—Obama co-sponsors bill to move forward deadlines of developer-friendly housing bill.

Mar. 16, 2004—Obama wins Democratic primary for U.S. Senate.

June 22, 2004—Jack Ryan's full divorce file released to the public.

June 25, 2004—Ryan drops out of U.S. Senate race.

June 30, 2004—Obama writes a public letter praising a 2004 Killerspin ping-pong tournament.

July 2004—Killerspin SPINvitational tournament at UIC.

Jul. 27, 2004—Obama delivers keynote address at the 2004 Democratic National Convention in Boston.

Nov. 2, 2004—Obama elected to U.S. Senate.

Dec. 17, 2004—Obama signs $1.9 million deal for three books.

Feb. 25, 2005—Eight city workers indicted in hired truck scandal, bringing the total number indicted to 23.

May 26, 2005—*Chicago Tribune* profiles **Tony Rezko**, noting that he has been subpoenaed in a criminal investigation.

May 27, 2005—Visits Thornton Township High School, decries short school day.

Jun. 12, 2005—*Sun-Times* publishes piece on the conspicuous level of political patronage hiring in city government. **David Axelrod** defends **Mayor Daley.**

Jun. 15, 2005—In the morning, Obama votes for ethanol mandate in the U.S. Senate, twice. On the same day, he and **Tony Rezko** close on adjacent properties in Hyde Park.

July 18, 2005—First two Daley aides indicted for fraud related to illegal patronage hiring.

Aug. 5, 2005—Obama expresses initial hesitation about endorsing Daley for re-election, only to change his mind an hour later.

Sept. 1, 2005—**Tony Rezko** subpoenaed in Teachers Retirement System pension investigation.

Oct. 20, 2005—Obama votes to fund the Bridge to Nowhere instead of sending money to rebuild New Orleans.

Dec. 7, 2005—Obama endorses **Alexi Giannoulias** for state treasurer.

January 2006—Obama purchases part of neighbor **Tony Rezko's** lot.

Mar. 14, 2006—Cook County Board President **John Stroger** has a stroke.

Mar. 21, 2006—**John Stroger** defeats **Forrest Claypool** in Democratic primary.

June 21, 2006—Obama speaks against withdrawal from Iraq.

Jul. 6, 2006—Four Daley aides convicted on charges related to illegal patronage hiring.

Jul. 19, 2006—**Todd Stroger** replaces his father on the ballot.

Sept. 8, 2006—Senate passes Coburn-Obama Federal Funding Accountability and Transparency Act.

Oct. 11, 2006—**Tony Rezko** indicted on 24 counts.

Oct. 17, 2006—Obama publishes *The Audacity of Hope*.

Nov. 2, 2006—Liberal columnist **Eric Zorn** criticizes Obama's endorsement of **Todd Stroger** for President of the Cook County Board of Commissioners.

Nov. 7, 2006—**Todd Stroger** defeats **Tony Peraica** for Cook County board president. Democrats seize control of U.S. Congress.

Nov. 20, 2006—Obama announces that it is time to withdraw from Iraq.

Jan. 30, 2007—Introduces legislation to withdraw all troops from Iraq by March 2008.

Jan. 22, 2007—Obama endorses Mayor **Richard M. Daley**.

Feb. 8, 2007—Obama challenges Republican presidential candidates to pledge to take public financing for 2008 general election.

Feb. 28, 2007—Mayor Daley re-elected.

Mar. 23, 2007—Obama endorses Ald. **Dorothy Tillman** in runoff election.

Apr. 17, 2007—**Dorothy Tillman** narrowly loses re-election.

May 26, 2007—Father **Michael Pfleger** threatens to "snuff out" a gunshop owner.

Aug. 1, 2007—I-35W Bridge collapses in Minnesota.

Sept. 11, 2007—Obama votes to preserve funding for bike paths instead of redirecting it to bridge safety.

Sept. 12, 2007—Obama lays out a plan for withdrawal from Iraq.

Nov. 11, 2007—Obama concedes to **Tim Russert** that he muted war criticism to help John Kerry in 2004.

Jan. 3, 2008—Obama wins Iowa caucuses.

March 18, 2008—Obama gives speech in Philadelphia defending Rev. Jeremiah Wright.

Apr. 6, 2008—Obama makes "bitter" comments at San Francisco fundraiser.

Apr. 28, 2008—Rev. **Jeremiah Wright** accuses Obama of political posturing, Obama disowns him.

May 15, 2008—Obama votes in favor of the farm bill.

May 22, 2008—Votes to override veto of farm bill.

May 25, 2008—Father **Michael Pfleger** taunts Hillary Clinton, whites in sermon.

May 30, 2008—Obama quits Trinity Church.

Jun. 4, 2008—**Antonin Rezko** convicted on 16 felony corruption charges.

Jun. 7, 2008—**Hillary Clinton** withdraws from the presidential race.

Jun. 19, 2008—Obama opts out of public financing for the 2008 election after repeatedly pledging to take public financing and challenging the Republican nominee to do the same.

NOTES

Introduction

1   John Kass, "Obama Unstained by Chicago Way," *Chicago Tribune*, May 10, 2008.

2   Keila Szpaller, "Missoula crowd cheers, weeps for Barack Obama," *Montana Standard*, Apr. 6, 2008.

3   Michael Whack, "The 'BAM'... The Obama Handshake," Michael Whack's Blog, January 12, 2008, http://my.barackobama.com/page/community/blog/michaelwhack.

4   David Mendell, *Obama: From Promise to Power*, (NY: Amistad , 2007), 229.

5   John Nichols, "Obama Gets Farm Bill Right," TheNation.com, May 21, 2008.

6   Steve Holland, "Tough Talk on Pakistan from Obama," *Reuters*, August 1, 2007, http://www.reuters.com/article/domesticNews/idUSN01322 06420070801.

7   Mendell, 203–204.

8   Frank James, "Sean Penn talks, strangely, about Obama," *Chicago Tribune Online*, May 15, 2008, http://blogs.trb.com/news/politics/blog/2008/05/sean_penn_talks_strangely_abou.html.

9   Dave McKinney, "Obama would not pardon Rezko if elected president," *Chicago Sun-Times*, June 5, 2008.

10   "Obama strongly denounces former pastor," Associated Press, April 29, 2008.

11   The Fiscal Year 2009 Budget for which Obama voted dictated that the 25% income tax rate reset to 28% when Bush's 2001 tax cuts expire in 2012. For 2008, the 25% bracket applies to everyone earning more than $32,550.See Jim Geraghty, "If Obama Doesn't Think $31,850 Is Rich, Then Take Back the Vote," *National Review Online's* "Campaign Spot," June 11, 2008, http://campaignspot.nationalreview.com/post/?q=ODBjMjAxOGYzYTRhN2Q3ZDk5NzNmMTIyOWM1MjJmMmM=

Chapter 1

1   Except where noted, the details of Obama's disqualifying his opponents from the ballot comes from David Jackson and Ray Long, "Showing his Bare Knuckles," *Chicago Tribune*, April 4, 2007.

2   Barack Obama, *The Audacity of Hope* (New York: Random House, 2006), 2.

3   David Jackson and Ray Long, "Showing his bare knuckles," *Chicago Tribune*, Apr. 4, 2007

4   Ibid.

5   Sunya Walls, "Alice Palmer Withdraws from Race for Re-election," *Chicago Weekend*, January 21, 1996.

6   CNN Newsroom, May 31, 2008.

7   David Jackson and Ray Long, "Showing his bare knuckles," *Chicago Tribune*, Apr. 4, 2007

8   Gretchen Reynolds, "Vote of Confidence," *Chicago Magazine,* January 1993.

9   David Jackson and Ray Long, "Obama knows his way around a ballot," *Chicago Tribune*, April 3, 2007.

10   Bruce Bentley, "Chicago new Party Update," *New Ground* 42, September – October, 1995, http://www.chicagodsa.org/ngarchive/ng42.html.

11   Data from FEC: Report of Receipts and Disbursements, Jesse Jackson, Jr. for Congress, year-end report, filed December 12, 1995; and Report of Receipts and Disbursements, Friends of Alice Palmer, amended year-end report, filed June 28, 1996.

12   Hank De Zutter, "What Makes Obama Run?" *Chicago Reader,* December 8, 1995.

13   Chris Fusco and Tim Novak, "Rezko cash triple what Obama says," *Chicago Sun-Times*, June 18, 2007.

14   Mendell, 109.

15   Mendell, 109.

16   Christopher Wills, "Obama faced tough choice in first legislative race," *WTOP News*, April 24, 2008.

17   See John Kass, "Anti-Daley Forces Start to Beat Campaign Drums," *Chicago Tribune,* July 29, 1994; and Steve Neal, "2nd District Race May Get Crowded," *Chicago Sun-Times,* July 30, 1995.

18   Editorial, "Another Black Mayor for Chicago," *Chicago Weekend*, August 21, 1994.

19   David Jackson and Ray Long, "Obama knows his way around a ballot," *Chicago Tribune*, April 3, 2007.

20   "Second Semi-Annual Report of the Compliance Administrator," *Shakman* v. *Democratic Organization of Cook County*, U.S. District Court for the Northern District of Illinois, Eastern Division, 69 C 2145, 16. Available online at http://www.countyshakman.com/downloads/cc_shakman_CAReport02.pdf, (accessed May 27, 2008).

21   Ibid, 15.

22   Ibid, 15.

23   Ibid, 13.

24   Ibid, 12.

25   Ibid, 14–15.

26   Ibid, 18

27   Ibid, 15

28   The letter is available at http://blogs.chicagotribune.com/news_columnists_ezorn/2006/11/obama_endorses_.html.

29   "Second Semi-Annual Report of the Compliance Administrator," 8.

30   Ibid, 7.

31   Ibid, 7.

32   Ibid, 3.

33   Hal Dardick, "Court monitor tells Cook board of patronage-hiring allegations," *Chicago Tribune*, April 9, 2008.

34   Scott Fornek, "First black county president built hospital; From Arkansas shack to dean of black politics in Chicago," *Chicago Sun-Times*, January 19, 2008.

35   "BGA Investigation Finds Stroger Fundraising Practices Alarming," *Better Government Association*, January 11, 2006, http://www.bettergov.org/news_20060111_01_stroger_release.html.

36   Steve Patterson, "Stroger hires best friend's wife: she will earn more than $126,000 in county job," *Chicago Sun-Times*, January 5, 2007.

37   Steve Patterson, "Todd's new PR guy has a PR problem; Mullins was a childhood friend to board president," *Chicago Sun-Times*, February 29, 2008.

38   Hal Dardick, "Cook County Realtor hired by Stroger demoted after questions of his qualifications,"*Chicago Tribune*, Apr. 29, 2008.

39   Mickey Ciokajlo, "More county jobs cut in latest budget figures," *Chicago Tribune*, February 27, 2007. See also Eric Herman, "Prosecutors: County budget cuts let crooks off hook," *Chicago Sun-Times*, Mar. 2, 2007.

40   Hal Dardick, "Stroger Dismisses Patronage Claims," *Chicago Tribune*, March 7, 2008.

41   Neil Steinberg, "Stroger may be ill, but save your sympathy for taxpayers," *Chicago Sun-Times*, March 15, 2006.

42   Editorial, "Michael Quigley's show of class," *Chicago Tribune*, December 20, 2005.
43   Mickey Ciokajlo and Robert Becker, "Stroger suffers stroke," *Chicago Tribune*, Mar. 15, 2006.
44   Tom Bevan, "Obama's 'No, I Can't' Moment," *The Real Clear Politics Blog*, June 10, 2008, http://timeblog.com/real_clear_politics/2008/06/obamas_no_i_cant_moment.html.
45   Video available at http://www.youtube.com/watch?v=i9l0BdfkaUU.
46   Gary Washburn, "John Stroger: 1929 - 2008; Gentleman politician always 'about people'," *Chicago Tribune*, January 19, 2008.
47   Jim Slusher, "When Leaders Fall Ill, Health of Democracy Must Be Considered," *Chicago Daily Herald*, June 15, 2006.
48   Carol Marin, "Hiring freeze? Cook County seems to be adding jobs," *Chicago Sun-Times*, July 18, 2006.
49   *Chicago Tribune*, "A fraud on Cook County voters," July 9, 2006
50   Ibid.
51   Mickey Ciokajlo, "Claypool refuses to give endorsement to Stroger; March primary loser will support no one," *Chicago Tribune*, September 8, 2006.
52   The letter is reprinted in full on ChicagoTribune.com: http://blogs.chicagotribune.com/news_columnists_ezorn/2006/11/obama_endorses_.html
53   Eric Zorn, "Letter to voters a letdown for Obama idealists," *Chicago Tribune*, November 2, 2006, http://blogs.chicagotribune.com/news_columnists_ezorn/2006/11/obama_endorses_.html.
54   John Kass, "Obama magically unstained by grime of Chicago way," *Chicago Tribune*, May 11, 2008.
55   John Kass, "Obama Unstained by Chicago Way," ChicagoTribune.com, May 10, 2008, http://weblogs.chicagotribune.com/news/politics/blog/2008/05/obama_unstained_by_chicago_way.html
56   David Jackson and John McCormick, "Critics: Obama endorsements counter calls for clean government," *Chicago Tribune*, June 12, 2007.
57   Fran Spielman: "Daley blasts Tillman for waiter request," *Chicago Sun-Times*, July 20, 2001.
58   Michael Gougis, "Chicago's Gun-Toting Aldermen Under Fire," Associated Press, November 21, 1991.
59   Board of Election Commissioners for the City of Chicago: http://www.chicagoelections.com/wdlevel3.asp?elec_code=60
60   Gary Washburn, "Smell of scandal challenges Daley Re-election," *Chicago Tribune*, August 21, 2005.
61   Fran Spielman, "Daley Defends Hired Truck Chief," *Chicago Sun-Times*, February 12, 2004.
62   John Kass, "'Quarters' is small change compared to other insiders," *Chicago Tribune*, October 8, 2004.

63 Rudolph Bush and Dan Mihalopoulos, "Daley jobs chief guilty: Jury convicts 4 in city hiring fraud," *Chicago Tribune*, July 7, 2006.

64 Patrick J. Fitzgerald, "U.S. charges two city of Chicago officials with fraudulently rigging hiring and promotions," U.S. Department of Justice, July 18, 2005, available at http://www.bettergov.org/pdfs/ 071805usattorneyrelease.pdf.

65 Laurie Cohen, Todd Lightly, and Dan Mihalopoulos, "Feds link close pal of Daley to hiring," *Chicago Tribune*, September 23, 2005.

66 Monica Davey, "Corruption Case Draws Interest in Chicago," *New York Times*, May 11, 2006.

67 Laurie Cohen, Todd Lightly, and Dan Mihalopoulos, "Feds link close pal of Daley to hiring," *Chicago Tribune*, September 23, 2005.

68 Fran Spielman, "Obama endorses Daley," *Chicago Sun-Times*, January 22, 2007.

69 Ibid.

70 Mendell, 97.

71 Mark Konkol et al., "HDO Grows into Political Powerhouse," *Chicago Sun-Times*, June 12, 2005.

72 Jane M. Von Bergen, "Graft probe mushrooming in Chicago," *Philadephia Inquirer*, Aug. 11, 2005.

73 Fran Spielman, "Mayoral challenger attacks cronyism," *Chicago Sun-Times*, September 3, 2002.

74 "Chicago Mayor Wrestles with 'Embarrassing' Epidemic of Corruption," Associated Press, February 9, 2005.

75 Ibid.

76 Steve Warmbir, "Hired Truck Scandal: John Daley's brother-in-law heading to prison," *Chicago Sun-Times*, June 1, 2006.

77 Patrick J. Fitzgerald, "Seven new trucking firm defendant and expanded charges added to hired truck indictment against former city water department officials and others," U.S. Department of Justice, February 24, 2005, available at http://www.ipsn.org/hired_truck_scandal/tomczak/tomczaksupersed2-24-05final.rel.pdf.

78 Steve Warmbir, "Hired Truck figure aided Daley," *Chicago Sun-Times*, May 2, 2005.

79 John Kass, "Videotapes speak volumes despite 'Quarters' silence," *Chicago Tribune*, August 25, 2005.

80 Matt O'Connor, "Ex-Hired Truck boss cops plea, stays mum," *Chicago Tribune*, March 19, 2005.

81 Fran Spielman, "Daley: Laski has 'a lot of personal problems,'" *Chicago Tribune*, February 14, 2008.

82 Tim Novak and Steve Warmbir, "Paid to do nothing," *Chicago Sun-Times*, Jan. 23, 2004.

83 Steve Warmbir and Tim Novak, "Driver gets probation in theft of city asphalt: Prosecutors wanted heavier penalty in Hired Truck guilty plea," *Chicago Sun-Times*, September 1, 2005.

84   Fran Spielman, "Daley dumps Hired Truck Program," *Chicago Sun-Times,* February 9, 2005.
85   Gary Washburn, "Daley Ban Exempts Key Ally." *Chicago Tribune,* February 10, 2005.
86   Fran Spielman, "Obama endorses Daley," *Chicago Sun-Times,* January 22, 2007.
87   Ryan Lizza, "Barack Obama's unlikely political education," *The New Republic,* March 19, 2007.
88   Michael Barone, "Mayor Daley Re-elected," *U.S. News and World Report,* Mar. 2, 2007.
89   Fran Spielman, "Mayoral challenger attacks cronyism," *Chicago Sun-Times,* September 3, 2002.

Chapter 2

1   Mendell, 180.
2   Christopher Wills, "Obama's career was boosted by his 'godfather,' Emil Jones Jr.," *Associated Press,* March 31, 2008.
3   "Obama's Political 'Godfather' in Illinois," Associated Press, March 31, 2008.
4   Ben Smith, "Emil Jones Blowback," *The Politico,* February 5, 2007, http://www.politico.com/blogs/bensmith/0207/Emil_Jones_Blowback.html.
5   Chris Fusco and Dave McKinney, "Secret deals enrich Jones stepson's firm; Work for gov's budget office as subcontractor valued at $700,000," *Chicago Sun-Times,* July 9, 2007.
6   Dave McKinney, "'This is politics'; State Senate boss backs gov's tax plan – and son lands $57K job," Chicago *Sun-Times,* April 15, 2007.
7   Chris Fusco and Dave McKinney, "Secret deals enrich Jones stepson's firm; Work for gov's budget office as subcontractor valued at $700,000," *Chicago Sun-Times,* July 9, 2007.
8   Mike Riopell, "Senate president Jones zaps effort to freeze electric rates," *Journal Gazette, Times-Courier,* April 21, 2008, http://www.jg-tc.com/articles/2007/04/21/news/doc46297e42688d8071464602.txt.
9   Dave McKinney, Chris Fusco, and Carol Marin, "Joneses plugged in to power; Stepson does business with firm that gets lots of help from senator," *Chicago Sun-Times,* May 3, 2007.
10   Dave McKinney, "State cleared way for Jones' wife to get job: Rule change let her become mental health chief," *Chicago Sun-Times,* April 11, 2007.
11   Dave McKinney, Carol Marin, Abdon M. Pallasch, and Steve Patterson, "Free loans for Jones; Senate president Emil Jones has taken tens of thousands of dollars from his campaign kitty," *Chicago Sun-Times,* May 22, 2008.
12   Chris Fusco and Dave McKinney, "Secret deals enrich Jones stepson's firm: Work for gov's budget office as subcontractor valued at $700,000," *Chicago Sun-Times,* July 9, 2007.

13 David Mendell, *Obama: From Promise to Power.* New York: Harper Collins, 2007, 147.
14 Mendell, 207.
15 Mendell, 206–7.
16 Todd Spivak, "Barack Obama and Me," *Houston Times,* February 28, 2008.
17 "Obama's Political 'Godfather' in Illinois," Associated Press, March 31, 2008.
18 Mendell, 124.
19 Mendell, 181.
20 Illinois Governor's office, http://www.illinois.gov/PressReleases/Show PressRelease.cfm?SubjectID=3&RecNum=359.
21 Ray Long, Ray Gibson, David Johnson, "State pork to Obama's district included allies, donors," *Chicago Tribune,* May 3, 2007.
22 Mendell, 180.
23 Raymond Hernandez and Christopher Drew, "Obama's Vote in Illinois Was Often Just 'Present'," *New York Times,* December 20, 2007.
24 Press release, "Obama Announces FY08 Federal Funding Requests," Sen. Barack Obama, June 21, 2007, available at http://obama.senate.gov/press/070621-obama_announces_3/
25 "State Spending Directed to Chicago State University Raises Questions, Highlights Need for Transparency," *Americans for Prosperity,* 2006, available at http://www.afphq.net/index.php?id=4013&state=il.
26 Tony Allen-Mills, "Barack Obama: Toxic mentors start to corrode pristine campaign," *The Sunday Times,* March 23, 2008, http://www.timesonline.co.uk/tol/news/world/us_and_americas/us_electi ons/article3602710.ece.
27 SB 1305, More on Rezko in Chapter 11.
28 Eric Zorn, "Obama missing chance to cut bad local ties," *Chicago Tribune,* August 2, 2007.
29 HB 824.
30 95th General Assembly, SB 87, SB 742, SB 1305, SB 1599, SB 1601. SB 1305 is the one that would have affected Levine, Rezko's ally on a state pension board.
31 Votes in the Illinois Senate are done electronically by pressing a button, and they typically last just 10–18 seconds.
32 Mendell, 126.
33 Mendell, 125.
34 Rich Miller of the *Capitol Fax,* quoted in Mendell, 122.
35 Ted Kleine, "Is Bobby Rush in Trouble?" *Chicago Reader,* March 17, 2000.
36 Ted Kleine, "Is Bobby Rush in Trouble?" *Chicago Reader,* March 17, 2000.
37 Ted Kleine, "Is Bobby Rush in Trouble?" *Chicago Reader,* March 17, 2000.

Chapter 3

1 David Freddoso and Timothy P. Carney, "The Girl Who Sank Hillary," *National Review Online*, January 4, 2008.
2 Survey results available at http://www.realclearpolitics.com/articles/docs/InsiderAdvantage_Majority_Opinion_Iowa_DEM_Poll_dec_31.html
3 Chris Matthews, News Transcript, "Iowa Caucus Coverage for Jan. 3," http://www.msnbc.msn.com/id/22505399/.
4 Original analysis of election data from CNN.com and delegate data from RealClearPolitics.com.
5 Keli Goff, "He's Gotta Have It," *Uptown*, Summer 2008, 75.
6 FEC data from the Center for Responsive Politics: http://opensecrets.org/pacs/expend.php?sort=A&cmte=C00409052&cycle=2008&Page=1
7 Jeff Zeleny, "Obama Asks Funders to Relieve Clinton's Debt," NYTimes.com, June 24, 2008, http://thecaucus.blogs.nytimes.com/2008/06/24/obama-asks-funders-to-relieve-clintons-debt/index.html?nl=pol&emc=pola1.
8 Scott Fornek, "Obama for president? That's 'silly'," *Chicago Sun-Times*, Nov. 4, 2004.
9 CNN YouTube Video, http://www.youtube.com/watch?v=Iqnmo6U8YpQ.
10 Winston Kenney, "A Normal Family," *Hyde Park Herald*, February 14, 2007, 6.
11 Janny Scott, "In 2000, A Streetwise Veteran Schooled Bold Young Obama," *New York Times*, September 9, 2007.
12 Center for Responsive Politics, OpenSecrets.org, http://www.opensecrets.org/politicians/summary.php?cycle=2000&cid=N00004690.
13 Illinois State Board of Elections, http://www.elections.state.il.us/ElectionInformation/VoteTotalsList.aspx?officeid=1305.
14 Tribune reporters, "Witness: Hastert linked to alleged plot to dump Fitzgerald," *Chicago Tribune*, April 28, 2008.
15 David Mendell, *Obama: From Promise to Power* (NY: Amistad, 2007), 212.
16 Andrew Herrmann and Scott Fornek, "Wealthy Hopeful lead Senate Race," *Chicago Sun-Times*, February 22, 2004.
17 Frank Main, "Hull's Dirty Laundry on the Line," *Chicago Sun-Times*, February 28, 2004.
18 David Mendell, "Hull's ex-wife called him violent man in divorce file," *Chicago Tribune*, February 28, 2004.
19 Mendell, 171.
20 Mendell, 171.
21 His liberal fans at the Daily Kos online community have done so already, unless this was a satire by a Hillary supporter: "Obama was born with his sun in Leo, and his story exemplifies the quest of the Solar Hero. ...Perseus had help from the gods. Does it not feel as if some special hand

is guiding Obama on his journey, I mean, as he has said, the utter
improbability of it all?...What is Obama's shield, in essence? I propose it
is his belief in hope, redemption, and his ability to channel the essential
goodness of the American people." http://www.dailykos.com/story/
2008/4/26/83118/7371/654/503796

22   "Poll: Obama Leads Ryan in Ill. Senate Race," Associated Press, June 1,
      2004.
23   I withhold the name because I believe that this consultant was genuinely
      deceived by his own candidate, as was most of the Illinois Republican
      Party.
24   John Gizzi and David Freddoso, "Lyin' Ryan," *Human Events*, June 24,
      2004.
25   "Ditka: Second Thoughts Until the Day I Die," NBC5Sports, July 15,
      2004,
      http://www.nbc5.com/sports/3528603/detail.html?z=dp&dpswid=22659
      94&dppid=65194
26   Barack Obama, *The Audacity of Hope*, (NY: Three Rivers Press, 2006), 211.
27   *Audacity*, 18.
28   Gromer Jeffers, Jr., "Obama's Star Power Shines Beyond Illinois," *Dallas Morning News*, October 16, 2004.
29   Chris Cillizza and Lauren W. Whittington, "DSCC Gets Late Help from
      the Fortunate," *Roll Call*, October 28, 2004.
30   *Audacity*, 354.
31   *Audacity*, 106.
32   *Dreams*, 133.
33   Adam Fleisher, "Testing Obama's Hope: Hyde Park Hero," *New York
      Sun*, January 15, 2008.
34   Ben Wallace-Wells, "Destiny's Child," *Rolling Stone*, February, 2007.
35   This false idea about Obama must take its origin from Democratic Congressman Keith Ellison (D-Minn.), the first Muslim member of Congress
      and an African-American. He was elected in 2006 to replace Democratic Rep. Martin Sabo and sworn in on Thomas Jefferson's copy of the
      Koran. Although there is a long tradition of federal lawmakers swearing
      on a Bible, there is no such explicit requirement.
36   At an Iowa steak fry in October 2007, Obama was photographed not
      properly saluting the flag during the national anthem. Conservatives on
      the Internet argued this was a deliberate snub, but there is no reason to
      believe it was part of a habit or anything other than inattention.
37   *Audacity*, 32–33.
38   Kiron K. Skinner, Annelise Anderson, and Martin Anderson, eds., *Reagan in His Own Hand*, (NY: Touchstone, 2002).
39   Mendell, 6–7.
40   Bruce Reed, quoted in Ben Wallace-Wells, "Destiny's Child," *Rolling
      Stone*, February 22, 2007.
41   *Audacity*, 33.

42   *Audacity*, 11.
43   Jonathan Weisman, Shailagh Murray and Peter Slevin, "Strategy Was Based on Winning Delegates, Not Battlegrounds," *Washington Post*, June 4, 2008.

Chapter 4

1   Psalm 146:3, King James Version.
2   Keila Szpaller, "Missoula crowd cheers, weeps for Barack Obama," *Montana Standard*, April 6, 2008.
3   Keila Szpalla, "Missoula crowd cheers, weeps for Barack Obama," *Montana Standard*, April 6, 2008.
4   Michael Powell, "On Center Stage, a Candidate Letting His Confidence Show," *New York Times*, February 24, 2008.
5   Jessica Van Sack, "The Monday Morning PRESIDENTIAL BRIEFING," *Boston Herald*, February 18, 2008.
6   John McCormick, "Even blowing his nose, Obama gets applause," The Swamp, February 20, 2008, http://www.swamppolitics.com/news/politics/blog/2008/02/even_blowing_his_nose_obama_ge.html.
7   Keli Goff, "He's Gotta Have It," *Uptown*, Summer 2008.
8   David Yepsen, "What Triggers the Big Buzz around Obama? It's Hope," *Des Moines* Register, September 26, 2006.
9   Felix Gillette, "Primary Scream," *New York Observer*, February 5, 2008.
10 Obamessiah, http://obamameessiah.blogspot.com.
11 Ezra Klein, "Obama's Gift," *The American Prospect*, January 3, 2008.
12 Martin Snapp, "Obama Making Mythical Journey," *Contra Costa Times*, March 8, 2008.
13 Lili Haydn, "Why Obama is Like a Desert Lover," *The Huffington Post*, February 29, 2008.
14 Mark Morford, "Is Obama an Enlightened Being?" *San Francisco Chronicle*, June 6, 2008.
15 Steve Davis, "Letter: Barack's appeal is actually messianic," *Journal-Gazette Times-Courier*, March 31, 2008, http://www.jg-tc.com/articles/2008/03/31/opinion/letters/doc47f0586a2ff1b441328510.txt.
16 Rev. Earlmont Williams, "The Hope of Obama," *Jamaica Gleaner*, March 1, 2008.
17 Mendell, 361.
18 http://my.barackobama.com/page/community/post/terrym/gGgMZs (accessed July 2, 2008).
19 Cf. Matthew 9:20; Luke 8:44; Matthew 14:36; Mark 6:56.
20 Acts 5:15.
21 Michael Whack, "The 'BAM'... The Obama Handshake," Michael Whack's Blog, January 12, 2008, http://my.barackobama.com/page/community/blog/michaelwhack.

22   Maya Soetoro-Ng, quoted in "Obama's Sister: 'Belly Dance for Obama'," Politics West, The Denver Post, June 24, 2008, http://www.politicswest.com/26256/obamas_sister_belly_dance_obama.
23   Jacob M. Victor, "The Ron Paulization of Obama," Harvard Crimson, February 27, 2008.
24   Noah Norman, quoted in Jose Antonio Vargas, "Obama Fever Is Breaking on the Web," Washington Post, February 23, 2008.
25   1 Corinthians 9:22.
26   Mendell, 6.
27   Keli Goff, "He's Gotta Have It," Uptown, Summer 2008.
28   Jake Tapper, "Bubba: Obama Is Just Like Jesse Jackson," ABC News, Political Punch, January 26, 2008, available at: http://blogs.abc-news.com/politicalpunch/2008/01/bubba-obama-is.html.
29   John 3:30.
30   Democratic Presidential Candidates Debate, Sponsored by CNN and Univision, University of Texas at Austin, February 21, 2008.
31   Mark Hemingway, writing on National Review Online's Corner blog, February 19, 2008: "Does anyone know where David Axelrod is? He, after all, would seem to be the obvious culprit on this "plagiarism" issue. He's been a consultant for both campaigns... it's an open secret that he's the one likely responsible for the similarities in language. You'd think he might want to clear the air. He can't, of course, because such honesty would involve admitting that Obama's praised-to-the-heavens rhetoric isn't so divinely inspired, but rather calculated and focused-grouped over the course of several campaigns by a highly paid political consultant."
32   109th Congress, 1st Session, roll call Vote No. 20, March 3, 2005.
33   Democratic Presidential Candidates Debate, The Palace Theatre, Myrtle Beach, South Carolina, January 21, 2008.
34   Robert Novak, "McCain Stakes His Turf," Washington Post, May 22, 2008.
35   Rich Lowry, "Obama Rules," National Review Online, May 13, 2008, http://article.nationalreview.com/?q=MDVkMWIzOGQ0MzdmMzg4N WE0YzFlNzQ0OTE0ZmQ0ODE=
36   Douglas W. Kmeic, "Reaganites for Obama?" Slate, February 13, 2008, http://www.slate.com/id/2184378/.
37   David Freddoso, "Pelosi Premium Pain," National Review Online, April 25, 2008, http://article.nationalreview.com/?q=N2M4NzNkMDQ4Y jZjZjFkZWE4YWJjODUzMDZiYTcyOWM=
38   Mendell, 89.
39   Mendell, 248.
40   His backhanded compliment on Clinton's "likeability" ("I think you're likable enough"), thrown out in a New Hampshire debate, January 5, became a moment of mirth on the Right.

41   Richard Wolffe and Evan Thomas, "Sit Back, Relax, Get Ready to Rumble," *Newsweek*, May 19, 2008.

Chapter 5
1   Barack Obama, *The Audacity of Hope*, (NY: Three Rivers Press, 2006),, 160. For a contemporaneous news story on the visit: Kati Phillips, "Youth is served," *Daily Southtown*, May 28, 2005.
2   Teachers' compensation for 2005 in Thornton Township District (Illinois School District 205) was compiled by Illinois Loop (www.IllinoisLoop.org/salary), whose searchable database contains information based on teacher service records from the Illinois State Board of Education. The figure given includes pension contributions and overtime/per diem payments, but not other benefits such as health care. Thornton Township students are described to be 40 percent poor in Diane Rado, "School day falls short in poorer districts," *Chicago Tribune*, Sept. 29, 2002.
3   Chicago Public Schools website, http://www.cps.k12.il.us/AtAGlance.html
4   Tracy Dell'Angela, "After years of cooping up kids, city schools flirt with recess," *Chicago Tribune*, October 23, 2006.
5   Andy Shaw, "Chicago Teachers Union approves Tentative Contract," abc7News, August 29, 2007, http://abclocal.go.com/wls/story?section=news/local&id=5615704
6   Jo Napolitano, "Election Dispute Leads to Impasse for Teachers Union," *New York Times*, July 2, 2004.
7   Based on 38.6-week schedules for 2008–2009 and 2012–2013 school years. CTU Teacher Salary Schedules are available at http://www.ctunet.com/contract_information/documents/new_07-12_teacher_salaries.pdf.
8   According to the U.S. Census, median income in Chicago is $41,015, http://www.census.gov/PressRelease/www/releases/archives/facts_for_features_special_editions/009486.html.
9   Lori Olszewski, "City graduation rate disputed," *Chicago Tribune*, February 3, 2005.
10   Jodi S. Cohen and Darnell Little, "Of 100 Chicago Public School Freshmen, Six Get a College Degree," *Chicago Tribune*, April 21, 2006.
11   "State of the Strategies: A Report on District Core and Supporting Strategies," Chicago Public Schools, Office of Strategy and Planning, March 2007.
12   David Mendell, *Obama: From Promise to Power*, (New York: Amistad, 2008), 203.
13   *Audacity*, 119.
14   Alexander Russo, "Chicago Teachers Go with Obama, Not Clinton," *Education Week*, October 4, 2007, http://blogs.edweek.org/edweek/thisweekineducation/2007/10/chicago_teachers_go_with_obama.html.

15 Thomas Fitzgerald, "Obama tells teachers he supports merit pay," *Philadelphia Inquirer*, July 5, 2007.

16 *Audacity*, 163.

17 SB 376, Mar. 29, 2006.

18 Remarks of Senator Barack Obama: "A More Perfect Union," Philadelphia, March 18, 2008, available at http://www.barackobama.com/2008/03/18/remarks_of_senator_barack_obam_53.php

19 http://www.cps.k12.il.us/AtAGlance.html

20 Barack Obama, *Dreams from my Father*, (New York: Three Rivers Press, 2004), 256–7.

21 David Brooks, "Obama, Liberalism and the Challenge of Reform," *New York Times*, June 13, 2008.

22 http://www.barackobama.com, as of July 2, 2008.

23 Jim Kuhnhenn, "Obama bypasses public money - 1st since Watergate," Associated Press, June 20, 2008.

24 Barack Obama, "Opposing view: The system is broken," *USA Today*, June 20, 2008.

25 Barack Obama, Remarks at a constituent breakfast, June 29, 2006, http://www.youtube.com/watch?v=IU5V3fO7B1U

26 David K. Kirkpatrick, "Obama Proposes Candidates Limit General Election Spending," *New York Times*, February 8, 2007.

27 David D. Kirkpatrick, "McCain and Obama In Deal On Public Financing," *New York Times*, March 2, 2007.

28 "Presidential Candidate Questionnaire," Midwest Democracy Network, November 27, 2007, quoted in "Common Cause Letters," February 15, 2008, www.commoncause.org.

29 "Presidential Candidate Questionnaire," Midwest Democracy Network, November 27, 2007, quoted in "Common Cause Letters," February 15, 2008, www.commoncause.org.

30 Barack Obama, "Opposing View: Both Sides Must Agree," *USA Today*, February 20, 2008.

31 FOX News, "FOX News Sunday," April 27, 2008, http://www.youtube.com/watch?v=GsOnmKK5j6Y.

32 Jim Kuhnhenn, "Obama opts out of public campaign finance system," Associated Press, June 19, 2008.

33 Ibid.

34 Ibid.

35 Shailagh Murray and Perry Bacon Jr., "Obama to Reject Public Funds for Election," *Washington Post*, June 20, 2008.

36 Center for Responsive Politics, http://opensecrets.org/527s/527cmtes.php?level=I&cycle=2004

37 Center for Responsive Politics, http://opensecrets.org/527s/527cmtes.php?level=I&cycle=2008

38 Barack Obama on CNN Larry King Live, January 24, 2007.

39   Barack Obama, *The Audacity of Hope*, (NY: Three Rivers Press, 2006), 318.

40   110th Congress, 2nd Session, roll call vote No. 130, May 15, 2008.

41   Net worth data from "Agriculture Income and Finance Outlook," United States Department of Agriculture, AIS-84, November 2006, 63, and consisting of a weighted average of large and very large farms' net worths, at http://usda.mannlib.cornell.edu/usda/current/AIS/AIS-11-30-2006.pdf.

42   110th Congress, 2nd Session, roll call vote No. 151, June 18, 2008.

43   Paul Krugman, "The Conscience of a Liberal," New York Times, February 22, 2008, http://krugman.blogs.nytimes.com/2008/02/22/demon-ethanol/.

44   "Barack Obama's Plan to Make America a Global Energy Leader," available at http://www.barackobama.com/issues/pdf/EnergyFactSheet.pdf, accessed June 25, 2006.

45   *Audacity*, 326.

46   *Audacity*, 169–170.

47   Ben Lieberman and Nick Loris, "Time to Repeal the Ethanol Mandate," The Heritage Foundation, May 15, 2008, http://www.heritage.org/research/energyandenvironment/wm1925.cfm

48   "Ethanol and Water Don't Mix," *The Economist*, February 28, 2008.

49   Ben Lieberman and Nick Loris, "Time to Repeal the Ethanol Mandate," The Heritage Foundation, May 15, 2008, http://www.heritage.org/research/energyandenvironment/wm1925.cfm

50   Seth Borenstein, "Ethanol may cause more smog, more deaths," Associated Press, April 18, 2007, http://www.msnbc.msn.com/id/18162493/.

51   Mark Clayton, "Carbon cloud over a green fuel," Christian Science Monitor, March 23, 2006.

52   Available at http://bioenergy.ornl.gov/papers/misc/energy_conv.html.

53   Ibid.

54   Department of Energy, "Annual Energy Review 2007," Energy Information Administration, June, 2008.

55   Available at http://www.eia.doe.gov/neic/quickfacts/quickoil.html.

56   Jason Hill, Erik Nelson, David Tilman, Stephen Polasky, and Douglas Tiffany, "Environmental, economic, and energetic costs and benefits of biodiesel and ethanol biofuels," Proceedings of the National Academy of Sciences of the United States of America, July 12, 2006.

57   Doug Koplow, "Biofuels – At What Cost?" The Global Subsidies Initiative, October, 2006, http://www.globalsubsidies.org/files/assets/pdf/Brochure_-_US_Report.pdf.

58   David Freddoso, "Children of the Corn," *National Review Online*, May 6, 2008.

59   J. Taylor Rushing, "Ethanol part of food crisis, says Durbin," *The Hill*, April 28, 2008.

60 "Obama pushes for increased ethanol production," Associated Press, March 14, 2005.
61 Energy Policy Act, HR 6,109th Cong., 1st Sess., *Congressional Record* (June 15, 2005): S6601–S6602.
62 109th Congress 1st Session, roll call votes Nos. 138 and 139, June 15, 2005.
63 Barack Obama Senate website, September 8, 2006. Available at http://obama.senate.gov/press/060908-senate_passes_c/.
64 See Chapter 2.
65 The two occasions came in the 110th Congress, 1st Session, roll call votes Nos. 121 (March 28, 2007) and 123 (March 29, 2007).
66 110th Congress, 1st Session, roll call votes Nos. 164 (May 15, 2007) and 335 (September 12, 2007).
67 109th Congress, 1st Session, roll call vote No. 262, October 20, 2005.
68 110th Congress, 1st Session, roll call vote No. 335, September 11, 2007.
69 109th Congress, 2nd Session, roll call votes Nos. 99 (April 26, 2006), 100 (April 27, 2006), and 105 (May 2, 2006), 109th Congress.
70 109th Congress, 2nd Session, roll call votes Nos. 108 (May 3, 2006) and 104 (May 2, 2006).
71 109th Congress, 1st Session, roll call votes Nos. 230 (September 14, 2005) and 260 (October 20, 2005).
72 109th Congress, 1st Session, roll call vote No. 192, July 19, 2005.
73 109th Congress, 1st Session, roll call vote No. 238, September 21, 2005.
74 109th Congress, 1st Session, roll call vote No. 160, June 28, 2005.
75 Ray Long, Ray Gibson and David Johnson, "State pork to Obama's district included allies, donors," *Chicago Tribune*, May 3, 2007.
76 David Heath, "Candidates exhibit different appetites for political pork," *Seattle Times*, February 7, 2008.
77 Mike Dorning, "Employer: Michelle Obama's raise well-earned," *Chicago Tribune*, September 27, 2006.
78 Dennis Byrne, "Something's Fishy about Pork Debate," *Chicago Tribune*, March 24, 2008.
79 Manu Raju and Kevin Bogardus, "Clinton: $2.3 Bil in earmarks," *The Hill*, April 28, 2008, http://thehill.com/leading-the-news/clinton-2.3b-in-earmarks-2008-04-28.html.
80 This was several months before Lieberman lost his Democratic primary and became an "Independent Democrat."
81 "The McCain/Obama Tick-Tock," The Hotline, February 7, 2006, http://hotlineblog.nationaljournal.com/archives/2006/02/the_mccainobama.html.
82 Ibid.
83 Ibid.
84 John McCain, quoted in "McCain criticizes Obama on lobbying ethics reform," *USA Today*, February 6, 2006.

85   Barack Obama, "Letter on Ethics Reform to John McCain," February 2, 2006, available at http://obama.senate.gov/letter/060206-sen_obama_and_sen_mccain_exchange_letters_on_ethics_reform/

Chapter 6

1   Barack Obama, *The Audacity of Hope*, (NY: Three Rivers Press, 2006), 354.
2   Barack Obama, *Dreams from my Father*, (NY: Three Rivers Press, 2004), 47–48.
3   David Mendell, *Obama: From Promise to Power*, (NY: Amistad, 2007), 285.
4   Barack Obama, keynote address delivered at the Democratic National Convention, July 27, 2004.
5   Ibid.
6   Ibid.
7   Ibid.
8   Ibid.
9   "Transcript of the Keynote Address by Ann Richards, the Texas Treasurer," *New York Times*, July 19, 1988.
10   Mendell, 281.
11   Mendell, 203–204.
12   Mendell, 226.
13   *Newsweek*, January 3, 2005.
14   Brian Friel, Richard E. Cohen, and Kirk Victor, "Obama, Most Liberal Senator in 2007," National Journal's vote ratings, *National Journal*, January 31, 2008, http://nj.nationaljournal.com/voteratings/.
15   Bruce A. Dixon, "In Search of the Real Barack Obama: Can a Black Senate Candidate Resist the DLC?" *Black Commentator*, June 5, 2003.
16   Dana Milbank and Jim VandeHei, "No Political Fallout for Bush on Weapons," *Washington Post*, May 17, 2003.
17   Barack Obama, letter to Black Commentator, quoted in Cover Story, "Not 'Corrupted' by DLC, Says Obama," *Black Commentator*, June 19, 2003, http://www.blackcommentator.com/47/47_cover.html
18   Publisher of *Black Commentator*, letter to Sen. Barack Obama, in Cover Story, "Not 'Corrupted' by DLC, Says Obama," *Black Commentator*, June 19, 2003.
19   Cover Story, "Not 'Corrupted' by DLC, Says Obama," *Black Commentator*, June 19, 2003, http://www.blackcommentator.com/47/47_cover.html.
20   Cover Story, "Obama to Have Name Removed from DLC List," *Black Commentator*, June 26, 2003, http://www.blackcommentator.com/48/48_cover.html.
21   *Audacity*, 24.

22   David Mendell, "Democratic hopefuls vary a bit on death penalty,"
      Chicago Tribune, February 20, 2004.
23   Ibid.
24   See *Audacity,* 132 and Mendell, 251.
25   HB 1812, May 15, 2001.
26   SB 1846, May 21, 1998.
27   *Audacity,* 244.
28   *Audacity,* 230. Obama was already denouncing the temporary suspen-
      sion of the Davis-Bacon Act in an interview with National Public Radio
      on   Sept.   21,   2005,   http://www.npr.org/templates/story/
      story.php?storyId=4857237
29   110th Congress, 1st Session, roll call vote No. 227, June 26, 2007.
30   *Audacity,* 182.
31   "Business-Labor Ideology Split in PAC & Individual Donations to Can-
      didates and Parties," OpenSecrets.org, http://opensecrets.org/bigpict
      ure/blio.php?cycle=2006
32   *Audacity,* 176.
33   *Audacity,* 57.
34   *Audacity,* 182.
35   Rick Klein, "No Lip Service: Dems Trade Higher Taxes For Social Pro-
      grams," ABCNews.com, May 29, 2007.
36   Steve Stanek, "Illinois Medicaid Takes on New Costs: Governor accused
      of ignoring unpaid bills," *Budget & Tax News,* June 1, 2006.
37   Mendell, 137.
38   92nd General Assembly, SB 1606.
39   90th General Assembly, SB 1850.
40   "January 2008 Census Shows 6.1 Million People Covered by HSA/High-
      Deductible Health Plans," Center for Policy and Research, April 2008,
      http://www.ahipresearch.org/pdfs/2008_HSA_Census.pdf
41   *Audacity,* 179.
42   Sarah Rubenstein, "Obama Likens McCain's Health Plan to Bush the
      Sequel," *The   Wall   Street   Journal,*   May   19,   2008,
      http://blogs.wsj.com/health/2008/05/19/obama-likens-mccains-health-
      plan-to-bush-the-sequel/.
43   *Audacity,* 342.
44   *Audacity,* 168–9.
45   U.S. Energy Information Administration.
46   90th General Assembly, SB 1668.
47   90th General Assembly, SB 1668; 91st General Assembly, HB 2167;
      92nd General Assembly, SB 619.
48   90th General Assembly, HB 204, passed May 31, 2008.
49   Corey Hall, "State Sen. Barack Obama Announces For Congress," *Hyde
      Park Citizen,* September 30, 1999.
50   90th General Assembly, Senate Transcript for May 31, 1997, 42–44.

51   Teddy Davis and Gregory Wallace, "Obama Shifts On Welfare Reform,"
      ABC News *Political Radar*, July 1, 2008.
52   *Audacity*, 125–6.
53   *Audacity*, 223.
54   Barack Obama, speech quoted in Ben A. Franklin, "The Fifth Black Sen-
      ator in U.S. History Makes F.D.R. His Icon," *The Washington Specta-
      tor*,   June   1,   2005,
      http://www.washingtonspectator.com/articles/20050601obama_1.cfm
55   David Perlmutt, "Obama meets Working Moms," *The Charlotte
      Observer*, April 9, 2008.
56   Raymond Hernandez and Christopher Drew, "Obama's Vote in Illinois
      Was Often Just 'Present,'" *New York Times*, December 20, 2007.
57   Nathan Gonzales, "The Ever-'Present' Obama," Real Clear Politics, Feb-
      ruary   13,   2007,
      http://www.realclearpolitics.com/articles/2007/02/the_everpresent_obam
      a.html.
58   SB 609, March 29, 2001.
59   SB 759, March 25, 1999.
60   Dana Milbank, "A Thank-You to 18 Million Cracks in the Glass Ceil-
      ing," *Washington Post*, June 8, 2008.
61   Byron York, "Michelle's Struggle," *National Review Online*, February
      29,   2008,
      http://article.nationalreview.com/?q=MmEyN2RkNzcwYzgyZDY2MDB
      iY2U5MjJlZGMwNDM2ODg=.
62   U.S.   Census   Bureau:
      http://quickfacts.census.gov/qfd/states/39/39119.html
63   Obama's   tax   returns   are   available   online   at
      http://my.barackobama.com/page/-/Press/Taxes_2000-2006.pdf
64   Mike Dorning, "Employer: Michelle Obama's raise well-earned,"
      Chicago Tribune, September 27, 2006.
65   Seema Mehta, "Obama's backyard economics session," *Los Angeles
      Times*, January 17, 2008.
66   http://www.demographia.com/db-stateinc2000.htm
67   U.S. Census table, *Selected Measures of Household Income Dispersion:
      1967   to   2001*,
      http://www.census.gov/hhes/www/income/histinc/ie1.html.
68   Mark Silva, "Obama on elitism: 'silly season,'" *The Swamp*, April 15,
      2008,
      http://www.swamppolitics.com/news/politics/blog/2008/04/obama_on_el
      itism_silly_season.html.
69   Ray Gibson, John McCormick and Christi Parsons, "How broke were
      the Obamas? Hard to tell," *Chicago Tribune*, April 19, 2008.
70   110th Congress, roll call vote No. 142, June 4, 2008.
71   *Audacity*, 191–2.
72   *Audacity*, 114.

73   *Audacity*, 47.

74   SB 1725, March 27, 2003.

75   See BarackObama.com. http://www.barackobama.com/issues/fiscal/

76   93rd General Assembly, SB 1634. Obama voted "yes" on Mar. 27, 2003.

77   Jeanne Sahadi, "Cap gains tax: How high can Obama go?" CNN-Money.com,   June   20,   2008, http://money.cnn.com/2008/06/20/news/economy/obama_capgains/index.htm?postversion=2008062007.

78   William W. Beach and Gareth E. Davis, "Social Security's Rate of Return,"   The   Heritage   Foundation,   January   15,   1998, http://www.heritage.org/Research/SocialSecurity/CDA98-01.cfm.

79   *Audacity*, 179.

80   *Audacity*, 179.

81   *Audacity*, 182.

82   James Pethokoukis, "Obama Plans a Massive Hike in Social Security Taxes,"   *U.S.   News   &   World   Report,*   June   13,   2008, http://www.usnews.com/blogs/capital-commerce/2008/6/13/obama-plans-a-massive-hike-in-social-security-taxes.html

Chapter 7

1   William Ayers, *Fugitive Days*, (Boston: Beacon, 2001) 256.

2   Hearings before the Subcommittee to Investigate the Administration of the Internal Security Act and Other Internal Security Laws of the Committee on the Judiciary, United States Senate, "Terroristic Activity Inside the Weatherman Movement, Part 2," October 18, 1974.

3   *Fugitive Days*, 258.

4   Ben   Smith,   "Ax   on   Ayers,"   *Politico,*   February   26,   2008, http://www.politico.com/blogs/bensmith/0208/Ax_on_Ayers.html

5   Don Terry, "The calm after the storm," *Chicago Tribune Magazine*, September 16, 2001, 10.

6   Hearings before the Subcommittee to Investigate the Administration of the Internal Security Act and Other Internal Security Laws of the Committee on the Judiciary, United States Senate. "Terroristic Activity Inside the Weatherman Movement, Part 2," October 18, 1974.

7   Ibid.

8   Ibid.

9   "Storm Clouds for Weathermen," *Time*, Monday, August 3, 1970.

10   Bernardine Dohrn, quoted in Timothy Noah, "Radical Chic Resurgent," *Slate,* August 22, 2001, http://www.slate.com/id/1008160/

11   Bill Ayers, quoted in Timothy Noah, "Radical Chic Resurgent," *Slate,* August 22, 2001, http://www.slate.com/id/1008160/

12   Bill Ayers, quoted in Hope Reeves, "The Way We Live Now: 9-16-01: Questions for Bill Ayers; Forever Rad," *New York Times Magazine*, September 16, 2001.

13   Mayor Richard Daley, quoted in editorial, "Guilt by association,"
      Chicago Tribune, April 18, 2008.
14   "Democratic Presidential Candidates Debate," Philadelphia, April 16,
      2008.
15   Ben Smith, "Obama once visited '60s radicals," *Politico,* February 22,
      2008, http://dyn.politico.com/printstory.cfm?uuid=3FC289D8-3048-
      5C12-009AD5180C22FF0B
16   Hendrik Hertzberg, "You (really) don't need a weatherman," *The New
      Yorker,* April 22, 2008.
17   "Should a child ever be called a 'super predator?'," University of
      Chicago   News   Office,   November   4,   1997,   http://www-
      news.uchicago.edu/releases/97/971104.juvenile.justice.shtml
18   Democratic Debate, April 16, 2008, Philadelphia.
19   *The Sean Hannity Show,* May 28, 2008.
20   Barack Obama, *Dreams from my Father,* (NY: Three Rivers Press,
      2004), 100–101.
21   *W. E. B. DuBois, "Joseph Stalin," 1953, reprinted in The Oxford W. E.
      B. DuBois Reader,* ed. Eric J. Sundquist, (Oxford: Oxford University
      Press, 1996) 287.
22   *Dreams,* 85–86.
23   *Dreams,* 197–206.
24   Barack Obama, quoted in Hank De Zutter, "What Makes Obama
      Run?" *Chicago Reader,* December 8, 1995.
25   Black Press Institute, "An Afro-American journalist in the USSR," *Peo-
      ple's Daily World,* June 19, 1986.
26   Black Press Institute, "An Afro-American journalist in the USSR," *Peo-
      ple's Daily World,* June 19, 1986.
27   Ben Smith, "Obama once visited '60s radicals," *Politico,* February 22,
      2008, http://www.politico.com/news/stories/0208/8630.html
28   See Chapter 6.
29   Bruce Bentley, "Chicago New Party Update," *New Ground* 42, Septem-
      ber–October   1995,
      http://www.chicagodsa.org/ngarchive/ng42.html#anchor792932
30   *New Ground,* March–April issue, 1996.
31   *Dreams,* 77
32   *Dreams,* 90–91
33   *Dreams,* 97.
34   Gerald Horne, "Rethinking the History and Future of the Communist
      Party,"   *Political   Affairs   Magazine,*   March   28,   2007,
      http://www.politicalaffairs.net/article/articleview/5047/1/32/
35   John Edgard Tidwell, *Frank Marshall Davis: Black Moods,* (IL: Univer-
      sity of Illinois Press, 2007), p. xxviii.
36   "Hearings before the Subcommittee to investigate the administration of
      the Internal Security Laws Act and other internal security laws, Com-

mittee of the Judiciary, United States Senate," "Scope of Soviet Activity in the United States." December 5–6, 1956, 2519.

37 Letter from the Communist International, Moscow, to members of the Communist Party USA in Hawaii. ComIntern Archives, Moscow, Fond. 495, Opus 20, Delo 541. Reproduced on page 36 of Herb Romerstein and Cliff Kincaid, "Communism in Hawaii and the Obama Connection." Available online at http://www.usasurvival.org/docs/hawaii-obama.pdf.

38 Ibid. "Like many other converts, [Davis] felt betrayed when Stalin signed the infamous nonaggression pact with Hitler on 24 August 1939." Davis himself wrote of the incident in his posthumously published autobiography *Livin' the Blues* (Madison, WI: University of Wisconsin Press, 1992): "Considering myself a freethinker, I openly disagreed with what I thought was wrong. I was skeptical after the Nazi attack on Russian caught the U.S. party with its ideological pants down." Yet as his actions at the time demonstrate, he may have been embellishing whatever objections he raised. See below.

39 Davis, then a writer for the Marxist *Chicago Star*, was among the sponsors of a forum by the Communist-backed National Negro Congress urging war resistance. "Negroes and the whole American people are being called to 'sacrifice for the national defense,'" a flier for the 1940 event states. "Our country may soon be actively engaged in another war. Facing the crisis, the people are forced to think and act lest, under the wave of war hysteria, they be bludgeoned into situations against their best interest."

40 Bermann's letter was later added to the record of April 1950 testimony before the House Un-American Activities Committee. *Hearings Regarding Communist Activities in Hawaii, Part 3*. The Congressional Record, April 1950, 2066–2068. In his testimony, Bermann also described how Communists had previously taken over another liberal civic association in a similar fashion.

41 House Committee on Un-American Activities, *Hearings Regarding Communist Activities in the Territory of Hawaii*, and a white member of the NAACP's executive board, Ed Berman, had written the national NAACP headquarters for assistance when Davis and others showed up.

42 Manfred Berg, "Black Civil Rights and Liberal Anticommunism: The NAACP in the Early Cold War," *Journal of American History*, June 2007, 94.

43 *The Atlantic Monthly*, August 1944.

44 Frank Marshall Davis, *Livin' the Blues*, (Madison, WI: University of Wisconsin Press, 1992), 277.

45 Davis, *Livin' the Blues*, 279. Davis wrote of this poem, "I was positive by now that I had attracted the special attention of the House Committee on Un-American Activities... it would indicate I was beginning to

upset the white power structure. What I had not anticipated was equal success in upsetting associates who were dedicated Communists."

46　Reprinted in *Livin' the Blues.*

47　"Obama suggests GOP will use race to scare voters," FOXNews.com, June 21, 2008, http://elections.foxnews.com/2008/06/21/obama-suggests-gop-will-use-race-to-scare-voters/

48　Tim Weiner, "Lake pulls out as nominee for C.I.A., assailing process as endless political circus," *New York Times,* March 18, 1997.

49　*Meet the Press,* November 24, 1996

50　Transcript of March 12, 1997, Day Two of Hearings on the Nomination of Tony Lake As Director of Central Intelligence.

51　James A. Barnes, "Obama's Inner Circle," *National Journal,* March 31, 2008, http://news.nationaljournal.com/articles/080331nj1.htm

52　Elias Crim and Matthew Vadum, "Barack Obama: A Radical Leftist's Journey from Community Organizing to Politics," *Foundation Watch, Capital Research Center,* 5.

53　FOX News Channel, *Hannity and Colmes,* January 6, 2006.

54　James A. Barnes, "Obama's Inner Circle," *National Journal,* March 31, 2008, http://news.nationaljournal.com/articles/080331nj1.htm.

55　Domenica Montanaro, "Informal Obama advisor steps aside," *First Read,* May 9, 2008, http://firstread.msnbc.msn.com/archive/2008/05/09/1005411.aspx

56　"Gaza Shelling Prompts Hamas to Call for Attacks Against U.S.," Associated Press, November 8, 2006.

57　Elias Crim and Matthew Vadum, "Barack Obama: a Radical Leftist's Journey from Community Organizing to Politics," *Foundation Watch,* June 2008: 5–6.

58　Bio of Jodie Evans on Women's Media Center web site: http://www.womensmediacenter.com/ex/bio/Jodie_Evans_main.html

59　Catherine Moy, "Code Pink 'Bundles' for Barack," *Human Events,* April 14, 2008.

60　Peter Slevin, "For Clinton and Obama, a Common Ideological Touchstone," *Washington Post,* March 25, 2007.

61　Ibid.

62　Ibid.

63　Saul Alinsky, *Rules for Radicals,* (NY: Vintage Books, 1989), dedication to the March 1972 edition.

64　Saul Alinsky, *Rules for Radicals* (NY: Vintage Books, 1989), 118–120.

65　Alinksy, 91–92.

66　Alinksy, 29, 25.

67　Alinksy, 18.

68　Elias Crim and Matthew Vadum, "Barack Obama: a Radical Leftist's Journey from Community Organizing to Politics," *Foundation Watch,* June 2008, 11.

69   Alinksy, 43.
70   Alinksy, 127.
71   Ryan Lizza, "Barack Obama's unlikely political education," *New Republic*, March 19, 2007.
72   Alinksy, 94.
73   Alinksy, 188, 190.
74   Barack Obama, quoted in Bonney Kapp, "Obama draws fire for comments on small-town America," FOX News, April 11, 2008.
75   Margery Frisbie, *An Alley in Chicago: The Ministry of a City Priest*, (Kansas City: Sheed & Ward, 1991).
76   Nicholas Lemann, *The Promised Land*, (NY: Vintage Books, 1991), 344.
77   Lemann, 101.
78   Lemann, 122.
79   David Mendell, *Obama: From Promise to Power*, (NY: Amistad, 2007), 82.
80   *Dreams*, 248.
81   *Dreams*, 169–170.
82   *Dreams*, 167–168.
83   Kenneth T. Walsh, "On the Streets of Chicago, a Candidate Comes of Age," *U.S. News*, August 26, 2007.
84   *Dreams*, 438.
85   See Chapter 6.
86   Corey Hall, "State Sen. Barack Obama announces for Congress: Candidate says he brings message and organization to position," *Hyde Park Citizen*, September 30, 1999.
87   Hank De Zutter, "What Makes Obama Run?" *Chicago Reader*, December 8, 1995, http://www.chicagoreader.com/obama/951208/.
88   Byron York, "The Organizer," *National Review*, June 30, 2008.
89   "Fact Check: Obama's relationship with William Ayers," Associated Press, April 17, 2008, http://elections.foxnews.com/2008/04/17/fact-check-obamas-relationship-with-william-ayers/.
90   Elias Crim and Matthew Vadum, "Barack Obama: a Radical Leftist's Journey from Community Organizing to Politics," *Foundation Watch*, June 2008: 7.
91   Tim Novak, "Obama helps ex-boss get $1 mil. from charity," *Chicago Sun-Times*, November 29, 2007.
92   Center for Tax and Budget Accountability, http://www.ctbaonline.org/
93   http://www.ctbaonline.org/HB%20750.htm
94   http://www.discoverthenetworks.org/funderProfile.asp?fndid=5184
95   http://www.aaan.org/oral.html
96   Stanley Kurtz, "Inside Obama's Acorn," *National Review Online*, May 29, 2008, http://article.nationalreview.com/?q=NDZiMjkwMDczZWI5ODdjOWYxZTIzZGIyNzEyMjE0ODI=&w=MA==

97   "ACORN's Hypocritical House of Cards: How one 'community' group
      helped the housing crisis harm taxpayers," Consumer Rights League,
      June, 2008.
98   "ACORN's Hypocritical House of Cards: How one 'community' group
      helped the housing crisis harm taxpayers," Consumer Rights League,
      June, 2008.
99   Stanley Kurtz, "Inside Obama's Acorn," *National Review Online*, May
      29,   2008,
      http://article.nationalreview.com/?q=NDZiMjkwMDczZWI5ODdjOWY
      xZTIzZGIyNzEyMjE0ODI=&w=MA==
100   Toni Foulkes, "Case Study: Chicago-The Barack Obama Campaign,"
      Social Policy, Winter 2003, Vol. 34, No. 2, Spring 2004, Vol. 34, No. 3.
101   Glen Stout, letter to the editor, *Albuquerque Journal*, May 22, 2007.
      Glen Stout's son's identity was allegedly stolen by ACORN:
      http://www.abqjournal.com/opinion/letters/564784opinion05-22-
      07.htm;   see   also
      http://www.abqjournal.com/news/metro/377098metro08-03-05.htm
102   Review and Outlook, "The ACORN Indictments," *The Wall Street Jour-
      nal*, November 3, 2006.
103   Terrence Scanlon, "Is ACORN disenfranchising the process itself?"
      Washington Examiner, November 6, 2006, http://www.examiner.com/a-
      381567~Terrence_Scanlon__Is_ACORN_disenfranchising_the_process_i
      tself_.html
104   Toni Foulkes, "Case Study: Chicago-The Barack Obama Campaign,"
      Social Policy, Winter 2003, Vol. 34, No. 2, Spring 2004, Vol. 34, No. 3.

Chapter 8

1   Reverend Jeremiah Wright, quoted in Roland S. Martin, "The full story
      behind Wright's 'God Damn America' sermon," CNN News, March 21,
      2008,   http://ac360.blogs.cnn.com/2008/03/21/the-full-story-behind-
      wright%E2%80%99s-%E2%80%9Cgod-damn-amer-
      ica%E2%80%9D-sermon/
2   Jonah Goldberg, "Tall Tales About Tuskegee," *National Review Online*,
      May 2, 2008.
3   Brian Ross and Rehab El-Buri, "Obama's Pastor: God Damn America,
      U.S. to Blame for 9/11," ABC News, March 13, 2008, abc-
      news.go.com/Blotter/Story?id=4443788
4   Stanley Kurtz, "Context, you say?" *National Review*, May 19, 2008.
5   Transcript, "Reverend Jeremiah Wright; Obama's Pastor Now a Cam-
      paign Liability?" *Good Morning America*, March 13, 2008.
6   Transcript, "Reverend Jeremiah Wright; Obama's Pastor Now a Cam-
      paign Liability?" *Good Morning America*, March 13, 2008.
7   Barack Obama, *Dreams from my Father*, (NY: Three Rivers Press,
      2004), 293. Ellipsis in original.
8   *Dreams*, 295.

9 David Mendell, *Obama: From Promise to Power*, (NY: Amistad, 2007), 75.
10 Mendell, 75, and Sara Karp, "Sen. Barack Obama's Pastor Frames Progressive Issues Through Lens of Faith," *Religion News Service*, March 10, 2005.
11 Allison Samuels, "Something Wasn't Right: Why Oprah Winfrey left Rev. Jeremiah Wright's church," *Newsweek,* May 12, 2008.
12 Ibid.
13 Barack Obama, *The Audacity of Hope*, (NY: Three Rivers Press, 2006), 204.
14 *Audacity*, 204.
15 *Audacity*, 224.
16 *Dreams,* 154–5.
17 *Dreams*, 274.
18 Available at http://www.cnn.com/ELECTION/2008/primaries/results/epolls/#PADEM
19 Bob Secter, "For Obama, charity really began in the U.S. Senate," *Chicago Tribune*, April 25, 2007.
20 Elias Crim and Matthew Vadum, "Barack Obama: A Radical Leftist's Journey from Community Organizing to Politics," *Foundation Watch*, June 2008, 11.
21 Robert M. Franklin, "Obama's Faith: A Civil and Social Gospel," Trinity United Church of Christ Bulletin, June 10, 2007, 12–13.
22 Larry Elder, "The Wright Cost of Anger," Human Events.com, May 1, 2008.
23 Trinity United Church of Christ website, http://www.tucc.org/talking_points.htm
24 Rev. Andrew Greeley, quoted in James Cone, *A Black Theology of Liberation* (NY: Orbis Books, 1986), xii–xiii.
25 Cone, 9.
26 Cone, 8.
27 Cone, 41.
28 Cone, 41–42.
29 Cone, vii.
30 Trinity United Church of Christ website, http://www.tucc.org /talking_points.htm
31 Akiba Online Store, http://www.tucc.org/store/index.cfm?action= cat-browse&catid=69
32 You can watch this video on YouTube at: http://www.youtube.com/watch?v=iPjVp3PLnVs, accessed July 1, 2008.
33 Amy Chozick, "Obama Quits Controversial Church," *Wall Street Journal*'s "Washington Wire" blog, May 31, 2008, available at http://blogs.wsj.com/washwire/2008/05/31/obama-quits-controversial-church/.

34   You can watch the video on YouTube, at http://www.youtube.com/watch?v=TWigzBClEk8, accessed July 3, 2008.
35   Cathleen Falsani, "I have a deep faith," *Chicago Sun-Times*, April 5, 2004.
36   Ibid.
37   Corey Hall, "State Sen. Barack Obama Announces for Congress: Candidate says he brings message and organization to position," *Hyde Park Citizen*, September 30, 1999.
38   Ray Long, Ray Gibson, and David Johnson, "State pork to Obama's district included allies, donors," *Chicago Tribune*, May 3, 2007.
39   "The Reverend Jeremiah Wright, the former Obama pastor, surprises a Chicago Church with appearance," Associated Press, March 29, 2008.
40   Transcript, "Sticking up For Wright and Farrakhan," *The O'Reilly Factor*, FOX News Channel, April 3, 2008.
41   See "Both Sides in State Commission Controversy Speak Out," NBC5.com, March 7, 2006, http://www.nbc5.com/news/7782149/detail.html?rss=chi&psp=news, and "Farrakhan Gets Award from Chicago Catholics," *St. Louis Post-Dispatch*, January 9 1990.
42   Thomas J. Craughwell, "Abraham, Martin, and John...and Barack," *American Spectator*, January 24, 2007.
43   Ibid.
44   Susan Hogan/Albach, "Cardinal rebukes Pfleger for 'threat'; Priest says words against gun shop owner misconstrued," *Chicago Sun-Times*, June 8, 2007. Audio of Pfleger's threat available at: http://www.isra.org/quick/pfleger_calls_for_murder_052607.mp3, accessed June 20, 2008.
45   Ben Wallace-Wells, "Destiny's Child," *Rolling Stone*, February 22, 2007.
46   Cathleen Falsani, "Obama: I have a deep faith" *Chicago Sun-Times*, April 5, 2004.
47   Theresa Fambro Hooks, "Frankie Beverly & Maze 'in concert' for Pastor Wright's tribute," *Chicago Defender,* March 5/March 6, 2007. According to the *Defender*, Obama halted campaigning to celebrate with his "mentor," Wright.
48   Barack Obama, "Transcript: Barack Obama's Speech on Race," NPR.org, March 18, 2008, http://www.npr.org/templates/story/story.php?storyId=88478467
49   Kenneth T. Walsh, "Obama 'typical white person' Comment Delights Clinton Aides," *U.S. News and World Report,* March 21, 2008.
50   *Dreams*, 18–19.
51   *Dreams*, 18–19.
52   *Dreams*, 19.
53   *Dreams,* 269–271.
54   Transcript: Reverend Wright at the National Press Club, April 28, 2008, available at http://elections.foxnews.com/2008/04/28/transcript-rev-wright-at-the-national-press-club/

55   Lynn Sweet, "After 'show of disrespect,' Obama denounces Wright," SunTimes.com, http://blogs.suntimes.com/sweet/2008/04/after_show_of_disrespect_obama.html

56   Brian Ross and Rehab el-Buri, "Obama's Pastor: God Damn America, U.S. to Blame for 9/11," ABCNews.com, March 13, 2008, http://abcnews.go.com/Blotter/story?id=4443788&page=1

Chapter 9

1   Transcript, "Senator Hillary Clinton Discusses Her Campaign and Stands on Issues," *Meet the Press*, January 13, 2008.

2   Gary T. Dempsey, "Reasonable Doubt: The Case against the Proposed International Criminal Court," Cato Institute *Policy Analysis*, July 16, 1998.

3   SB 26, March 3, 1999.

4   SB 27, March 3, 1999. The Senate journal for that day is available at http://www.ilga.gov/senate/journals/sfinaljrnls91/pdf/sjf91015_r.pdf

5   Rebecca Ephraim, "Looking for a Knockout: U.S. Senate Candidate Barack Obama would like to score one in the first round.," *Conscious Choice*, February 2004.

6   Bob Egelko, "Presidential candidates diverge on U.S. joining war crimes court," *San Francisco Chronicle*, January 2, 2008.

7   Don Kraus, "2008 Presidential Candidate Questionaire: Response from Barack Obama," Citizens for Global Solutions.

8   "World: Americas: Bush no whiz on foreign quiz," *BBC News*, November 6, 1999.

9   "Part I: CNN/YouTube Democratic presidential debate transcript," *CNN.com/politics*, July 24, 2007.

10   Ibid.

11   Ibid.

12   Transcript, "North Korea test-fires 7th missile," *CNN.com*, July 5, 2006.

13   NBC, *Meet the Press* May 18, 2008.

14   ABC *This Week*, May 18, 2008.

15   CNN, *America Morning*, May 20, 2008.

16   IVI-IPO 2004 US Senate Questionnaire, available at http://www.iviipo.org/2004queries_primary/Obama-response.pdf.

17   CNN *Situation Room*, May 19, 2008.

18   MSNBC, *Race for the White House with David Gregory*, May 27, 2008.

19   Transcript, Jack Tapper, "Political Punch: Interview with Barack Obama," ABCNews, May 20, 2008, http://blogs.abcnews.com/ politicalpunch/2008/05/interview-with.html.

20   Transcript, Jack Tapper, "Political Punch: Interview with Barack Obama," ABCNews, May 20, 2008, http://blogs.abcnews.com /politicalpunch/2008/05/interview-with.html.

21   David Reinhard, "Nuance or Confusion?" *The Oregonian*, May 22, 2008.
22   BarackObama.com, http://www.barackobama.com/issues/iraq/.
23   David Mendell, *Obama: From Promise to Power*, (NY: Amistad, 2007), 174.
24   Bettylu Saltzman, "Going Back a Few Years with Obama," *Chicago Tribune*, July 3, 2007.
25   Transcript, "Remarks of Illinois State Sen. Barack Obama Against Going to War with Iraq," October 2, 2002, on BarackObama.com, http://www.barackobama.com/2002/10/02/remarks_of_illinois_state_sen.php.
26   Mendell, 208.
27   Mendell, 175.
28   Mendell, 175.
29   David Mendell and Jeff Zeleny, "Obama says war to decide election," *Chicago Tribune*, July 27, 2004.
30   Transcript, *Meet the Press*, November 11, 2007
31   *Congressional Record* June 21, 2006, S 6233
32   Transcript, "Remarks of Senator Barack Obama," November 20, 2006, Chicago Council on Global Affairs, available at http://www.barackobama.com/2006/11/20/a_way_forward_in_iraq.php
33   BarackObama.com, http://www.barackobama.com/issues/iraq/.
34   Barack Obama, *The Audacity of Hope*, (NY: Three Rivers Press, 2006), 298.
35   *Audacity*, 302.
36   Amanda Carpenter, "Obama Never Tried To Meet Petraeus," *Townhall*.com, May 29, 2008.
37   *Audacity*, 58.
38   Amanda Carpenter, "Obama Never Tried To Meet Petraeus," *Townhall*.com, May 29, 2008.
39   *Audacity*, 127
40   Jane M. Von Bergen, "Graft probe mushrooming in Chicago," *Philadelphia Inquirer*, August 11, 2005.
41   "Military Deaths by Year/Month," Iraq Coalition Casualty Count, http://icasualties.org/oif/
42   You can watch this video here: http://www.youtube.com/watch?v=l4vlBgh7KLg, accessed July 1, 2008.
43   *Morning Joe*, May 30, 2008, MSNBC. Video available, http://www.youtube.com/watch?v=l4vlBgh7KLg
44   MSNBC *News Live* July 1, 2008.
45   Democratic Presidential Candidates Debate, Cleveland, Ohio, February 26, 2008.
46   Zachary Roth, "The U.S., Iraq, and 100 Years: Press needs to call Obama on distortion of McCain's statement," *Columbia Journalism Review*, April 1, 2008

47 "Cleveland Clinkers," FactCheck.org, February 27, 2008 http://www.factcheck.org/elections-2008/cleveland_clinkers.html

48 Frank Rich, "Tet Happened, and Noone Cared," *New York Times,* April 6, 2008

49 Zachary Roth, "The U.S., Iraq, and 100 Years: Press needs to call Obama on distortion of McCain's statement," *Columbia Journalism Review,* April 1, 2008

50 *Audacity,* 26.

51 *Audacity,* 286.

52 *Audacity,* 39.

53 Note that Obama has been falsely accused of making this statement.

54 Remarks at the Annual Convention of the National Association of Evangelicals, March 8, 1983.

55 Patricia Koza, "Washington News," United Press International, March 24, 1983.

56 ABC News Transcript, *World News Tonight,* March 24, 1983.

57 Don Phillips, "O'Neill: Mondale must attack 'cold, mean' Reagan" United Press International, July 19, 1984.

58 James Reston, "Q&A; 'The President Is Going down the Wrong Road'," *New York Times,* November 1, 1983.

59 See Kevin Mooney, "KGB Letter Outlines Sen. Kennedy's Overtures to Soviets, Prof Says," CNSNews.com, Oct. 20, 2006, and Herb Romerstein, "Ted Kennedy was a 'Collaborationist'," *Human Events,* Dec. 5, 2003. See also Paul Kengor, *The Crusader: Ronald Reagan and the Fall of Communism* (New York: Harper Collins, 2006).

60 Melvin R. Laird, "Iraq: Learning the Lessons of Vietnam," *Foreign Affairs,* November/December 2005. (http://www.foreignaffairs.org/20051101faessay84604-p0/melvin-r-laird/iraq-learning-the-lessons-of-vietnam.html)

61 *Audacity,* 289.

62 "Navy: Missile defense test a success," ABC7, June 6, 2008, http://abclocal.go.com/kabc/story?section=news/national_world&id=61 89438.

63 Available at http://www.youtube.com/watch?v=7o84PE871BE.

64 109th Congress, 1st Session, roll call vote No. 311, November 8, 2005.

65 David Freddoso, "John Kerry, Bush's Advisor on Iraq," *Human Events,* March 16, 2004.

Chapter 10

1 Liz Townsend, "Survivors of Second-Trimester Abortions Left to Die in Illinois Hospital, Nurse Alleges." *National Right to Life News,* Oct. 12, 1999.

2 Dennis Byrne, "A new low in heartlessness," *Chicago Sun-Times,* Sept. 29, 1999.

3   Christ Hospital is owned by Advocate Health, which states on its web-site that it is "[r]elated to both the Evangelical Lutheran Church in America and the United Church of Christ." http://www.advocatehealth.com/system/about/overview.html.

On the website of United Church of Christ, you can find a document titled "Reproductive Health and Justice," which includes this statement: "The United Church of Christ has affirmed and re-affirmed since 1971 that access to safe and legal abortion is consistent with a woman's right to follow the dictates of her own faith and beliefs in determining when and if she should have children." Available at http://www.ucc.org/justice/advocacy_resources/pdfs/reproductive-health-and-justice/reproductive-health-and-justice.pdf

4   Dennis Byrne, "A new low in heartlessness," *Chicago Sun-Times*, Sept. 29, 1999.

5   Letter from Illinois Attorney General Jim Ryan to Karen Hayes, July 17, 2000.

6   "Fortunately for me, the abortionist was not in the clinic when I arrived alive, instead of dead, at 6:00 a.m. on the morning of April 6, 1977." Testimony of Gianna Jessen before the Constitution Subcommittee, House Committee on the Judiciary, Apr. 22, 1996.

7   Transcript of the Illinois 90th General Assembly, Mar. 30, 2001.

8   Michael Dobbs, "Obama's Voting Record on Abortion," WashingtonPost.com, February 6, 2008, http://blog.washingtonpost.com/fact-checker/2008/02/obamas_voting_record_on_aborti.html

9   SB 1661 and SB 1662, April 4, 2002.

10   107th Congress, S. Amdt. 814 to S. 1052.

11   Congressional Record, 107th Congress, "Bipartisan Patient Protection Act, S. 1052: Consideration of Senate Amendment 814." Jun. 29, 2001, S7128.

12   93rd General Assembly, SB 1082. Chairman Obama "postponed" the bill and held it from Mar. 6, 2003, until the session's end on Jan. 11, 2005. On March 14, 2003, he sent the amendment that made it identical to the federal bill, back to the Senate Rules Committee in order to kill it.

13   John Chase, "A big split over abortion, stem cells; Polar opposites wage campaign for U.S. Senate," *Chicago Tribune*, October 4, 2004.

14   Barack Obama, *The Audacity of Hope*, (NY: Three Rivers Press, 2006), 132.

15   NARAL.org, http://www.naral.org/choice-action-center/in-congress/congressional-record-on-choice/california.html

16   Planned Parenthood, http://www.ppaction.org/ppvotes/person-vote.html?person_id=14232

17   Frances Kissling, "The Best Candidate for Choice," *Huffington Post*, February 14, 2008, http://www.huffingtonpost.com/frances-kissling/the-best-candidate-for-ch_b_86762.html

18   Press Release, "NARAL Pro-Choice America Endorses Sen. Barack Obama," May 14, 2008. Becky Carroll, National Director of Women for Obama, wrote that the endorsement was unanimous: http://women.barackobama.com/page/community/post/beckycarroll/gG Bl2G

19   Terence P. Jeffrey, "Obama Is the Most Pro-Abortion Candidate Ever," CNSNews.com, January 9, 2008.

20   Transcript of the Illinois 92nd General Assembly, Mar. 30, 2001.

21   HB 1900, May 16, 2001.

22   HB 383, May 21, 1998, HB 709, April 7, 2000. Obama voted "no" on both bills, which would have limited Medicaid funding of abortions.

23   Ronald Powers, "Moynihan, in Break with Clinton, Condemns Abortion Procedure," Associated Press, May 14, 1996.

24   E-mail from Obama for Illinois, "A Message from Michelle Obama," February 17, 2004. You can see a screen capture of this e-mail at http://www.jillstanek.com/Slide%201%20michelle%20obama%20pba %20letter.jpg

25   Illinois 90th General Assembly, SB 230 and HB 382.

26   "Obama Response to Supreme Court Decision,' April 18, 2007, http://my.barackobama.com/page/community/post_group/ObamaHQ/C ZsK

27   SB 230, Mar. 18, 1997, and HB 382, May 13, 1997.

28   Obama voted against SB 230 in the Judiciary Committee on Mar. 5, 1997.

29   *Audacity*, 84.

30   This is from an advertisement PHACT placed in the *National Journal Convention Daily* on August 12 and 13, 1996, during the Republican convention, as quoted in "Ad Watch; PHACT Places Ads in Convention Dailies," *Abortion Report*, August 15, 1996.

31   Ruth Padawer, "Clinton May Back Abortion Measure," *Bergen Record*, May 14, 1997.

32   *Audacity*, 222.

33   Video available at http://www.imoneinamillion.com, at 30:45

34   "FOCA will supersede anti-choice laws that restrict the right to choose, including laws that prohibit the public funding of abortions for poor women or counseling and referrals for abortions. Additionally, FOCA will prohibit onerous restrictions on a woman's right to choose, such as mandated delays and targeted and medically unnecessary regulations." Source: National Organization for Women website, http://www.now.org/ issues/abortion/070430foca.html. Accessed June 6, 2008.

35   "The 'Freedom for Partial-Birth Abortionists Act'," National Right to Life, April 25, 2007, http://www.nrlc.org/FOCA/ LawmakersPropose-FOCA.html

36   *Gonzales v. Carhart*, (200 U.S. 321) April 18, 2007.

37   Mark Sherman, "Court Upholds Part of Child Porn Law," The Associated Press, May 19, 2008.
38   Charles Lane, "Justices Affirm Property Seizures," *Washington Post*, June 24, 2005
39   "Supreme Court Says Boy Scouts Can Bar Gay Troop Leaders," CNN.com, June 28, 2000, http://archives.cnn.com/2000/LAW/06/28/scotus.gay.boyscouts/.
40   *Audacity*, 89.
41   *Audacity*, 91.
42   *Audacity*, 90.
43   You can read the memo on the website of the Coalition for a Fair Judiciary, http://fairjudiciary.com/cfj_contents/press/theycallthemnazis.pdf, accessed July 4, 2008.
44   *Audacity*, 99.
45   *Audacity*, 82.
46   *Audacity*, 195–198.
47   *Audacity*, 59.
48   David Freddoso, "Did God Misspeak?" *Doublethink Online*, April 27, 2007, http://americasfuture.org/doublethink/2007/04/did-god-misspeak/.
49   For an example of this approach, see http://lewiscrusade.blogspot.com/2007/08/nrlc-is-not-pro-life.html.
50   Hank De Zutter, "What Makes Obama Run?" *Chicago Reader*, Dec. 8, 1995, http://www.chicagoreader.com/features/stories/archive/barackobama/.
51   Alinsky, *Rules for Radicals*, 188.

Chapter 11

1   David Jackson, "Obama: I trusted Rezko," *Chicago Tribune*, March 15, 2008.
2   Dave McKinney, "Madigan: Fire Hospital Board," *Chicago Sun-Times*, June 30, 2004.
3   Tim Novak, "GOP Wastes No Time Hitting Obama Angle," *Chicago Sun-Times*, June 5, 2008.
4   Mark Brown, "Obama's Dealings with Rezko Buy a Parcel of Questions," *Chicago Sun-Times*, November 2, 2006.
5   Timothy J. Burger, "Obama Bought Home Without Rezko Discount, Seller Says," Bloomberg.com, http://www.bloomberg.com/apps/news?pid=20601103&sid=a_9sOMpy91Js&refer=us.
6   Timothy J. Burger, "Obama Bought Home Without Rezko Discount, Seller Says," Bloomberg.com, http://www.bloomberg.com/apps/news?pid=20601103&sid=a_9sOMpy91Js&refer=us.
7   Peter Slevin, "Obama Says He Regrets Land Deal with Fundraiser," *Washington Post*, December 17, 2006.

8   Jeff Coen, Ray Gibson, and Bob Secter, "Rezko's gambling troubles: Checks bounced, Vegas officials say," *Chicago Tribune*, May 30, 2008.
9   Rick Pearson, "Obama on Obama," *Chicago Tribune*, Dec. 15, 2006.
10   Tim Novak, "Obama's letters for Rezko; As a state senator, he went to bat for now-indicted developer's deal," *Chicago Sun-Times*, June 13, 2008.
11   Binyamin Appelbaum, "Grim Proving Ground for Obama's Housing Policy," *Boston Globe*, June 27, 2008.
12   Tim Novak, "Obama's letters for Rezko; As a state senator, he went to bat for now-indicted developer's deal," *Chicago Sun-Times*, June 13, 2008.
13   Illinois Senate transcript, May 13, 1998.
14   90th General Assembly, SB 401.
15   92nd General Assembly, SB 53 and SB 1135.
16   See also, Binyamin Appelbaum, "Grim Proving Ground for Obama's Housing Policy," *Boston Globe*, June 27, 2008.
17   93rd General Assembly, HB 2345.
18   Bill synopsis on the website of the Illinois General Assembly: http://www.ilga.gov/legislation/BillStatus.asp?DocNum=2345&GAID=3&DocTypeID=HB&LegId=3654&SessionID=3&GA=93
19   Illinois General Assembly, http://www.ilga.gov/legislation/ BillStatus.asp?DocNum=625&GAID=3&DocTypeID=HB&LegId=1041&SessionID=3&GA=93
20   See the document at http://www.ihda.org/admin//Upload/Files//6ef5b189-a34f-4e21-9e42-c55fe12639e2.pdf
21   93rd General Assembly, HB 625.
22   93rd General Assembly, SB 2724.
23   93rd General Assembly, SB 569.
24   92nd General Assembly, SB 2039.
25   Binyamin Appelbaum, "Grim Proving Ground for Obama's Housing Policy," *Boston Globe*, June 27, 2008.
26   Ibid.
27   Ibid.
28   Ibid.
29   Mema Ayi, "New Development Launched at Roberty Taylor Homes," *Chicago Defender*, May 5, 2006 - May 7, 2006
30   Binyamin Appelbaum, "Grim Proving Ground for Obama's Housing Policy," *Boston Globe*, June 27, 2008.
31   Tim Novak, "Broken Promises, Broken Homes," *Chicago Sun-Times*, April 24, 2007.
32   Tim Novak, "Broken Promises, Broken Homes," *Chicago Sun-Times*, April 24, 2007.
33   Tim Novak, "Obama and his Rezko Ties," *Chicago Sun-Times*, April 23, 2007.

34 "Sun-Times' Questions, and Obama Campaign's Answers," *Chicago Sun-Times*, April 23, 2007.
35 Binyamin Appelbaum, "Grim Proving Ground for Obama's Housing Policy," *Boston Globe*, June 27, 2008.
36 David Jackson, "Obama: I trusted Rezko," *Chicago Tribune*, March 15, 2008.
37 Chris Fusco and Tim Novak, "Rezko Cash Triple What Obama Says," *Chicago Sun-Times* June 18, 2007.
38 "Obama; Rezko Raised $250,000 for Him," Associated Press, March 14, 2008.
39 Dave McKinney et al. "Obama Surface in Rekzo's Federal Corruption Case," January 20, 2008. (Rezko's name is misspelled in the headline on SunTimes.com.)
40 Quoted in Alexander Bolton, "Sen. Obama Finesses His Lobbyist Ties," *The Hill*, April 19, 2007.
41 Alexander Bolton, "Sen. Obama Finesses His Lobbyist Ties," *The Hill*, April 19, 2007.
42 Mark Hemingway, "Lobbying for Obama," *National Review Online*, May 28, 2008.
43 Abdon M. Pallasch, "Caught in a Feud," *Chicago Sun-Times*, May 27, 2007.
44 Paul J. Nyden, "Senator Gives Big Boost to Byrd," *Charleston* (W. Va.) *Gazette*, Mar. 31, 2005.
45 David D. Kirkpatrick et al., "Obama's Camp Cultivates Crop in Small Donors," *New York Times*, July 17, 2007.
46 "Johnson Resigns From Team Vetting Obama Veep," MSNBC, June 11, 2008 http://www.msnbc.msn.com/id/25101650/.
47 Ibid.
48 David Mendell, *Obama: From Promise to Power*, (NY: Amistad, 2007), 155.
49 Susan Chandler and John Keilman, "18-year-old Pritzker rattles $15 billion family empire," *Chicago Tribune*, Dec. 15, 2002.
50 Source: Federal Election Commission.
51 Ken Dilanian, "Campaign Advisers Tied to Lending Crisis," *USA Today*, April 3, 2008.
52 Abdon Pallasch, "Obama's subprime pal," *Chicago Sun-Times*, Apr. 28, 2008.
53 Press Release, "OTS Closes Superior Bank FSB; Hinsdale, Ill. Thrift is Insolvent," Office of Thrift Supervision, July 27, 2001, available at http://www.ots.treas.gov/docs/7/77151.html.
54 Ken Dilanian, "Campaign Advisers Tied to Lending Crisis," *USA Today*, April 3, 2008.
55 Abdon Pallasch, "Obama's subprime pal," *Chicago Sun-Times*, Apr. 28, 2008.

56   Ken Dilanian, "Campaign Advisers Tied to Lending Crisis," *USA Today*, April 3, 2008.

57   Ibid.

58   David Mogberg, "Breaking the Bank," *In These Times*, November 8, 2002.

59   Ibid.

60   Ken Dilanian, "Campaign Advisers Tied to Lending Crisis," *USA Today*, April 3, 2008.

61   "Ernst & Young to Pay U.S. Over Bank Collapse in '01," *New York Times*, December 25, 2004.

62   Ann Sanner, "Treasurer candidates split Democratic endorsements " Associated Press, March 6, 2006.

63   FEC data from the Center for Responsive Politics: http://opensecrets.org/ indivs/search.php?name=Giannoulias&state=&zip=&employ=&cand=o bama&c2004=Y&sort=N&capcode=ntdtk&submit=Submit.

64   David Jackson and John McCormick, "Critics: Obama Endorsements Counter Calls for Clean Government," *Chicago Tribune*, June 12, 2007.

65   Mark Hemingway, "Lobbying for Obama." *National Review Online*, June   25,   2008 http://article.nationalreview.com/print/?q=NGNhMmU0YjAyYmI4ZG M4NmQ0NzcyYmRkODI5ZWNmNjg=

66   Courtney Flynn and David Jackson, "Loans to crime figure haunt state treasurer hopeful," *Chicago Tribune,* March 15, 2006.

67   David Jackson, "Giannoulias speaks up on loans; 'I made mistakes,' he says of past remarks," April 27, 2006.

68   Scott Fornek, "Giannoulias: I take it back: Treasurer candidate says loans to crime figures were bad idea," *Chicago Sun-Times,* April 27, 2006,

69   David Jackson, "Loans cast pall over candidate," *Chicago Tribune*, April 9, 2006.

70   "Obama demands answers from candidate," *Chicago Tribune*, April 13, 2006

71   Steve Warmbir and Frank Main, "The Face of the New Mafia," *Chicago Sun-Times*, February 24, 2008.

72   "Treasurer Candidate: Loans Were Business Only." Associated Press, April 8, 2006.

73   Andy Shaw, "Opponent Questions Giannoulias Connections to Mob," ABC9,   September   28,   2006,   http://abclocal.go.com/ wls/story?section=news/local&id=4609432.

74   Andy Shaw, "Opponent Questions Giannoulias Connections to Mob," ABC9,   September   28,   2006,   http://abclocal.go.com/ wls/story?section=news/local&id=4609432.

75   Chuck Neubauer and Tom Hamburger, "Obama Donor Received a State Grant," *Los Angeles Times*, April 27, 2008.

76 Barack Obama, *The Audacity of Hope*, (NY: Three Rivers Press, 2006), 354.
77 Mendell, 144: "He had maxed out his credit card, partly on campaign expenses...."
78 Chuck Neubauer and Tom Hamburger, "Obama Donor Received a State Grant," *Los Angeles Times*, April 27, 2008.
79 Ibid.
80 Review of Federal Election Commission filings at FEC.gov.
81 Chuck Neubauer and Tom Hamburger, "Obama Donor Received a State Grant," *Los Angeles Times*, April 27, 2008.
82 Raoul V. Mowatt, "Sport of table tennis gets a local spin," *Chicago Tribune*, January 1, 2003.

INDEX

A
"A Time for Choosing", Reagan's
address on behalf of Goldwater,
56
abortion,
and Born Alive Infant Protection
Act, 197–198
born-alive protection bill speech,
199–200
definition of "birth" and "life",
195–196
and Freedom of Choice Act,
203–204
Obama's voting position on abortion, 196–197
partial-birth abortion, 201–203,
210
premature births from, 191–193
respecting other positions on, 208
ACORN (Association of Community Organizations for Reform
Now), 149–150

affirmative action, 110
Ahmadinejad, Mahmoud, 71,
175–176
Alinsky, Saul, 122, 139–143, 142,
210
Altgeld Gardens, 196
Ambinder, Marc, 98–99
American Prospect, 62
American Society of International
Law, questionnaire, 171–173
Arab American Action Network,
149
Archer Daniels Midland, 93
Askia, Gha-is, 3
Association of Community Organi-
zations for Reform Now
(ACORN), 149–150
The Audacity of Hope (Obama), 1,
53, 79–80, 89, 90, 109, 111–112,
155, 181, 182–183, 186, 188,
198, 203, 205, 208, 229
Aventine Renewable Energy, 92

oil exploration, on American soil,
113–114
O'Malley, Patrick, 169–171, 194,
196
O'Neill, Tip, 120, 188
Oregonian, 176
Owen, Priscilla, 208

P
PAC, Hopefund, 43
Pakistan, incursions into, xii
Palmer, Alice, 2, 4, 5, 36, 37,
128–130
partial-birth abortion, 116,
201–203, 210
Patrick, Deval, 70
patronage system, 28
"Friends and Family Plan", 29
Paul, Ron, 65–67
peace dividend, 119
Penn, Sean, xii
People's Daily World, 128
Peraica, Tony, 17, 18
personal accounts, Social Security,
119–120
"petitions guru", 2, 3
Petraeus, David, 182, 183
Pfleger, Michael, 161–164
Physicians Ad Hoc Coalition for
Truth, on partial-birth abortions,
202–203
Ping-Pong patronage, 229–232
Planned Parenthood, 197, 199, 201
Political Affairs, 133
Potter, Trevor, 88
Powell, Colin, 163
Prairie State Achievement Examina-
tion, 81
prescription drugs, price-controls
for, 112–113
Pritzker, Penny, 226–227
"Project Vote", 3, TK
The Promised Land (Lemann), 144
Proteus fund, 149
Pryor, Bill, 208

Public Affairs, 15
public financing of campaigns,
85–89

Q
Quayle, Dan, 54
Quigley, Michael, 13

R
racial profiling bill, reducing, 30
radical faith, 157–164
Radogno, Christine, 32–33
Rauschenberger, Steve, 34–35, 83,
209
Reagan, Ronald, 55–56, 120,
186–187
"Reagan Democrats", 77
Reid, Harry, 52
Reinhard, David, 176
Reynolds, Mel, 4
Rezko, Antoin "Tony", 5, 32, 46,
233, 234
and dealings with Obama,
211–220
as fundraiser for Obama state
senate seat, 223
and low-income public housing,
221
and Obama campaign contribu-
tions, 222
other candidate contribution
from, 222
Rice, Condoleeza, 107, 164
Rice, Susan, 175, 185
Rich, Frank, 185
Richards, Ann, 105
Richardson, Bill, and Iowa caucus,
41
Roe v. Wade, 196, 197, 209
Rogers-Brown, Janice, 208
Rolling Stone, 55, 164
"Ron Paulization" of Barack, 65–66
Roosevelt, Franklin D., 115–116
Roseland (Chicago), 147
Roth, Zachary, 185